CW00505996

The Peasantry of Europe

THE MAKING OF EUROPE

Series Editor: Jacques Le Goff

The Making of Europe series is the result of a unique collaboration between five European publishers – Beck in Germany, Blackwell in Great Britain and the United States, Critica in Spain, Laterza in Italy and le Seuil in France. Each book will be published in all five languages. The scope of the series is broad, encompassing the history of ideas, as well as including their interaction with the history of societies, nations and states, to produce informative, readable, and provocative treatments of central themes in the history of the European peoples and their cultures.

The Peasantry of Europe

Werner Rösener

Translated by
Thomas M. Barker

BLACKWELL
Oxford UK & Cambridge USA

First published in 1994 by Blackwell Publishers and simultaneously by four other
Publishers: © 1994 Beck, Munich (German); © 1994 Critica, Barcelona (Spanish); © 1994
Editions du Seuil, Paris (French); © 1994 Laterza, Rome and Bari (Italian).

Blackwell Publishers
108 Cowley Road
Oxford OX4 1JF
UK

238 Main Street
Cambridge, Massachusetts 02142
USA

British Library Cataloguing in Publication Data
A CIP catalogue record for this book is available from the British Library.

Library of Congress Cataloging-in-Publication Data
Rösener, Werner.
[Bauern in der europäischen Geschichte. English]
The peasantry of Europe: from the sixth century to the present/
Werner Rösener; translated by Thomas M. Barker.
p. cm. — (The Making of Europe)
Includes bibliographical references and index.
ISBN 0–631–17503–2 (acid-free paper)
1. Peasantry – Europe – History.   I. Title.   II. Series.
HD1531.5.R67313   1994
305.5'633'094–dc20
93–39086
CIP

Typeset in 11 on 12$\frac{1}{2}$ pt Garamond by Best-set Typesetter Ltd., Hong Kong
Printed in Great Britain by T.J. Press, Padstow, Cornwall
This book is printed on acid-free paper

Contents

Illustrations

Maps

Figures

Table

Series Editor's Preface

Europe is in the making. This is both a great challenge and one that can be met only by taking the past into account – a Europe without history would be orphaned and unhappy. Yesterday conditions today; today's actions will be felt tomorrow. The memory of the past should not paralyse the present: when based on understanding it can help us to forge new friendships and guide us towards progress.

Europe is bordered by the Atlantic, Asia and Africa, its history and geography inextricably entwined, and its past comprehensible only within the context of the world at large. The territory retains the name given it by the ancient Greeks, and the roots of its heritage may be traced far into prehistory. It is on this foundation – rich and creative, united yet diverse – that Europe's future will be built.

The Making of Europe is the joint initiative of five publishers of different languages and nationalities: Beck in Munich; Blackwell in Oxford; Critica in Barcelona; Laterza in Rome; and le Seuil in Paris. Its aim is to describe the evolution of Europe, presenting the triumphs but not concealing the difficulties. In their efforts to achieve accord and unity the nations of Europe have faced discord, division and conflict. It is no purpose of this series to conceal these problems: those committed to the European enterprise will not succeed if their view of the future is unencumbered by an understanding of the past.

The title of the series is thus an active one: the time is yet to come when a synthetic history of Europe will be possible. The books we shall publish will be the work of leading historians, by no means all European. They will address crucial aspects of European history in every field – political, economic, social, religious and cultural. They will draw on that long historiographical tradition which stretches back to Herodotus, as well as on those conceptions and ideas which have transformed historical enquiry in the recent decades of the twentieth century. They will write readably for a wide public.

Our aim is to consider the key questions confronting those involved in Europe's making, and at the same time to satisfy the curiosity of the world at large: in short, who are the Europeans? where have they come from? whither are they bound?

Jacques Le Goff

1

The Rural Way of Life: Opposing Views

European agriculture is in crisis. Its agrarian policy and the growing problems of family farms dominate the debate about the peasant population. European agriculture is experiencing a transformation that will accelerate with the creation of an internal European market. Threats to livelihood, overproduction and environmental degradation are among the chief problems of economic and societal change. Farmers, consumers, politicians and scholars are confronted by challenges which will be very difficult to meet. It should also be borne in mind that the disappearance of farmsteads, irrational overproduction, despoliation of nature and agrarian exploitation of the Third World are interrelated phenomena with the same roots. They constitute the inevitable consequences of the last 200 years or so of revolution in farming technology – an event marked by mechanization, the employment of chemicals and the industrialization of the agrarian economy. Agrarian economic progress, which once seemed so promising because it led to a great increase in yields, has become counterproductive. The resultant economic, social and ecological costs for the principal countries of Europe far outweigh the initial benefits and raise the question of the origins of a development so harmful to Europe's peasantry.

The rural way of life has long held the interest of both the public at large and the scholarly research community. Clearly, it was above all the endangered existence of the traditional husbandman, the impending loss of ancient villages and deteriorating surroundings that drew the attention of broad segments of the population to the problems of the rustic world. Scholarly concern for the tiller of the soil and for village society has arisen against the background of modern urban society and the process of industrialization which fundamentally altered Europe's economy in the nineteenth and twentieth centuries. In this context two sharply divergent positions may be distinguished. The first is a conservative view of the peasantry; the other is a critical approach that stresses the negative features of village life.

The conservative perspective evolved under the influence of the humanities, history and sociology. It sees modern urban life as the expression of a process of absorption into a mass mode of existence, anonymity, alienation and commercialization in contrast to the contemplative mentality, mutual caring and closeness to nature of traditional peasant life. In accordance with the now famous distinction of Ferdinand Tönnies, the primordial village environment is regarded as the quintescence of 'community' (*Gemeinschaft*) and demarcated from a negatively perceived 'society' (*Gesellschaft*) represented by the modern metropolitan milieu. Changes in village life are portrayed critically and sadly as a transition from 'community' to 'society'. The concomitant uprooting of human beings and the destruction of their original, firm ties to kinsmen and neighbours are underlined.*

Europe's traditional peasantry was frequently the centrepiece of writing by conservative, nineteenth-century ideologues who yearned to restore the good old days. The rustic way of life was idealized and compared to the allegedly decadent novelties of the urban industrial world. Thus, in opposition to liberal and socialist critics of the era, Wilhelm Riehl lauded the conservative influence of peasants during the 1848 Revolution and ascribed the salvation of Germany's princely thrones to it.

In our fatherland the peasant has a political impact, as in few other European countries. The peasant is the future of the German nation; he constantly refreshes and rejuvenates the life of our people. If we can avoid an uncontrolled expansion of the rural proletariat, then we need have little fear of businessmen and literati. . . . The greatest mistake made by the bureaucratic state of the last half century has been its total failure to grasp the inherent virtues of the peasantry. It has forgotten the supreme principle that the strength of a conservative polity resides in the countryman. The 1848 Revolution has shown us how grave that error was.[1]

This idealization of the rural way of life and of the persistence of the peasantry in the face of the decadent currents of modern times is not

---

* Translator's note: for Tönnies' dichotomy of *Gemeinschaft* and *Gesellschaft*, see Ralf Dahrendorf, *Society and Democracy in Germany* (London, Weidenfeld, 1968), pp. 120–2.

encountered only in the work of German folklorists such as Riehl. In the French, German and Italian literature of the nineteenth and twentieth centuries there are also numerous testimonials in which the rural world is compared nostalgically to the mad pace of industrial towns. Disgusted by the demands and pressures of urban life, many saw redemption in a return to the land. Immersed in a metropolitan society which they considered to be inhuman, they pined for a simpler, less circumscribed way of life and believed that it could be found in a bucolic setting. This longing was echoed in the works of many novelists, folklorists and social scientists, who claimed that traditional peasant village culture was more humane and served the well-being of the individual better than modern industrial society, which had undermined the venerable tissue of village life.

Pitted against this conservative interpretation of peasant life was a critical tendency. Its roots may be found in the eighteenth-century Enlightenment, and it extends via the social reformers of the nineteenth century down to the proponents of modern critical theory. It depicts the village and the peasant family in an alliance arising from necessity and compulsion, as the matrix of authoritarian behaviour, structurally incapable of maturation. Village society by its very nature blocks its own emancipation and spiritual progress. In such a framework even outside impulses do not contribute to qualitative transformation.

Theodor Adorno, a leading advocate of critical theory, goes so far, in regard to the village, as to speak of 'a duty to deprovincialize'. The picture which results from this philosophic stance often casts peasants and villagers in a distorted and sombre light. The social edifice of the village deforms peasant character and reinforces the grim attributes of their life. One cannot trust the village and its inhabitants to effect social structural change that would have a 'deprovincializing' outcome. The stimulus must be external, in the form of education and enlightenment. When the village world is described in such a way, it follows without question that urban bourgeois society constitutes the better part of civilization.

Socialist literature of the nineteenth and twentieth centuries also generally denies peasants any reforming political capacity and autonomous social competence. With their *idée fixe* of liberating the progressive working class, neither Karl Marx nor Friedrich Engels concerned themselves to any great extent with the peasant stratum, for they were fully convinced that this obsolete, pre-industrial segment of the population would quickly disappear. As early as 1848, in their famous Communist Manifesto, they extolled the progressive qualities of the urban bourgeoisie *vis-à-vis* the ignorance of country folk. Indeed, the middle class had already managed to disengage an important segment of the peasantry from 'the idiocy of rural life'. Marx and Engels likewise considered peasant land ownership to be a relic of a previous age and certain to vanish gradually. Since they belonged to the centre of the social spectrum, peasants were a conservative, in fact a reactionary group: they opposed the progressive element of the bourgeoisie in order to protect their own status. In the first volume of *Das Kapital* (1867) Marx depicts the peasantry as a bulwark of the old order of society, doomed to destruction as the consequence of historical development.[2] He denigrates the peasant family as an economic unit, describing it as 'the most habitually indolent and most irrational type of enterprise imaginable'; the advance of modern agrarian technology would soon, he thought, result in its welcome demise. Marx had of course little knowledge of the realities of the agrarian economy and judged it mainly from the vantage point of his urban ivory tower.

In the writings of Marx and Engels about current affairs one can sometimes even discern outright hatred of the peasantry. Marx was especially outraged by the French peasants who supported the conservative regime of Napoleon III that resulted from the 1848–9 Revolution. In his opinion, the behaviour of French peasants on that occasion had revealed their identity as a barbarian, reactionary class.

> The Bonaparte dynasty does not represent the revolutionary but the conservative peasant, not the rustic who struggles to escape the conditions of his social existence, namely, his little plot of land, but rather the one who wishes to consolidate it; not the country folk who seek with their own reserves of energy and in alliance with cities to overthrow the old order but rather the fuzzy-minded ones who are entangled in it and fancy that the spectre of the empire guarantees salvation and advantage for themselves and their parcel of soil. The reigning house does not symbolize the peasant's enlightened intellect but his superstitiousness, not his judgement but his prejudice.[3]

Engels also castigated in similar fashion the 'thick-headed ignorance, blindness' and 'obtuse stupidity' of peasants. Like Marx he branded them as barbarians in the modern world. In both Germany and France they were 'barbarians in the midst of civilization'. This strange situation caused Engels to stress the distinctiveness of the rural way of life, for which he used stereotypical explanatory models.

The peasant's isolation in a remote village with a sparse population that changes only through the succession of generations, the self-denying, monotonous work which binds him more tightly to the glebe than serfdom ever did and which from father to son always remains the same, the static nature and routine character of all aspects of his life, the limited horizons of a family that has become for him the most important and decisive social relationship – all these things reduce the peasant's realm of vision to the narrowest parameters possible in modern society. The great movements of history bypass him. Although they may drag him along from time to time, he has no idea of the nature of the propellant force, of how it originated or which way it is headed.[4]

Alongside such unmistakable expressions of antipathy and disdain for peasants in the work of Marx and Engels, certain references to the progressive role which rustics can play in history can also be found. However, the two writers argue that the proletariat must first awaken the revolutionary potential of the rural populace, for up to the present it has been beguiled by the false promises of the reactionary element of society. Still, one searches vainly in the thought of the two classic socialist writers for a fair assessment of the circumstances of rural life. Not only was the latter entirely alien to them but they also they considered it unimportant, for the peasants would soon be swept aside by social progress. After all, the small peasant farm was – to quote a then much read polemic co-authored by Marx (*Eccarius*) – a barrier to social and economic development, a 'leaden weight' that restrained the working-class movement everywhere. It had failed the test in every instance and could not be a reliable partner for modern industry and social progress.

Marxism was quick to apply to the agrarian sector both the general thesis that big business was superior to small ventures and the corollary, that the former would inevitably supplant the latter in the world of industry and commerce. When rural problems were discussed at the 1864 London congresses of the International Workers' Association, the proposition that large-scale agrarian enterprise was bound to prevail over small peasant farms became a hard and fast component of socialist doctrine. The Geneva Manifesto therefore stated dogmatically: 'small-scale peasant agriculture is irrevocably and implacably condemned to a gradual death by the omnipotence of capital, the role of science, the course of events, and the interests of society as a whole.' Hence, Socialist parties would face the task of convincing peasants and rural workers of the absolute correctness of this argument. If country people would only hurry to join forces with city workers, peasant emancipation could be achieved more quickly. However, the effect of Socialist agitation among rustics was nil. Peasant freeholders indignantly rejected the new doctrine of social ownership of the land. The Socialist movement not only found no support among the rural populace but in many regions it even engendered an anti-Socialist attitude.

However, the French socialist thinker, Pierre-Joseph Proudhon, who likewise belonged to the International, took it upon himself to challenge the agrarian tenets of Marx and his followers. Ridiculed by Marx as 'petty bourgeois', Proudhon subscribed to the ideal of a future rural society made up of small peasant farmers who supported themselves by working independently on soil that was their own. A reaction to this ringing endorsement of the peasant family farm with its flat contradiction of Marxist dogma was not long in coming: the Second Congress of the International in Lausanne (1867) was the scene of acrimonious disagreement. Notwithstanding the protests of the Proudhon faction, the next two congresses approved a resolution that straightforwardly advocated nationalization. Marx had won out over his rival, Proudhon.

When, towards the end of the nineteenth century, there was renewed criticism of the Marxist position with respect to the agrarian issue, and when it had become clear that the peasant family farm was surviving despite all predictions to the contrary, Engels added his voice to the discussion. In his article 'The Peasant Question in France and Germany' he passed negative judgement on Socialist demands for a government programme to protect the peasantry and emphasized that it was the duty of Socialists to seek continually to convince the rustics of the hopelessness of their situation. 'There can be no question but that capitalist mass production will trample over the impotent, antiquated small farm just as a train crushes a push cart.'[5] It follows from this that Engels saw no future at all for peasant agriculture.

Clearly, the dogmatic Marxist stance concerning agrarian matters is linked to the urban background of most Socialists and their limited knowledge of the factors that affected the peasant's ability to make a living. In the context of a mainly urban industrial society it was very difficult for academics and factory workers to analyse fairly the conditions of country life and to grasp the day-to-day realities of the rural environment. Thus most economists, sociologists and historians focused their investigations primarily upon changes in urban industrial civilization. They gave precedence to phenomena such as the genesis of modern political and social patterns, the march of industrialization, the growth of cities, and the unfolding of new norms and value systems. They devoted less attention to themes associated with pre-industrial society and peasant culture. The latter came to be viewed as extraneous and the tendency was to ignore it.

As a consequence of Third World crises, there nevertheless arose in the decades after World War II a new interest in the structures of agrarian societies and the history of the European peasantry. Above all, social and cultural anthropology evolved in a number of countries into a recognized research discipline. This led to a new way of viewing peasant society which differed greatly from both the conservative idealization of the village and the enlightened critical approach. The net effect was a more equitable presentation of all facets of the peasant way of life. The social anthropological shift of direction towards peasant society was marked by the formation of a broad spectrum of issues and a fruitful, interdisciplinary collaboration of anthropologists, ethnolologists, sociologists and historians. The resultant concept of 'peasant society' – from the work of Robert Redfield, Lloyd A. Fallers and Eric R. Wolf on the lands of Latin America, Africa and Asia – fitted especially well the structures of rural society and was also quite applicable to European circumstances.

What, then, are the chief characteristics of a 'peasant society'? The simplest answer is that it lies in between primitive tribal and modern industrial society. Peasants form the main group of a society in which there is a division of labour but in which not everyone is involved with agriculture: alongside them are various kinds of artisans and merchants. Thus one encounters not only villages but also market towns and cities, as a result of which there are reciprocal urban-rural relationships. Agrarian products constitute the major share of required consumer goods and are made on relatively autarkic peasant family farms. The peasant segment of society as a whole is marked by a strong attachment to tradition and – unlike modern industrial society – by solid ties to local groups. A further characteristic of peasant societies is control by non-rural individuals: the ploughmen depend upon mighty lords to whom they must pay taxes and render various services.

According to Wolf, the historic importance of peasant societies resides above all in the fact that in the last analysis they provide the foundations for modern industrial society. They differ from primitive societies particularly on the basis of well-defined market relationships: peasants bring their surplus products to market centres which tend to develop later into cities. They are also assimilated into a political unit, the non-peasant members of which seek to rule them, the lords applying sanctions in order to effect their pretensions. Fallers has studied in detail the connections of peasants to the rest of society. Households, the basic units of peasant society, while semi-autonomous economically because they are largely self-sufficient, nevertheless need to market their goods and to trade. Politically speaking, peasant families and village units are likewise semi-autonomous, and their folk culture exists alongside a more advanced, urban variety.

Certainly the social anthropological concept of peasant society encompasses significant aspects of rural life and it can also be applied to the agrarian world of the Middle Ages and the Early Modern Era, in which a peasant demographic majority subsisted from agriculture, was bound up in a traditional order of things and was characterized by specific economic forms, mentalities and ways of life. This new perspective both accounts for the relative autonomy of village relationships and takes seriously the special thought and behavioural patterns of a peasant population. Thus it is easier to understand different phenomena such as the peasant family economy, manorial dependency, traditional value systems, and particular forms of resistance to lordship and bring them together as a whole. Still, the autonomy of peasant life should not be exaggerated since the peasantry of the Middle Ages and the Early Modern Era was subject to feudal rule until its emancipation in the late eighteenth and earlier nineteenth centuries.

The growing problems of the predominantly agrarian Third World have unquestionably promoted the interest of European industrial societies in their own rural past and have stimulated scholarly investigation of Europe's peasants. Phenomena such as population pressure, poor harvests, famines, diminution of cultivable terrain and peasant migratory movements, typical of many developing countries, were also to be found in the agrarian societies of pre-industrial Europe. One need only look at Asia, Africa and Latin America to realize that the overwhelming majority of the earth's inhabitants continue to be peasants and subsist from agriculture and animal husbandry. Dependent upon weather, climate and varying soil yields, their standard of living is frequently only marginal.

The euphoria which development aid policy-makers felt in the 1950s and 1960s has been dampened most recently by grave failures. Above all, the abortive tactics used to confront Third World agrarian problems were obviously based upon wrong deductions and insufficient knowledge of the traditional forms of peasant economies. For a long time economic planners favoured rapid inustrialization, which meant that the agrarian sector was subordinated to business. In so far as the former received any attention, huge, showy projects such as dams and irrigation systems were given preferential financial treatment. The idea was to modernize a 'backward' variety of agriculture and cause traditional economic and social patterns to melt away.

Only in the 1980s, in the light of the population explosion, the growth of the environmental movement and clear signs of failure, was there greater stress upon agrarian issues in development aid policy-making. Disturbing trends such as the destruction of forests, deterioration of the soil and devastating erosion were partly the consequences of erroneous decisions. The last of these particularly reflected wrong judgements about peasant smallholders whose receptivity to change was underrated. For many years peasant farming, the norm in most developing countries, was automatically considered to be obsolete by specialists in the subject. However, more recent investigation has shown that, even in the case of small operations, which are almost entirely at subsistence level, there is much flexibility and openness to market relationships. Since peasant families account for approximately 85 per cent of Third World agricultural activity, rural development policy should concentrate upon encouraging their interests. Small farms are manifestly more productive than big ones, and it follows that fostering them promises greater success than before. The new awareness of the value of peasant family farms is to a large extent owing to the writings of the Russian agrarian scholar, Alexander Chayanov, who has conducted numerous studies of the different forms of peasant agriculture and has developed an impressive theoretical framework for understanding the family model. He stresses the peculiar structures of the peasant economy and the fact that families work on the basis of specific, strictly internal laws of production and consumption.

The ecological movement has also provided stimuli for new thinking about the foundations of Europe's peasantry. Reports of environmental damage, the death of forests, natural catastrophes and the depopulation of rural areas have reverberated strongly in the public mind and have led to a powerful, organized effort to preserve the environment in a way worthy of mankind, one in which the traditional family farm has an important role to play. The ecological repercussions of the food-processing industry and of an ever more intensive form of agricultural production can no longer be overlooked. 'Nitrate deposits in groundwater', 'pesticide residues in groceries', 'torture of animals in factory farms' – these were some of the headlines of the past few decades when newspapers wrote about agricultural and environmental topics. Taken together, these phenomena led to growing criticism of previous agrarian policies and to a demand for an ecologically orientated approach to agriculture. People recognized that in

some regions peasant farming is simply indispensable if the face of the
countryside and natural resources are to be preserved. The peasant thus
becomes the caretaker of nature and the guarantor of a kind of agriculture
that harmonizes production and the environment. However, this gives rise
to further questions: what are the bases of Europe's traditional peasantry
and what factors must be considered if the goal is to safeguard the peasant
variety of farming and a cultural landscape that has been shaped by the
tiller of the soil?

To complicate matters, it must be noted that agrarian policy has under-
gone not only an ecological crisis but an economic one as well. Increases in
productivity have brought about massive surpluses within the European
Community. Mounting farm subsidies accompanied by declining peasant
income have been the result of this development. The European agrarian
market has meanwhile generated such high costs that it is no longer
financially sustainable in its present form. Policy-makers must change
direction – whether they want to or not. Hardly any realm of the economy
has changed so quickly and fundamentally as has Europe's agrarian sector.
In 1960, when the Community counted only six members, 15 million
persons were still employed in agriculture; this figure shrank to 5 million
in 1987, in other words by two-thirds. The decline of the agrarian sector
was matched by a sharp drop in the number of farms – from 6.4 million in
1960 to 4.8 million twenty years later. At the same time the demise of
small farms encouraged the formation of larger-scale units, as well as
specialization and mechanization. Farmers concentrated more and more
upon a few branches of production which they believed offered greater
prospects of success because of either favourable soil conditions or better
market outlets.

Through structural change many villages face the possibility of extinction: aging populations, empty farm buildings, the departure of younger
people and accelerating infrastructural decay, accompanied by a loss of
local and regional identity on the part of those who have remained. In the
light of this transformation of agriculture and of the countryside, the
question arises of whether it is possible to continue sticking to the conven-
tional leitmotif of European agrarian policy, namely, to preserve a form of
agriculture that is characterized by the predominance of the peasant family
farm. Should a balanced social edifice and a cultural landscape of peasant
configuration be maintained? Is it clear beyond doubt that a variety of
farming distinguished by huge cultivated surfaces is wrong? Because the
grave threat to the existence of family farms since 1945 has to do above all
with the large number of small and medium-sized units, there is a further,

more basic question to be asked: under what conditions, if at all, can the peasant mode of agriculture survive?

The crisis confronting Western European agriculture is in no way mitigated by the fact that its Eastern European counterpart is suffering even worse economic and social difficulties. Ever since Stalin's precipitate forced collectivization and the liquidation of the kulaks, Soviet agriculture has had to overcome production and distribution problems under the aegis of a central authority. The predicament faced at present by Russian agriculture consists primarily of bottlenecks in food distribution, the need for extensive grain imports and high agrarian subsidies. The low productive capacity of Russia's agrarian economy is best illustrated by a comparison with the United States. Whereas 20 per cent of Russian workers are still employed in agriculture, the equivalent American figure – and there are huge commodity surpluses as well – is but 3 per cent. The standard of life in the Russian countryside is relatively low, while village supply and distribution facilities are extremely poor. The inadequate infrastructure means not only that a considerable portion of the crop is lost at the time of the harvest, but also that much of it is spoiled by a faulty system of storage.

While it is true that the social position of kolkhoz peasants and rural workers improved under both post-Stalinist party leadership and Gorbachev, the rustic population continues to be the weakest stratum of Russian society. Alongside state farms (*sovkhozi*) and agricultural cooperatives (*kolkhozi*) privately tilled garden plots are still – astonishingly – a major prop of the system for supplying the nation with raw foodstuffs. Although these non-public 'collateral farms' made up merely 1.2 per cent of all Russia's agriculturally exploitable land in 1976, they furnished 64 per cent of the country's potatoes and 22 per cent of its meat and dairy products. With regard to the foreseeable future, it is impossible to conclude that simple enhancement of work-force productivity on state farms and kolkhozes can ensure what in fact seem to be Russia's rather uncertain chances for agricultural self-sufficiency and a rise in the overall standard of living. The time-honoured practice of refusing to grant kolkhoz peasants internal passports was an unmistakable sign that unchecked emigration from rural areas could have turned into a flood; without such a barrier the countryside could have become a desert. The prolongation of government-imposed soil bondage proved that the Soviet economy was far from achieving an equilibrium that would allow people the choice of employment in either the agrarian or the industrial sector. It also showed that the living standards of country dwellers have remained at an abysmally low level.

After World War II the Soviet model of collectivized agriculture was introduced to the states of East Central Europe occupied by Moscow's troops. However, the system was not applied as consistently in Poland, Czechoslovakia and Hungary as it was in the territory of the USSR. Hailed with great passion as the solution to all agrarian problems, the combination of land reform and nationalization encountered solid resistance almost everywhere. The harder the authorities pushed for collectivization, the more hostile was the reaction – at least in general – of the peasants affected by it. Thus, for the most part, the rural population assumed a defensive posture *vis-à-vis* the Stalinist power elite. Collectivization was energetically pursued with all the force at the disposal of the state and for many decades characterized conditions in the countryside. Nevertheless, the results were disappointing – a consequence of a mixture of peasant opposition, poor organization of cooperative farms, insufficient capitalization and the vigorous suppression of individual initiative.

Notwithstanding all its defects, collectivization remained for a long time the official objective of agrarian policy. This brought about a fundamental transformation of agrarian structures and rural life in the countries in question, so any return to private farming – the goal of reforms over recent years, in part anyway – has been made extremely difficult. As a result of the departure from the scene of the most efficient, old-style peasants, the aging of the residual agrarian population and the growing demands of youth for a higher standard of living, there is often no basis for a revival of agriculture in its traditional form. Most country regions in East Central Europe thus find themselves in a transitional phase that has two facets. On one hand, there is still a collectivized component of the agrarian economy which operates with mechanized equipment, receives states subsidies and is closely connected to agro-industry. The other side of the coin is a private sector that has become increasingly important and delivers a surprisingly large share of the basic supply of foodstuffs. To what extent this kind of farming has a future in Eastern Europe remains to be seen.

The crisis faced by agriculture and the peasantry in both halves of the continent demands an examination of the disparate agrarian history of individual regions and some study of the roots of Europe's rural population. Knowledge of the essential traits of the traditional peasantry and the chief features of its history in the different nations of Europe may provide some hints useful for safeguarding forms of country life that are genuinely worthy of preservation. An historical analysis of Europe's peasants opens new perspectives that can assist in overcoming very difficult contemporary problems. Thus the following chapters will attempt to illustrate some of the fundamental attributes of rural development in the principal European states all the way from the Early Middle Ages down to the present. Because the volume and quality of research vary considerably, and because of the myriad of basic geographic, economic and social determinants of peasant life throughout the continent, only certain main lines of historical development can be pursued. The goal is not, nor can it be, fully comprehensive treatment. What is required is the intellectual courage to penetrate the multiplicity of patterns encountered. The peasant environment – in medieval and early modern times ploughmen represented 80–90 per cent of the total population – has become largely foreign to the rest of us who are engrossed in a culture and society dominated by industry, but we must do our very best to understand it.

2

What is the European Peasantry?

European emigrants, who were cast upon America's shores before and during World War II, were confronted with a very different kind of economy and society. Among the characteristics of the United States was a peculiar form of agriculture: the emigrants noted with special interest the contrasts between the farmers they encountered in their new homeland and the peasants they had known in the old country. The agrarian activities of skilled businessmen-farmers were capitalist ventures, the chief goal of which was to maximize profits. They looked in vain upon the broad agricultural plains of North America for peasants with deep roots in the soil and strong attachments to family, village and a venerable plot of land.

Compared with agrarian circumstances in Europe, American agriculture was even then very specialized and heavily mechanized. The development of differentiated zones of cultivation and the speedy introduction of modern agrarian technology had led to high levels of productivity, as well as an irreversible decline in the proportion of the population engaged in agrarian pursuits. Unlike the European peasant, the American farmer was much more mobile, more strongly orientated to economic success, and quick to sell unremunerative parcels of land and to experiment in recently settled regions with improved varieties of fruits and plants. New approaches, work-saving machinery and modern marketing methods were enthusiastically embraced. Additional motivations were opportunities for large-scale production, a copious flow of investment capital and the fluidity of land-owning relationships.

One of the Europeans who went to the United States before World War II and drew interesting comparisons between American farm life and European peasant culture and, more generally, between the historical development of the New and Old Worlds, was the historian Dietrich

Gerhard. Like the Frenchman Alexis de Tocqueville, who had crossed the Atlantic a hundred years earlier and described in his books[6] an American society shaped by concepts of social equality, Gerhard sought to explain to the reading public of his own day both the shared and the mutually distinct traits of American and European civilization. Having attempted while in the United States to help his audiences understand the principal features and main ideas of European history, so too, once he was back in Germany, he tried to define for his students the different patterns of American politics, culture and society.

Compared to the relatively unstructured and extremely mobile society of the United States, social divisions and regional demarcations seemed to Gerhard to be the chief components of the European way of life.[7] American life was conditioned by equality, mobility and modern technology whereas being part of a particular landscape, with deep local roots and corporate cultural traditions, played an important role in Europe; this was especially noticeable in the case of the peasant population. As opposed to agrarian circumstances in America and Russia, the European peasantry was characterized by many centuries of attachment to the soil and a strong sense of corporate identity. It was obvious that Europe's peasants were sedentary in a very special way. The presupposition for this was the full evolution of the corporate order – the 'society of estates' that had prevailed during the *ancien régime* – and the European countryside.

When de Tocqueville, under the immediate shock of the July 1831 revolution in France, travelled to America in order to acquaint himself with an embryonic world of equality, he encountered an overwhelmingly agrarian if rapidly changing society, one already far removed from the old corporate order of Europe. Within rural settings the village – which had once existed in certain parts of New England – was now largely a thing of the past, thanks to real-estate speculators. In a land of immigrants and domestic colonization there was no room for attachment to the ancestral sod, and the immigrants themselves soon shook off such attitudes. The development of commercial agriculture in America thus transpired against the background of a dynamic, westward projection of settlement.

During the Frontier Period, the era of the daring nineteenth-century pioneers, the North American landscape changed very rapidly, a process that also affected the personality of the country population. In an age of expanding world trade the European peasants and immigrants who settled the virgin prairie and the plains soon became individualistic American farmers as a result of their totally new experiences. Having discarded the baggage of Old World peasant traditions, they were transformed into efficient, mobile agrarian entrepreneurs. Under the pressure of a veritable flood of immigrants from the overpopulated countries of Europe and influenced by both capitalistic forms of commerce and impulses conveyed by an emergent industrial economy, a profit-orientated variety of agriculture arose. It was a powerful force that accelerated the tempo of settlement and radiated across the wide-open agrarian spaces of America. Only in high-lying valleys and remote districts did largely self-sufficient farming households manage to survive for a while. The idea of independent farmers relying upon free labour triumphed in the North whereas the slavery-based plantation economy of the South disappeared as a result of the Civil War of 1861–5.

What were the resources that made it possible for an American farmer to become rich and climb from the lowly category of a settler to that of an agrarian entrepreneur? There were two principal means of reaching this goal. The first was simply to sell off newly acquired settlement land and make a substantial speculative profit from its increase in value. The other possibility did not involve such a high degree of risk: the surefire way to augment income was to produce sizeable surpluses for an expanding national economy, above and beyond the farmer's own family requirements. The construction of an up-to-date road network and railways, together with the growth of consumer demand in industrial and urban centres, provided immense outlet markets for agrarian products.

The emergence of this new, profit-minded variety of husbandman was helped by the fact that in many instances he did not come from a rural stratum of the population. The mere fact that he was not a typical representative of the old-fashioned peasantry made him an excellent frontiersman and pioneer. The farmer who was prepared to run risks knew how to adjust rapidly to changing economic conditions, to exploit land recently opened for settlement, to adopt innovative methods of cultivation, to apply inventive techniques and to benefit from rearing new breeds of cattle. He was constantly searching for ways to derive greater advantage from his work-force, to employ his skills on broader stretches of soil and to produce ever larger surpluses for the consumer market. There cannot be the slightest doubt that the American farmer belonged to a society convinced of the absolute precedence of private property, the merits of free enterprise and the unlimited possibilities of technological progress.

The establishment of zones specializing in the cultivation of wheat, maize and other crops, as well as the rapid introduction of mechanical implements, were two areas in which the American farmer demonstrated his ability to react to the stimuli of both domestic and foreign markets.

Specialized zones of cultivation and separate regions for dairying and the production of meat were a spatially related response to the growth of cities and the improvement of the transport infrastructure. The mechanization of farming showed most clearly how much potential modern agriculture had at its disposal for shortening work intervals within the high-tension context of modern industrial development. At a very early stage the American farmer sought to exploit every possibility for mechanizing work sequences and promptly put into everyday practice the fruits of scientific research relating to better methods of fertilization, cultivation and fattening cattle.

The development of an agrarian economy controlled by a modern, profit-orientated type of farmer was the consequence of social and economic circumstances quite different from those that obtained in Europe. Among the social forces that affected rural America were family structure and special kinds of relationships between neighbours. Although up to now there has been relatively little study of the evolution of the American farming family and the traits which distinguish it from its European counterpart, it is still possible to make certain interesting observations. The Americans obviously constituted a particularly cohesive unit, since the farmsteads were normally isolated and scattered about the land. The family was also less authoritarian, since every individual member made a contribution to the well-being of the whole. Since the farm represented a joint enterprise of man and wife, women were more independent than they would have been in a European peasant milieu. Moreover, farmers adhered to the same behavioural norms as the rest of American society, namely, a strict Puritan work ethic and a high regard for economic success.

Villages such as Europe had known them since time immemorial did not exist in rural America. Instead, there developed a system of social communications between individual farmers and a well-defined network of neighbours. It was not within the framework of a village community but rather that of their neighbours that country folk helped each other to carry out tasks that required collective effort: transporting logs, raising buildings, putting up fences and bringing in the sheaves. Threshing of grain was likewise an important realm of activity before the invention of a machine to do such work and it was an especially effective means of ensuring neighbourly cooperation. Collaboration of this kind was supplemented by important activities carried within the local church community. The parish served not only as a centre of worship but a place in which experiences and information could be exchanged. It also afforded the opportunity for making a great variety of social contacts.

Against the background of this sketch of the characteristics of American farm life, one may ask what the essential features of the European peasantry were? The account above has certainly made it clear to the reader that European rustics, both in the past and more recently, had traits that distinguished them from the rural population of America and other countries. Closely connected to this issue is the problem of defining the historical phenomenon of the peasant. What is a peasant anyway? What marks him off from the American farmer and separates him completely from the profit-orientated agrarian producer of modern industrial society? How do the characteristics of the peasantry diverge from those of the urban bourgeoisie and the nobility?

The peasant as a member of a legally defined social estate is recognizable from the beginning of the High Middle Ages. As he is described in the sources of that period, he does not seem to differ from the paradigm of the social anthropologists mentioned above, who have studied peasant societies in Asia, Africa and Latin America. According to this interpretation, tillers of the soil are the main group within a society characterized by a division of labour between themselves, craftsmen, traders and merchants. Peasants are for the most part dominated by outsiders, strongly attached to tradition and shaped by their membership in various types of local communities in the broad sociological sense of the term.

Reinhard Wenskus has proposed five criteria relating to the manner in which rustics engage in economic activity and establish work patterns. One may thus posit a Weberian ideal-type of peasant.[8] (1) He is a producer of vegetable and animal comestibles, i.e., he plants the fields and raises cattle; hence, he differs from both the cattle-raising nomad as well as the primeval fisherman, hunter and food-gatherer. (2) He produces his bounty within the framework of an autonomous economic entity; therefore, he is also distinct from the hordes of slaves on Roman latifundia and modern hired hands. (3) Peasant cultivation takes place with the aid of a plough; this is an essential trait of the European peasant in particular. (4) The peasant works his plot of land by himself; this distinguishes him from the lord who has turned over usufruct of all or part of his seigniory of peasants. (5) The ploughman participates personally in work and is assisted by family members and domestics. The criterion of personal physical involvement encompasses several other features associated with the extent of the landholding in question. On one hand, a rustic economic unit cannot be less than a certain size because it must be sufficient to ensure the family a decent living. On the other hand, it cannot exceed specific dimensions because this would mean that work would have to be organized on a larger scale, and this would exclude personal physical participation. Clearly, the ancient unit of the hide constituted this type of peasant economic unit, though its proportions could vary greatly, depending upon terrain and soil conditions.

In addition to these purely economic criteria there are traits that project an image of the peasant rooted in everday speech: they have to do above all with the way rustics live and behave. The peasant is perceived above all as a sedentary being. Attachment to the land is thus a part of the underlying popular concept of rural life. Max Weber concluded that the peasant's immobility was a consequence of economic-technological progress, of a more intensive form of agrarian economic activity and of settlement density. An ever greater concentration upon tilling the soil *ipso facto* increased the husbandman's reliance upon making his living that way. Greater settlement density brought about a shift from cattle-raising, which had predominated at first, to cultivation of the land, a more arduous form of livelihood. Thus, in regions where cattle-raising was paramount, the peasant's ties to the glebe were far less evident.

Attachment to the soil is also related to the notion of the pacific and unwarlike rustic. The fact that an ever-increasing number of economic tasks were thrust upon the peasant's shoulders, together with the growing importance of armies made up of knights on horseback, meant that he was more and more exempt from military service. Indeed, the Imperial Public Peace Edict of 1152 prohibited him altogether from owning weapons. Nor could a run-of-the-mill peasant farmstead bear the heavy expense of a cavalryman's armour and appurtenances for very long. The result was the formation of a special stratum of mounted warriors. The awkwardness of the peasant ban in contrast to the relative manoeuvrability of a knightly host was so disadvantageous that general popular levies gradually ceased to have any importance. Exceptions to this image of the peaceful rustic were certain peasant soldiers stationed on borders, namely, the Cossacks of southern Russia and the military settlements of the Habsburgs along the frontier with Ottoman Turkey.

Another characteristic of the peasant's mentality is his social conservatism. This tendency distinguishes him from the town burgher and an urban mode of thought and behaviour. The peasant insists upon a lifestyle that he has inherited from a long sequence of forebears and that seems antiquated to the city-dweller. The rustic is altogether more bound by tradition. Because of his conservative mind-set he is often regarded as backward and opposed to progress.

But was the peasant in fact an enemy of progress? How can one explain his conservative demeanour and at the same time avoid misconceptions? The cultivators of the High Middle Ages, unlike the agrarian freebooters of earlier centuries, were most certainly paragons of progress and produced a cornucopia of material, social and cultural innovations. Study of Third World rural societies has recently provided a fresh basis for understanding peasant conservatism and the logic of a traditional way of farming, and the new insights are also applicable to the peasant societies of European history. Husbandmen reacted quite positively to agrarian reforms and innovations in so far as it was obvious that the latter were economically advantageous. For example, the fact that India's peasants clung tenaciously to a field system of highly subdivided strips, the inefficiency of which they could not recognize, can be explained by their ability to protect themselves thereby against extreme harvest oscillations and to compensate better for the risks of differing soil quality. It was thus possible to avoid debt, the loss of land and a low rung on the village social ladder, even if this meant renouncing the possibility of harvest maximization. One should not automatically take peasant conservatism for granted but rather seek to explain its essential rationality. In any case, it is high time to reject the image of a reactionary peasant making decisions blindly because he is hidebound by tradition. What is necessary is to ask why he cleaves to specific behavioural norms.

Peasants in the full sense of the word – that is, persons possessing the economic, social and psychological traits described above – appear on the European stage only from the eleventh century onward, when an estate of peasants emerged and became an entity in its own right *vis-à-vis* an estate of knights. This corporate differentiation was based upon the evolution of a professional warrior stratum supported materially by the possession of fiefs and large tracts of land tilled by serfs. Noble vassals and the diffuse, nascent estate of knights stood out more and more from the bulk of the rustic population. The peasantry that made its appearance in the early High Middle Ages continued to exist for many centuries and put its stamp upon the later Middle Ages and Early Modern history of European countries altogether. What were the characteristics of this European peasantry, and in which lands and regions of Europe could it be encountered?

Europe as the term is understood here refers to historical as opposed to geographical space. The Europe of geographers has been clearly defined since the early eighteenth century, when Tsar Peter the Great opened his country to the West: it stretches from the Atlantic to the Urals, from the North Cape to the Rock of Gibraltar. Before that time the historical concept of Europe generally meant the Occident, that is, the realm of the Latin Church. Russian lands within the Orthodox Christian orbit, as well as Islamic regions such as Moorish Andalusia, did not belong to Europe in the strict sense of the word. The structure of the Muscovite state under Tsar Ivan the Terrible was fundamentally different from the West, and southern Spain shared few traits with the heartland of Europe until the Moorish kingdom of Granada was conquered by Castile in 1492. It is more difficult to establish a demarcation in the south-east, since the Byzantine Empire ruled large parts of the Balkans and Italy and Ottoman Turkey penetrated deep into Hungary in the course of the sixteenth century. Thus, in the following analysis of the features of the European peasantry, the focus of attention must be the West. The goal will be to search for certain peculiarities of Europe's peasants and at the same time to show how they contrast with others of their genre. In addition to making the above comparisons with American farmers, it will be useful to take note of agrarian relationships in Russia and the Orient.

The basic features of the European peasantry are already discernible in the heartland of the eighth- and ninth-century Frankish kingdom, that is, the region between the Loire and the Rhine. As the centuries passed, they became more pervasive and spread beyond their place of origin. Significant changes in agriculture and the agrarian system took place in the interior of the Carolingian Empire, which encompassed the main western and central European countries (see map 2). Some of the main chacteristics need to be touched upon briefly. Among them were increased cultivation of grain and a shift to a more intensive way of working the land. In many a place transition to the three-field method – the cultivation of acreage in a three-year cycle of winter planting, summer planting and then allowing ground to lie fallow – was already under way, though the practice was not common elsewhere until the High Middle Ages. Within the village milieu the introduction of the three-field system occurred in conjunction with a reordering of arable land held in common and the formation of three large fields. These parcels of land were called either clearings or, to use an obsolete Middle English term, fallows. They were cultivated according to a binding commons ordinance. The hide appeared at the same time: it was the standard peasant family endowment, made up of arable terrain, pasture and the right to utilize communal woodlands and meadows.

From the High Middle Ages onward the three-field system, the commons ordinance and the hide are the hallmarks of the European village and they influence the formation of village communities with their various rights of administrative autonomy. This agrarian system slowly spread across the major countries of Europe and, with some delay, also extended to marginal regions of the West, such as Scandinavia and the Baltic. Werner Conze's studies of the agrarian structure of Lithuania and Belorus

(White Russia) have shown that, by the turn of the seventeenth century, the three-field system had extended as far as the eastern section of the great Polish-Lithuanian kingdom, but that in the neighbouring Muscovite realm other types of agrarian relationships endured, at least to some degree. To cite Otto Brunner, the three-field system, the hide and villages with well-articulated communal arrangements were central features of Europe's agrarian constitution and they were of crucial importance in the historical evolution of Europe's peasants.[9]

As the next chapter of this book will demonstrate at greater length, manorial lords participated meaningfully throughout the Middle Ages in this fundamental transformation of Europe's agrarian structure. The new pattern required far-reaching changes in the form of village settlement, led to the establishment of common fields and mandated fixed dates for planting and harvesting, since the prospective fallow served as grazing land for everybody's cattle as soon as it had been cropped. Commons ordinances could normally be introduced only with the help of manorial lords, inasmuch as they often controlled the biggest segments of arable land, and any alteration of the manner in which it was worked could only be carried out with their assent. They were obviously decisive participants in the crucial process of change that the village peasant environment underwent and helped to lay the foundations of a specifically European agrarian structure, one that survived until the radical reforms of the eighteenth and nineteenth centuries. Manorial lords and peasants were involved in a mutual relationship of fruitful tension ever since the emergence of the servile labour system in France in the Early Middle Ages. The result of their cooperation over the centuries was the village and agrarian configuration of Europe.

The three-field system, the yields of which were substantially greater than those of earlier, primitive methods of exploiting the soil (the rotation of grain and grass crops or the two-field system), was for a long time a highly progressive agricultural technique, something that agrarian reformers of more recent times frequently overlooked. It demanded the harmonious collaboration of all peasants who resided within the village environment and it capitalized on the productivity of the land without abusing it. The result of the much augmented cultivation of grain in the core regions of Europe from the High Middle Ages onward was greater population density in places that had been inhabited since antiquity. Enhanced production of grain likewise led to the expansion of settled areas by means of clearance and the extension of cultivation. The intensification of the agrarian economy and the escalation of grain production on rearranged village common lands also brought about a stronger peasant attachment to the soil. Compared with previous forms of land utilization and the predominance of a cattle economy in the Early Middle Ages, the later medieval transition to the three-field system and intensive cultivation of grain made Europe's rural population more sedentary; the reason was that heavier demands were being placed upon the peasant work-force. Under these changed economic circumstances the peasant became ever more 'dispensable', as Max Weber once put it,[10] for political and military tasks beyond his own bailiwick. He thus remained confined to his village and the surrounding countryside.

Over what period of time did the basic characteristics of the European peasantry described above extend? The groundwork dates above all from the Early Medieval Frankish kingdom and from the principal countries of Europe during the High Middle Ages. Manorial lordship, the hide, the three-field system and the peasant communal order arose in the heartland of Europe and gradually spread to marginal regions. European rural society and the traits that distinguish it reach all the way from the Carolingian era in which servile labour originated to the emancipation of peasants in the nineteenth century and thus possess conceptual validity for more than a millennium. In all of this epoch it is possible to discern the collective root phenomena of Europe's peasants: manorial dependency, three-field tillage within the context of the village, predominance of peasant family farms, relative autonomy of village relationships and a striking homogeneity of value systems.

The fundamental features of Occidental husbandmen emerge more clearly if they are compared to agrarian conditions in other settings. The Near Eastern Islamic peasantry provides a nicely contrasting picture although one must be careful to take divergent regional circumstances into account. The venerable agricultural landscapes of Egypt, Syria and Mesopotamia, which support cultures reliant upon irrigation, involve natural spatial and climatic factors quite different from those that obtain in Europe. Marginal districts near the Mediterranean and river oases, in which winter rain is sufficient for cultivation or irrigation allows intensive agriculture, constitute especially productive terrain. In so far as the country is flat and the soil good, steppes serve adequately for growing grain; they also permit extensive rearing of sheep and goats. However, even in the best parts of the desert it is possible to pasture animals only temporarily: this is the land of bedouins, an entirely nomadic people.

The nomads were the antithesis of agrarian rustics and city-dwellers in the great river districts and zones near the Mediterranean. The success of agriculture in oases was due above all to a rational water-distribution system; the only practical means of installing irrigation devices and digging canals was unified direction of the peasant labour force. The virtual anarchism of semi-desert, bedouin-inhabited zones stood in sharp contrast to the strict state control of irrigated districts. Frequently, work in the countryside was supervised by an urban centre, but the price for this was a considerable share of the annual harvest. It was from this relationship of dependency that the fellahin, the true peasantry of the Near East, emerged within the belts of potamic oases, such as the long narrow bands of greenery adjacent to the Nile. The power of the cities ended, on one hand, at the edge of the desert, which always represented a threat to security, and on the other, at the beginning of mountainous regions, where favourable soil-tillage conditions permitted the formation of autonomous village communities. The fellahin, for their part, were a population stratum quite distinct from the bedouins and the city-dwellers. Because they were direct descendants of the autochthonous, pre-Arab population, the former had preserved much of their cultural heritage. Their social status was comparatively humble because they were renters dependent upon big landowners.

Cattle-raising played a smaller role in the fellahin setting than it did in Europe, for, even if animals were used to work the fields and operate the waterworks, they were less necessary in the Near East than in Europe. Admittedly, the heavy wheeled plough served in some places to break thick rich sod, but it was by no means the standard implement for doing this since, aside from gardens, the simple, wheel-less stick plough was the tool of choice. To be sure, the fecundity of the earth, especially in Egypt, made it possible to cultivate fields intensively. Many villages collectively tilled specific parcels of land in a fixed, rotating sequence. As with the hides of the West, the farming unit often corresponded to a single family work-force and a team of draft animals. Unlike European peasants, the fellahin were altogether more oppressed, enjoyed little in the way of village autonomy and were unable to develop much dynamism of their own.

There are also striking differences between the European peasant and the older variety of Russian ploughman although, by the very nature of things, agrarian relationships in Muscovy resembled those of the West more closely than those of the Near East. As late as the sixteenth century, the Russian peasants who inhabited the huge north-eastern forest regions were quite mobile. A floating, scattered, rural population – the agrarian practices of which were primitive judged by Western standards – subsisted in settlement pockets within the vast sylvan wilderness from the produce of tiny parcels of cleared land. After a few harvests the sites were abandoned and the settlers moved on to virgin terrain.

Russian villages were relatively small, lacked stable arrangements for the use of common lands and did not have a mature community structure, as in Western Europe. Cultivation often took the form of planting field grasses or was based upon slash-and-burn techniques. As soon as the soils were exhausted, the fields were deserted and allowed to revert to forest. Although the Russian village was a close-knit community in terms of everyday work and mutual help, it could easily be shifted to somewhere else, whether as a single unit or as individual pieces. Indeed, relocations occurred on a massive scale, initially during the period of extreme serfdom at the command of a noble proprietor or the Tsarist state and much later, after the reforms of Alexander II, as the result of decisions made by the village community itself.

Peasant dependency in Tsarist Russia was much harsher than in Western and Central Europe. It is difficult to compare Russian serfdom with the gentler subjection of Western European peasants to manorial lords. The Russian husbandman was not only adscript to the glebe but could be called upon arbitrarily for whatever work his master wished to have done. Whole villages could be resettled or individual families sold off. The unique evolutionary pattern of Russia's peasantry may be explained by the fact that, from the fourteenth to the late seventeenth century, when Peter the Great (reigned 1689–1725) opened the doors of his realm to the West, Muscovy was an almost hermetically sealed-off state. As Immanuel Wallerstein and Fernand Braudel have pointed out,[11] the tsarist state of the sixteenth and seventeenth centuries was a largely self-sufficient economy that developed in isolation from the Occident. During this era of Russian history serfdom became much worse, a process that the government itself fostered. Ivan the Terrible (reigned 1544–84), the father of the imperial Muscovite state, managed on one hand to force the nobility to obey him and on the other heightened the Russian peasant's dependency upon the nobility and the government. The nascent system of the Russian landed estate imposed upon the peasant a growing burden of work and compulsory services: he became a villein in the strictest possible sense of the word. However, the frequent migration of rustics from one place to another threatened the manorial order. In 1580 Ivan abolished the right of free movement entirely. Later edicts further tightened the rules: any change of location not sanctioned by a peasant's master was declared illegal.

The Russian husbandman was not only bound to his lord but also to the mir, a village community characterized by joint possession of land and cultivation by individual families. The terrain turned over to individual members of the community, according to the size of a family, was periodically taken back and redistributed. Whereas the Western European peasant had always been allowed to occupy his farmstead on an individual basis and, for the most part, became a freeholder in the course of the eighteenth and nineteenth centuries, his Russian counterpart had only a very limited right of possession within the framework of the mir. It was not until Peter Stolypin's agrarian reform legislation of 1906–7 that redistribution was done away with. Up to the year 1861, when it was finally suppressed, the Russian form of serfdom was altogether the most severe imaginable. The rustic had no firm legal recourse against his seignior, merely the argument of tradition. The bond to the soil outweighed the right to the land, whereby the community as a whole was responsible for services and payments to the landowner. In this way Russia's peasants were fundamentally distinct from their confrères in the West.

While it is true that Occidental peasants manifested a uniform set of basic traits compared with rural life in eastern Russia and the Near East, they were also characterized by great diversity. Substantial differences between the various regions and countries of Europe with respect to soils, climate, vegetation, methods of cultivation, agrarian economics and agrarian organization obviously affected peasant relationships in a major way. While the heterogeneity of European agriculture in past and present reflects divergent circumstances of nature, it is also related to the size of farms, land distribution patterns and traditions of inheritance. The fracturing of agriculture into numerous spatial realms is a consequence of miscellaneous factors. For example, there are definite temperature limits with respect to the cultivation of food plants such as wheat and wine grapes, which cannot flourish under excessively cold conditions. Other climatic determinants are the length of the growing season, the amount of warmth and air moisture required by the vegetation in question, and precipitation levels. Nor can the quality of soils, nearness to markets, export opportunities and consumer habits be overlooked (see map 1).

As far as the conditions of agrarian livelihood are concerned, it is possible to distinguish four principal zones: Northern Europe, Western and Central Europe, the Mediterranean, and Eastern Europe. As a result of the influence of the Gulf Stream, the cultivation border of grain extends far into the north. Barley is the leading crop of the northern zone, which encompasses most of Scandinavia. More southerly regions are suited prima-

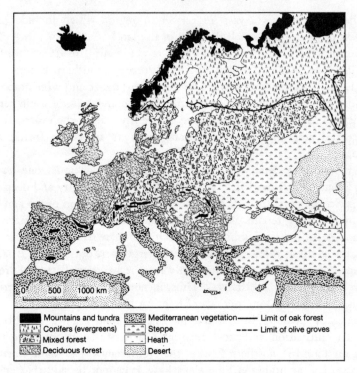

Map 1   The vegetation zones of Europe

rily for oats and rye; both need more hot weather than barley does.
Moreover, oats demand copious quantities of moisture. Northern Europe is
characterized altogether by a mixture of cattle-raising, agriculture and
forestry.

The huge agrarian zone of Western and Central Europe, comprised
mainly of England, France and Germany, can be distinguished by multifarious cultivated plants and a collection of agricultural economic sectors.
Adjacent to a belt of grassland near the sea is another in which rye and
potatoes predominate. It begins in the Netherlands as a narrow band and
broadens as it extends eastward: light soils, moderate summer temperatures and sufficient precipitation afford an ideal basis for root crops and
rye. To the south, running from east to west right through the centre of the
Continent, is a band of loess; on the northern side of the central elevations
lies a countryside of fertile plains. Loess soils are perfect for agriculture:
they easily sustain both wheat and sugar beet, plants that place heavy
demands upon the earth. This is in fact the most productive part of Europe.

To the south-west is a vast winter wheat region which includes large sections of France and small districts in England.

Southern or Mediterranean Europe is a gigantic, relatively uniform agrarian zone, made up mostly of Spain, Portugal, southern Europe, Italy and the Balkans. Its chief grain is winter wheat; maize and wine grapes are subsidiary crops. Compared to Central Europe and leaving aside certain districts in the Po valley, agriculture is extensive rather than intensive. In the coastal areas the most important products are citrus fruits, wine and olives.

It is harder to demarcate Eastern Europe. An enormous zone reaches from Poland across the Czech Republic, Slovakia, Hungary and deep into Russia. In the north it is distinguished by the cultivation of rye and oats and in the most fertile plains of the south by wheat and maize. The chernozem soils of the Ukraine are so rich that there has traditionally been a surplus of wheat there. It is used to feed large parts of central Russia, the inferior podsols of which produce only meagre harvests. Eastern Europe's climate is markedly continental. Thus, in north-eastern sections, agriculture is inhibited by long periods of freezing weather.

Generally speaking, in all four agrarian zones there is a neat equilibrium between cultivation and stock-raising. Districts that concentrate upon cattle are found in northern France, the Netherlands, Denmark, northern Germany and at higher Alpine elevations. It cannot be said that animal husbandry is restricted to territory that is less suited for agriculture because of poor soil quality and extreme altitude. Intensive cultivation and intensive stock-raising are frequently intertwined. Again, with respect to all four zones, vegetables and fruit are widely grown in more thickly settled and climatically favoured locations. As far as beef cattle are concerned, a distinction must be made between districts in which dairying prevails and others that focus upon feed and the production of meat. A belt in which dairying predominates stretches from northern France across the Netherlands to Poland. As a result of increasing mechanization the proportion of draught animals is dropping steadily; this has also had a tangible effect upon the growing of crops for stock feed.

3

Early Medieval Origins

The zenith of Europe's political, economic, and cultural hegemony was undoubtedly around the year 1900. Two world wars deeply undermined it. What were the reasons for the global predominance of a small continent? What forces shaped a Europe that brought the peoples of the planet closer to one another? Among the great nations of world history it was the Europeans who first brought about that unity of all mankind which is today the basic fact of earthly existence. Martial catastrophe and the rebirth of Europe's will to determine its destiny independently – thereby extricating itself from being trapped between two power blocs – raise the question of its historic roots. How could Europe become the centre of the civilized world, notwithstanding its modest foundations?

It is clear that Europe's rise to pre-eminence did not begin in the nineteenth century but rather in the Middle Ages, when the Occident proved capable of resisting the Byzantine Empire as well as other Near Eastern powers and began to develop its own form of civilization. More than a millennium passed before these events became politically relevant: it was only in the second half of the twentieth century that the problem of Europe's relationship to the Islamic world became critical. How was it possible for the wretched peoples who inhabited the north-western edge of Greater Asia in the Early Middle Ages to experience, from the High Middle Ages onward, an historically unique ascent to world domination and gradually to overshadow the brilliance of the spiritually and materially superior Islamic civilization?

The dynamism of Europe's economy, society and culture was not based merely upon cities and manifold endeavour in the realm of manufactures or trade, but also upon agriculture and the forces at work within the agrarian sector. The rise of European urban centres in the twelfth and thirteenth centuries, as well as the flowering of commerce and transportation, were preceded, strengthened and accelerated by important changes in the agrarian economy and rural society. But why, in High Medieval Europe, did a dense network of small and medium-sized towns arise? It is striking that this phenomenon did not occur in Islamic countries and in the territory of the Byzantine Empire, with which the Europeans maintained a lively exchange of goods! European cities were obviously based upon foundations that already existed in the feudal peasant environment of the Early Middle Ages and could not have arisen otherwise. The European town of the High Middle Ages developed within the context of a feudal society with which it was intimately linked in the person of an urban seignior. It was in the conflict between the burghers and their lord that the basic features of urban freedom evolved. The vigorous associative character of urban life – i.e., the activities of corporate bodies, especially craft guilds – and civic independence derived from older structures.

European towns of the High Middle Ages were able to unfold because of an amazing upsurge of the agrarian economy and tremendous growth in agricultural productivity. This meant that the expanding populations of towns could be supplied with the foodstuffs they required. The great extension of grain acreage and the overall intensification of soil tillage were in any case the elementary presuppositions for High Medieval urbanization. The shift in European agriculture to grain production was in the last analysis the reason for a powerful demographic concentration in long-inhabited landscapes and at the same time provided the human reservoir for migration to cities. From as early as the seventh century the settled territory of Europe increased steadily as the consequence of forest clearance and the breaking of virgin soil, a process that culminated in the twelfth and thirteenth centuries. The opening-up of new terrain and the population movements of this epoch shaped the character of Europe's peasant cultural landscape which existed for so long thereafter and only began to change as the result of the industrialization and urbanization of the nineteenth century. Thus European cities were able to develop within an intensively exploited agrarian environment: the evolution of Europe's rustics and the flowering of urban life were interrelated occurrences.

If we wish to broach the question of the spatial dimensions within which the medieval roots of the European peasantry took hold, we must look back mainly to the Frankish Empire. The Carolingian state was not merely the political centre of Early Medieval Europe; it also had an enduring effect upon the economic and social history of European countries. Elevated in AD 800 to the dignity of the *Imperium Francorum*, this polity was, as Josef Fleckenstein puts it, 'the connecting link between the divergent tribal kingdoms of the migratory Early Germans and – notwithstanding all the tensions and combat – the later, ever expanding collectivity of European peoples' that emerged on the territory or margins of the quondam Frankish entity.[12] The Carolingian Empire encompassed within its frontiers the main lands of the West and imparted to them common legal, economic and cultural traits. While the Frankish realm could not maintain its unity for very long, it was the matrix of the Occidental European community of nations, which in the course of succeeding centuries experienced further articulation.

Who were the peoples assembled by the Frankish rulers? On which regions did Frankish culture leave its mark? Let us glance first at the expansion that occurred under Kings Pepin and Charlemagne. Pepin conquered the last Saracen outposts in Septimania, brought all of ancient Gaul under his control by suppressing insurgency in Aquitania and was also able to prevail in the eastern parts of the realm. A tumultuous phase of empire-building ensued under Charlemagne, who subjected the Lombards and extended his influence across the states of the Church to southern Italy. Aquitania was firmly incorporated into his domains, and the Spanish March was established to ward off Islam. The fearsome Avars were surrounded from the west and the east. After Frankish suzerainty had been imposed upon them and the Alpine Slavs, the emperor reached out in the direction of the Balkans. The hardest challenge was the subjugation of Saxony, which could only be absorbed and forced to accept Frankish social and constitutional arrangements after years of brutal warfare. Further battles were fought in the north-east against the West Slavs and in the north against the Vikings in order to protect the empire against the assaults of the less evolved peoples who dwelt beyond Europe's momentary perimeter.

Charlemagne's empire reached its height around AD 800. It now included all of Gaul and Germany and extended via a system of border marches into both northern Spain and the Slavic east. By possessing the Lombard crown Charlemagne also ruled most of Italy. Thus he and his immediate successors controlled the main countries of modern Europe, i.e., France, Germany and Italy. England remained outside the Carolingian dominions but maintained close cultural and religious ties with them. These links proved useful to the Frankish monarchs in their effort to convert semi-pagan and heathen lands to Christianity. There were also various contacts with the Norsemen and the Slavs, which later brought both groups into the orbit of the Latin Church.

Charlemagne's coronation in Rome (AD 800) was one of the high points in the history of the full-blown Frankish Empire and at the same time illustrates the tense nature of its relationship to the neighbouring power of Byzantium. The bestowal of Roman dignity upon Charlemagne raised him above all other *regna* and created an *imperium* which from that time onward was Constantinople's direct rival. After long negotiations a compromise agreement was reached. Both governments had the right to claim the heritage of the ancient polity: the *imperium occidentale* was the counterpart of the *imperium orientale*. Charlemagne's domains were equivalent to the West which in turn corresponded to the sphere of the Latin Church. The correlation with Europe was complete: it was now a concept associated with the territory of the Carolingian Franks, which occupied the largest portion of the Continent (see map 2).

Diversity and homogeneity were from the beginning the two funda-mental principles of Europe. Both stem from the Carolingian state and

Map 2   The Carolingian Empire in the ninth century

apply to the period of its ascent as well as to that of its decline, which in the ninth and tenth centuries resulted in a division of the whole empire into several equal ones. Indeed, from the very time of its birth in the late fifth century the Frankish kingdom was a union that represented a medley of various peoples and regional entities. It encompassed not only Franks but also a number of other tribes and ethnic groups. Although the latter lost their political autonomy when they were incorporated into the Frankish realm, they preserved their legal identity; ancient common law codes also remained in effect.

In spite of this heterogeneity of tribes and regions, the Frankish state of the Carolingian era was a single entity, a reality that was expressed in different ways. Charlemagne's world-historical significance is not limited to territorial expansion and the conquest of new lands. A parallel phenomenon was his effort to accelerate the process of internal homogenization in order to impart to the empire's disparate structures a greater measure of unity. He took particular care to foster a collective approach in the fields of Church life and religion, in law and education, in the coinage system and trade, as well as in social and economic relationships. The rustic world and agriculture were also a focus of attention. Important common structures came into being, survived the empire's collapse, and affected the destiny of Europe's peasants for many centuries. The chief institutions were manorialism, the hide and feudalism, all of which, having originated in the central part of the Frankish realm, evince a pan-European character. Before proceeding to a detailed examination of Europe's agrarian system and the conditions of peasant life, it seems useful to offer certain observations about Western feudalism.

The wide-ranging concept of feudalism generally entails a close connection between the granting and possessing of fiefs and manorial relationships. In keeping with this linkage the feudal system involves not only the legal affiliation of feudal lords and their vassals but also the manorial order that applies to the dependent peasant population. Otto Hintze has characterized feudalism as a triad of military, political and socio-economic phenomena.[13] In his view feudalism had three functions. The first was to produce a well-trained, professional, warrior estate that was loyal to the ruler. The second was to engender a manorial economy that guaranteed the privileged warriors a work-free income. The third was to secure for such persons the exercise of local lordship. Thereby they could exercise paramount influence on a yet higher level of political association; the loose structure of the latter was in fact predestined for this. An economy in which most payments were made in kind and a poorly developed transport network like that of the Early Middle Ages favoured the rise of feudalism. Hintze maintains that these three functions were present in mature form only in the Frankish kingdom of Carolingian times and in the states that succeeded it in the High Middle Ages. Feudalism understood as encompassing the manorial peasant milieu belongs, along with capitalism and the European city, to those forces which many historians, sociologists and philosophers consider to have brought about the world-historical uniqueness of the Occident. The singularity of European rustics should likewise be viewed within the overall framework of Western feudal society.

Feudalism in the narrower sense of granting and receiving fiefs was undoubtedly an important structural ingredient of the Carolingian kingdom. The phenomenon originated in the centre of the Frankish realm and spread from there in one way or another across the West. In marginal territory it often did not include royal administrative districts, and it did not penetrate at all into the historically younger, eastern states of Poland and Hungary. Feudalism of this type reached Scandinavia in a more circumscribed way only in the High Middle Ages. From the mid-eighth century onward mounted warriors were increasingly prominent in the Frankish kingdom and became the veritable nucleus of its army. It was possible to maintain larger contingents of armoured cavalry only if the warriors were endowed with lands that provided them with an economic basis sufficient to defray the high costs of their equipment and to ensure their availability for military expeditions. This was the situation that created the fundamental attributes of feudal law. The feudal warrior, like the servile peasant, accepted the protection and entered the service of a lord (*commendatio*) and received land in compensation (*beneficium*). Just like the subject peasant on a manorial dominion, the feudal relationship involved both a personal and a material element.

Economically speaking, the Carolingian realm was overwhelmingly agrarian, and this meant that landed possessions played a great role in the organization of the state. Whoever sought to prevail or to become more effective politically had to have land and people at his disposal. This was the presupposition for establishing one's own comitatus, that is, a retinue of personal vassals. The Carolingians utilized the feudal system in order to bind the people who helped them govern the country as closely as possible to themselves. By Charlemagne's reign there were hardly any office-holders who were not feudally subordinate to the monarch. Dukes and counts, for their part, also had to rely upon vassals if they wished to maintain their positions and fulfil their duties to the Crown. Be this as it may, feudalism should not be seen merely as something that replaced the state. With

growing regionalization and the increasing weakness of kingship the autonomy of vassals became ever greater: this meant that the decentralizing
effect of feudalism was enhanced.

Manorial lordship was another significant phenomenon that arose in the
heartland of the Frankish kingdom and extended into neighbouring territories. From that era onward it was a factor that strongly influenced the
social and economic lives of the rustic population in most European
countries, and as such it endured for almost a thousand years. Along with
the hide, manorial lordship in its classical guise was a peculiarity of the
Western agrarian system and contributed fundamentally to the dynamism
of European agriculture. The term itself connotes a basic kind of rule, that
is, 'control over fellow human beings who dwell upon a specific parcel of
land and are therefore encompassed by the seigniory' (Friedrich Lütge).[14]
Manorial lordship is thus a form of dominion which concerns the relationship between someone who has power over land and the peasant who is
dependent upon him. The observation that this affiliation contains elements of mutuality by which the lord is obliged to afford shelter and
protection and the subservient peasant to provide counsel and help in no
wise justifies an idealized interpretation of their association. It was in fact
a relatively one-sided relationship of dependency; it was not a case of
voluntary divsion of labour. The antithesis of higher feudal proprietorship
and the peasant's right to exploit the soil in return for payments and
services led time after time to vehement argument and conflict between the
manorial lord and the ploughman.

Nevertheless, the relationship cannot be considered to have been an
arbitrary one. Nor can the rustic subservience of the Middle Ages be
equated with the slavery of the ancient world as it existed upon Roman
latifundia. Household law regulated the ties between the manorial lord and
the dependent peasant; individual cases were jointly decided by the seignior and rustic juries. A manorial lordship was normally endowed with
legal immunity and exercised judicial authority over the peasants who
resided within it. The rustic who possessed his own hide also enjoyed a
more or less autonomous position and was therefore quite distinct from the
slave of antiquity. The economic independence and the clearly perceptible
social activity of peasants who dwelt upon manorial lordships were essential components of European economic development.

Western manorial lordship sprang primarily from two sources: the
Roman legacy of an agrarian order rooted in landed property and a primeval Germanic one characterized more by personal relationships of patronage and clientage. This was the matrix of the unique economic and

seigniorial constitution produced by the Frankish kingdom of the sixth to
ninth centuries. It was a set of arrangements that assumed concrete shape
in a variety of magnitudes and in different forms of organization, legal
codes and economic activity. The archetype of Early Medieval manorial
lordship was what German scholars call the 'villatic system', a dual appor-
tionment of land (*domaine bipartite*) that is often labelled 'classical manorial
lordship'. Its chief feature was the centrality of the servile labour farm
(*villa*), a demesne whose soil (*terra salica*) was worked with the help of the
lord's own domestics and his tenants, that is, the peasants who occupied
hide-type farmsteads (*mansi*). Since servile labour farms differed in size and
economic structure, the extent of compulsory rustic services also varied.
The holdings of magnates were more tightly managed; servile labour land
was divided into primary and subsidiary farms. Bigger manorial lordship
precincts were likewise split into servile labour units supervised by *villici,
maiores* or *iudices*. The tenants and the unfree domestics of seigniorial farms
were lumped together in a manorial or household association, the *familia*,
and were both subject to manorial jurisdiction.

The genesis of the bipartite farming system, that is, classical manorial
lordship, is an interesting question. Where and under what conditions did
this system originate? The most convincing explanation has been provided
by Alfred Verhulst.[15] According to him, the servile labour farm, characterized by an interweaving of the lord's demesne and peasant hides, arose
above all in the fertile grain countryside of northern France and more
generally in the territory between the Loire and the Rhine during the
seventh and eighth centuries; it then spread, in varying degrees, to neighbouring regions. Verhulst maintains that this type of manorial lordship
was an innovation of the Early Middle Ages and had no connection with
the organization of Roman landed estates; favourable geographical circumstances, particularly soil well suited to grain cultivation, fostered the
system's growth in the Frankish heartland. Economic decisions made by
the Carolingians clearly contributed to its expansion. As already noted,
classical manorial lordship prevailed in the central part of the Frankish
realm that lay between the Loire and the Rhine. It extended in the eighth
and ninth centuries to adjacent districts and proved to be astonishingly
flexible and adaptable. The classical system coexisted in many regions with
other versions of manorial lordship, above all, the rental income seigniory,
the chief feature of which was payment in money and kind.

Closely linked to Early Medieval manorial lordship was the hide system;
it too became a major feature of Europe's agrarian structure. Peasants who
were dependents of a servile labour farm resided upon plots of their own

large enough to support them. The hide or *mansus* was thus defined as the standard endowment of a seigniorially dependent peasant; it consisted of a house, outbuildings, cultivable land and pasturage, as well as associated rights to utilize forest and meadow commons. The *mansus* and the hide were not originally of equal size, but with the passage of time they became identical within the context of the manor. Linguistic practice varied from one place to another, and so *mansus* and hide did not always have the same meaning. Diverse legal relationships and the particular status of the hide occupant within a manorial community played an important role: there was frequently a distinction between free hides (*mansi iugenuiles*) and servile ones (*mansi serviles*). It is calculated that the usual size of a hide was 30 rods (10 hectares). However, one must take into account the fact that the dimensions of a hide reflected the nature and quality of the soil and therefore differed from district to district.

The fundamental fact is that the hide constituted an autonomous farmstead within the manorial environment: the ploughman was given enough land to maintain himself and simultaneously allowed to work it freely. The norm was a full hide. Although only one part of the peasantry possessed this kind of plot, it long served as a model. The hide system gradually spread from its Carolingian nucleus mainly towards the east and the north; it penetrated strongly into some regions and less so into others. Its expansion was closely related to the growth of manorial lordship, and it was undoubtedlty promoted by the Frankish monarchs. According to Walter Schlesinger, Charlemagne, animated by the example of large monasteries, pursued a general policy of subdividing royal and ecclesiastical possessions into hides.[16]

Systematic notations in the records of different Church manors about the total size of holdings are expressed in terms of hides. A case in point is the *Brevium exempla* of the diocese of Augsburg from about AD 810 which lists 1427 occupied and 80 unoccupied hides (*Monumenta Germaniae Historica*, Cap. I, 128). Statistics of this kind, prepared by important Frankish ecclesiastical institutions in the form of polyptychs and hide registries, may be based in part upon the emperor's initiative. It seems likely that the government was promoting a more or less uniform assessment of cultivable land in the hands of rustic tenants in order to achieve an overview of the economic capacity of the realm. The basic unit of measurement was the hide, the term used to describe the average peasant farmstead. It was supposed to serve not only as the cornerstone for computing payents and services due to the manorial lord but also as the basic unit for general taxation purposes. Charlemagne likewise attempted to utilize the hide system for codifying the military obligations of the free population. Whoever personally disposed of three to five hides had to go to war himself; individuals whose possessions were smaller than that had to form muster committees and, as the need arose, collectively outfit a warrior (MGH, Cap. I, 48).

Even if the current status of research does not permit us to gauge the exact extent of Charlemagne's role in the establishment of the hide system, it is still clear that it spread rapidly in the Carolingian era and became a norm for peasant landholding. It also retained its importance in post-Carolingian times. Although many hides were subdivided as a consequence of demographic growth during the High Middle Ages and the quarter-hide became the standard peasant farmstead in fertile, long-settled regions, the hide itself remained the basic conceptual criterion. In places where field systems were more or less uniform, it lasted – in part at least – down to the eighteenth century. Within the context of High Medieval colonization, and especially in conjunction with the settlement of eastern lands, the function of the hide was crucial: it was a major consideration when lords handed out farmsteads to peasant families. Virgin territory was generally split into hides. The dimensions varied according to the provenance of the settlers or the colonial entrepreneurs: villages were laid out as either forest or marshland hides. Partition of naturally open terrain into hides was especially common in the eastern regions colonized by the Germans and served as an example for adjacent Eastern European countries. The practice of using the hide as a standard unit of surface measurement for assessing the value of peasant holdings, having originated in the Carolingian empire, persisted in many Central European states until much later.

The landed possessions of the king, the nobility, and clerical institutions were scattered throughout all of the Carolingian dominions. Larger manors were equipped not only with farms that raised cattle and grain but also with workshops manned by serfs who provided the lord with whatever he needed in the way of handicrafts. Many seigniors also possessed vineyards and so did not have to resort to the market-place for their wine. Charlemagne's famed *Capitulare de villis* tells us much about farming organization and management in the royal domains. The multifarious crown lands were divided into fiscal pracincts and *villae* grouped around servile labour farms administered by *villici*.

While we know little about the holdings of the nobility or about the life of peasants subject to seigniorial rule because of the poverty of the sources, the land and revenue inventories of certain great monasteries give us an excellent idea of the organization of their possessions and of rustic social structure on ecclesiastical manors. The renowned polyptychon of Abbot Irmino of St Germain-des-Près outside Paris, dating from the early ninth century, gives us the best and most detailed account that we have of a great Carolingian monastic domain. It contains an exact description of the division of the monastery's vast lands into servile labour farms and the peasant hides attached to them.[17] Also informative is the polyptychon (account-book) of St Bertin from the middle of the ninth century: it documents conditions on a monastic manor in Flanders.[18] The individual chapters of this registry depict minutely the principal components of a Carolingian manorial lordship that controlled over 11,000 hectares of land: the total circumference of the *villae*, the extent of *terra salica*, the number and size of farmsteads and the services owed by the peasants. Statistical analysis of the abbey's twelve *villae* shows that every servile labour farm averaged ten and a half hides or roughly 105 hectares. In each case the mean was eighteen and a half peasant farmsteads (*mansi*); hence, the ratio of the demesne to peasant hides was about one to two.

Whereas St Bertin lay in the Carolingian heartland, the Abbey of Staffelsee was located in the Alemannic border diocese of Augsburg. The so-called 'Staffelsee Inventory' (MGH, Cap. I, 128) from the early ninth century also describes the structure of a classical manorial lordship that engaged in large-scale seigniorial farming and included rustic hides whose obligatory services were entirely devoted to the monastery's economic activity. The main farm, situated on an island, encompassed 740 'workday' units of land measurement and amounted to an impressive 250 odd hectares. It embraced a total of forty-two hides that had to render very onerous services because of the extent to which the monastery was involved in farming. It is simply amazing how many buildings, implements and cattle the farm possessed: the figure of twenty-six draught oxen is indicative. The *villa* of Staffelsee also disposed of several buildings that served economic functions and a women's house (*genitum*) in which twenty-four maidservants wove textiles for their clerical lords.

In other parts of the Frankish realm the villatic system was far less developed than on the domains described above. This was as true of the Saxon territory only recently added to the empire as of the Mediterranean zones in southern France and northern Italy. In marginal regions the rental income seigniory tended to prevail, and even within the Frankish heartland in the vicinity of servile labour farms there were numerous small peasant farms that operated on their own. Thus the structure of the agrarian economy was more complex than might appear to be the case at first glance. Because we have more information about them and because they were more efficient, the huge *villae* seem to have taken centre stage, but the realities were somewhat different. The Manorial relationships similar to those in the Carolingian dominions could also be found in neighbouring countries, albeit in a less pronounced form. In Spain manorial structures were based upon late Roman and Visigothic institutions and evolved further under Moorish and Frankish influence. In Italy the demesne was less important than in the lands north of the Alps; at a very early stage rustic payments in money and kind played a major role. The rise of cities and the revival of trade were beginning to weaken the manorial order already in the tenth century. In England the forms of manorial lordship resembled those on the Continent, but, generally speaking, landed estates were more loosely organized prior to the Norman conquest of 1066. The lord worked one portion of the soil – the demesne – while the other was farmed by villeins understood for the most part as legally free persons who owed manorial services.

The lands to the north and east of the Frankish Empire and the peoples who inhabited them were distinguished for a long time by more venerable forms of peasant life and less by the structures of manorial lordship that had emerged in the central part of Europe. In Scandinavia rural society was characterized by medium and large-sized peasant farmsteads; the peasant cultivated the odal, i.e., land that he had inherited from his forefathers, or plots that he leased from others. Apart from the big estates of kings and Viking princes, there was nothing like a manorial lordship inhabited by dependent peasants. Around AD 900 Carolingian influence ended east of a line that ran from the Baltic island of Rügen down the Elbe and the Saale and into the eastern Alps and the Adriatic. In the tenth and eleventh centuries the line was crossed on a broad front, and the Slavs, Magyars and other peoples who dwelt beyond it were affected by the practices of the Occidental heartland. The social and economic order of the Slavic countryside can only be dimly perceived because of the paucity of historical sources; the material culture of settled cultivators in these regions has only come to light with the help of archaeology. The social system of what were relatively underpopulated rural landscapes was marked by patriarchal relationships. Only gradually did more advanced forms of lordship come into being. For the most part the process began in Poland, the Czech lands, Croatia, Serbia and Russia during the ninth century.

Between the ninth and the eleventh centuries manorial lordship became more common and firmly established. Its expansion meant that free peasants found themselves increasingly dependent upon secular and clerical seigniors. The steps that Charlemagne took with respect to the economic

1   *Farm work month by month, represented in an almanac from Salzburg made about 818*

and military functions of the simple freemen who peopled the Carolingian dominions suggest that initially the numerical strength of this type of peasant remained substantial. The growth of manorial lordship that continued within the Carolingian successor states was greatly fostered by the opening-up of new lands, a process that transpired rapidly in many European countries in conjunction with a demographic explosion. The manorial lords organized new servile labour farms, settled their bondsmen on indi-

vidual plots, and supervised the exploitation of virgin soil; the physical
tasks of land clearance were handed over to the ploughmen. Although the
extension of cultivation was a pan-European phenomenon that may be seen
all the way from the Mediterranean world to Scandinavia, colonization
developed most strongly in the northern Alpine regions of the Frankish
Empire, in which immense forests and remote rural zones still offered
many an opportunity for new settlements. The individual phases of this
great movement can only be elucidated by means of arduous scholarly
research on the history of small areas. After temporary stagnation owing to
the Viking and Magyar incursions, a new wave of land clearance began
towards the end of the tenth century. In the High Middle Ages this led in
practically all European countries to an enormous expansion of agriculturally exploited terrain.

The tremendous extension of cultivation in the nuclear regions of the
Frankish Empire – that is, in France and Germany – unquestionably
enhanced the economic power of northern Alpine zones, which were
opened up primarily on an agrarian basis. The decay of ancient urban
culture and the increasing significance of agriculture meant that central
Europe with its spacious grain-fields supplanted the historical functions
of the Mediterranean world. The employment of new agrarian technology
in the form of improved ploughs, more efficient hitching devices and
fresh ways of working the soil served above all to foster economic progress
in the central part of the Frankish realm. Whereas the Mediterranean
countries stuck to traditional methods of cultivation and crop sequences,
the more rational three-field system had prevailed in the north since
the Carolingian era; it spread gradually to other regions in succeeding
centuries.

In the course of an economic process that particularly involved the
agrarian sector, Europe's centre of gravity shifted from the Mediterranean
lands to the territory north of the Alps. The nucleus of the Carolingian
Empire was the region between the Loire and the Rhine and the
Carolingian successor states of France and Germany which, along with
England, later became the principal countries of the West. The gravita-
tional displacement from the south to the formerly barbarian lands of the
north was certainly also caused by the loss of the Mediterranean world's
economic cohesion, a consequence of the wave of Islamic conquest that
began around AD 750. Henri Pirenne has heavily stressed this point.[19] Lynn
White[20] has explained the incipient superiority of north-western Europe
over the south primarily in terms of technological innovation. In his view,
the use of new ploughs made possible the tilling of the heavier soils of the

lands north of the Alps, and the extension of the three-field system meant an increase in the products needed to feed a growing population. Hence, he maintains, the power centre of Europe's economy from the Carolingian period onward lay in the broad plains of north-western Europe. The problems with the White thesis are that the so-called medieval agrarian revolution is set at too early a point in time and technology is seen in too isolated a context. Agrarian economic advances can only be understood as one facet of Europe's overall historical evolution. However, the American author is correct in pointing out that Europe's hub was transferred from the south to the north and from the old lands of the Mediterranean to the Transalpine plains.

Be this as it may, we must in fact emphasize the social, economic and political forces that conditioned Europe's gradual rise to cultural pre-eminence in the Early and High Middle Ages. Manorial lordship, the hide system and the slowly crystallizing village community, along with the Western version of feudalism, were crucial factors in the process of medieval social evolution. Marxian historical scholarship is at least partly correct in stressing that feudal dynamism was the reason for medieval economic development. Conflicts between feudal lords and dependent peasants for a fair division of material goods accelerated economic progress; thus, feudalism must be regarded as the chief impulse of European economic expansion. For their part, demographers have argued that economic development and colonization were due to an increase in population that began in the Early Middle Ages. In so far as the demographic factor is separated from other historical forces, it is hardly an adequate explanation for the overall process.

In his study of economic and social development in the Early Middle Ages, Georges Duby has also broached the fundamental question of the reasons for growth. After weighing various factors he concludes that the pressure exerted by manorial lords upon servile peasants was the motor of expansion. Because of seigniorial encouragement peasant productivity was greatly augmented, and agrarian economic activity intensified altogether.[21] Undoubtedly, Early Medieval manorial lordship had a significant impact upon the economic evolution of the Occident. Seigniorial dynamism, which especially manifested itself in the establishment of servile labour farms, led to a perceptible acceleration of agrarian production. Within the cadre of Western manorial lordship, the rustic who occupied a hide enjoyed a relatively high degree of autonomy and was able to engage in an intensive form of economic activity. The creative tension engendered by the relationship of seigniorial and communal forces was especially evident in the judicial system of the domains: lords and peasants jointly laid legal disputes to rest.

It can thus be said that Europe's peasants, notwithstanding ties to the manor, disposed of a considerable measure of legal and economic freedom and were therefore quite distinct from the oppressed fellahin of the Islamic world. Within the framework of Early Medieval manorial lordship there was born an autonomous, economically orientated type of ploughman who also evinced a special work ethic. The great medieval work of settlement, the matrix of Europe's cultural landscape, was in the last analysis the achievement of the peasantry. It is difficult to judge to what extent the rural work ethic was influenced by Christianity. In any case, it is certain that the medieval Church invented a religious work ethic in which labour was hallowed not just externally, but also considered of moral worth in the sense of participation in God's act of creation. High evaluation of work was an outstanding trait of monasticism and could be encountered particularly on the manors of religious orders, where peasants and clerics were in frequent contact with one another. Max Weber sharply underlined the importance of the monastic work ethic in the formation of Europe's economic attitudes: the friar of the Middle Ages was 'the first human being of the epoch who lived rationally and methodically pursued a rational goal, namely, life in the Hereafter'.[22] The daily regimen of monks was systematically divided into hours of prayer and of labour, and the economic side of monastic life was also carefully planned. The rational economic management of religious establishments was particularly evident in the case of the twelfth-century Cistercians: they were so energetic that some scholars have claimed to discern in their manifold activities features of the early capitalist, entrepreneurial mentality. With this observation we have reached the High Middle Ages, which represent the first high point in the history of Europe's peasants.

4

Prosperity in the High Middle Ages

Historians believe that the social position of Europe's peasant population during the High Middle Ages was extremely favourable overall. The Austrian scholar, Alfons Dopsch, described the conditions of rural life at that time as follows:

This era was the period in which the peasant estate flourished . . . However, the mighty forward steps taken by German rustics also served to promote the economic breakthrough that occurred on large landed estates. The great secular and ecclesiastical seigniories exploited progress in the peasant world as a solid foundation for an expanding agrarian economy. The counterpart of German peasant advancement was the aulic culture fostered by manorial lords of princely rank who now disposed of the economic resources required for such purposes.[23]

The social historian, Robert Fossier, recently assessed the position of French peasants during the twelfth and thirteenth centuries in an equally positive fashion: 'None the less, I doubt that I am exaggerating if I say that up to the late nineteenth century – that is, at the very height of rural France's greatness around 1900 – the peasantry had not yet recovered the equilibrium that distinguished it during its initial, two medieval centuries of brilliance.'[24]

Do these positive readings of the status of European ploughmen in the High Middle Ages actually correspond to the facts? Do not the judgements of many historians amount to an overly idyllic picture of the conditions of rural existence in a society in which the great mass of the population continued to be subject in a variety of ways to manorial lords both secular and ecclesiastical? What impulses and changes in circumstances seem to justify the conclusion that the situation of peasants had in fact improved from the Early to the High Middle Ages, that is, from the time of Charlemagne to the era in which modern states began to emerge? We should not allow the grandeur of medieval churches and cathedrals and the magnificence of many a castle and city to mislead us into equating this superficial glory with the social life of rustics, all the more so because we know from the history of many lands and epochs that urban wealth and rural poverty tend to go hand in hand. Before we treat these critical questions it seems appropriate to mention some of the main factors that brought about change in the agrarian world of the High Middle Ages. To be sure, we must first discuss the question of whether it is possible in the first place to speak of a homogeneous European peasantry, in view of the great diversity of legal, social and economic conditions among the country population of the High Middle Ages.

By the beginning of the eleventh century the homogeneity of Western civilization was an established fact. Although the greater Frankish Empire had dissolved into several fractional realms and countries, Europe consti-tuted a whole, thanks to its common cultural, spiritual and political heritage. However, its unity was multilayered and consisted of a mixture of components, especially allegiance to Christianity, the all-encompassing authority of the Church hierarchy as well as traditional judicial and consti-tutional paradigms. Then there were the commonalities of social and economic life, such as feudalism, manorial lordship and the nobility, all of Carolingian provenance. On one hand, the uniformity of the rural social world rested upon analogous types of seigniorial dependency among the great mass of the population and, on the other, upon the congruous lifestyle and everyday customs of the peasantry.

Around the mid-eleventh century one can gradually discern forces, the consolidation of which was destined to give birth to a High Medieval corporate order determined by individual descent and social function: it consisted above all of knights, peasants and burghers. Rural social and legal relationships within the manorial cadre were by now much the same; the many gradations of formerly unfree status had produced a relatively uniform, if internally differentiated, peasant estate. Utilizing the proce-dures of household law, manorial lords had enegetically fostered the as-similation and levelling-off of the diverse rustic groups that inhabited their domains. Old-fashioned bondsmen, who now generally occupied and farmed plots of their won, rose to the condition of rustics with obligations rooted in the soil and were hardly distinct from the quondam legally free peasants who, for their part, had become the dependants of manorial lords. The social groups who lived on a manor, with their hodge-podge of rights and duties, slowly coalesced into a subordinate peasantry; the vestiges of outright slavery from the Roman and barbarian past vanished completely. The formation of knightly and peasant estates created the feudal, corporate society that was the hallmark of the High Medieval rural world. However, this phenomenon was not restricted to the old Carolingian heartland – that is, France, Germany and Italy – but also included neighbouring countries. A strict feudal system was imposed upon England and southern Italy as the result of Norman conquests; Spain was affected by the stage-by-stage progress of the *reconquista*; and German colonists put their stamp upon the eastern parts of Central Europe. In all of these instances domestic forms of lordship intermingled with extraneous structures and impulses.

The gradually unfolding uniform traits of Europe's peasantry should not lead us into ignoring the diversity of geographical circumstances that remained as relevant as ever. Inasmuch as peasant families and communities were often situated in remote places and villages that were barely in touch with the outside world, local and regional differences played a significant role, all the more so because of the inherent qualities of the rural setting. As a consequence of the peasant's close link with the realm of nature, heterogeneity of climate, soils, altitude and land-forms had a powerful impact upon the social and economic relationships of country folk, more in any event than was the case in the urban milieu. The influence of nature upon agriculture and peasant life in the Middle Ages was also much stronger, owing to an agrarian technology that was little developed in comparison with that of modern times. In considering the effect of geography upon the rural economy of High Medieval Europe three particular zones must be distinguished, namely, coastal, interior and mountainous terrain. Atlantic coastal belts were generally too moist for the cultivation of grain, and this meant that pasturage and cattle-raising prevailed. In mountainous regions – from the Pyrenees across the Massif Central to the elevated country of central Germany, from the Apennines across the Alps to the Carpathians – there were likewise relatively few areas suitable for grain crops; on the other hand, vast forests and broad meadowlands offered other kinds of agrarian opportunity. The enormous intermediate zone encompassed the great river valleys and plains that reached from southern England to Russia, for example, the northern German lowlands and similar terrain in eastern Europe, where there were simply vast tracts of cultivable land.

As far as the peasantry is concerned, the four larger expanses mentioned before may be distinguished within High Medieval Europe: the Mediterranean, the western and central heartland, Eastern Europe and Scandinavia. The Mediterranean zone extended from the Iberian peninsula across southern France and Italy to the southern Balkans: it was ideal country for viticulture, fruit trees, and southern, cultivated fruit but required good irrigation systems because of low or nonexistent summer rainfall. In the north-western part of the central zone the cultivation of grain became increasingly significant during the High Middle Ages and put its stamp upon a peasant economy that was normally characterized by a combination of soil tillage and cattle-raising. On the plains of Eastern Europe grain likewise became more important; however, in Scandinavia – that is, Denmark, Norway and Sweden – peasants devoted themselves to stock-raising.

The diversity that marked European peasant life in the High Middle Ages also reflected the uneven evolution of different regions. Much of the east and the north was only in an incipient stage of development around AD 1000; the peoples and tribes who dwelt there shifted to locally stabilized forms of agricultural enterprise relatively late. The Eastern European countries exhibited a broadly meshed, spatially scattered pattern of clustered farmstead and village settlements after the zone was caught up in the colonization wave of the High Middle Ages and subjected to intensive exploitation. The Mediterranean zone, which was much more developed, offers a sharp contemporaneous contrast. Its outstanding features were: the ancient agricultural practices of intensively farmed, landed estates, written leases, and a dense network of roads and market towns. Thus it can be said that an east–west line of development traversed a north–south gradient. The antithesis of more and less developed regions was the reason for chronological disparity in the evolution of Europe's agrarian economy. This dichotomy also explains the fact that the greatest and most enduring progress occurred in those regions that were initially the most retrograde. Let us cite the example of the Slavic districts to the east of the Elbe: the changes that took place there, owing to technological improvements, were the most revolutionary of all.

However, it was not only the east Elbe territories but the whole of Europe that passed through an amazing era of expansion and progress in the social, economic and cultural realms. The most obvious changes were a demographic explosion and the opening up of virgin land. According to the calculations of Josiah Russell,[25] population rose from 38.5 million in AD 1000 to 73.5 in 1340; this amounted to a numerical doubling. Differences in ratios between individual regions are noteworthy. Whereas the southern European countries – Iberia, Italy, Greece and the Balkans – increased from 17 to 25 million, the population of Western and Central Europe – chiefly, France, Germany and England – surged from 12 to 35.5 million; that is, it expanded by almost 300 per cent. These data tell us that north-western and Central Europe developed at a rapid pace and thus came to form the Continent's new centre of economic gravity, whereas the Mediterranean countries obviously lost ground. The populations of Scandinavia and Eastern Europe remained comparatively small by the end of the High Mediaeval growth phase.

Population increase was accompanied by a torrent of internal colonization and its concomitant of land clearance in every European country. Thus the High Middle Ages constituted an era in which the cultural face of the countryside was fundamentally altered. The landscape took on an appearance that it would retain for centuries. Exploitation of virgin terrain was especially pronounced in some areas as opposed to others. The structure of settlement in Central Europe was particularly affected. The expansion of cultivated land in long-inhabited regions went hand-in-hand with systematic peasant colonization of places newly open to agrarian enterprise. The pioneers who ventured into the mountains of the central zone had to chop down many forests, whereas the peasants who fought their way into coastal and potamic marshlands could only wrest agriculturally usable soil from waterlogged sites by constructing drainage networks and dikes. Traces of this gigantic work of settlement can be found in the epithets of many villages, in place-names with suffixes such as *-bourg* in Normandy, *-bastide* in south-western France, and *-berg*, *-rode* or *-reuth* in Germany. Even today the planned character of some localities is obvious, particularly marshland hide, forest hide and single-street villages by virtue of their systematic layout.

The expansion of settlement in Spain was decisively influenced by the *reconquista*, that is, the recovery by force of arms of those portions of the Iberian peninsula occupied by the Moors. It is difficult to say whether the repopulation of vast regions of western and central Spain occurred because they had previously lost almost all their inhabitants. Waves of colonization from Galicia, initiated by Christian rulers and the Church, had a lasting effect; many pioneers proceeded from the north-west into the interior of the peninsula. To the east French peasants bore the brunt of the work of resettlement. The great demand for human beings led to a marked improvement in the legal status of peasants. Often the act of acquiring land and cultivating it anew corresponded to a hereditary transfer of possession;

Castilian peasants in particular were the recipents of generous liberties in
the form of so-called *poblaciones*.

In keeping with the bipartite division of France into the flood plains of
the north and the high plateaux of the south, which fall within the
Mediterranean climate zone, it is not surprising that the process of internal
colonization was characterized by a diversity of forms and chronological
stages. In the north, the Paris basin and the broad Loire valley belonged to
those favoured regions in which peasants were quick to clear the land. A
new surge of settlement began in the late twelfth century, when various
southern French feudatories set about extending their domains. Systematic
planning thus led to the foundation of numerous new villages known in
the central part of the south as *bastides* and in the south-west as *sauvetés*. The
privileges granted to the rustics who cleared the land contributed in a
major way to the emancipation of the rural population and to the diminution of manorial prerogatives.

The pan-European character of the powerful settlement wave of the
High Middle Ages is also evident in the case of German colonization of the
Continent's eastern tier, a subject that – unhappily – was long studied
mainly from a nationalistic perspective. The fact of the matter is that this
movement, with respect to the techniques employed in opening up new
territories and establishing peasant colonies, took place in accordance with
the same basic patterns seen elsewhere in High Medieval Europe. Extensive
clearance and village construction occurred not only east of the Elbe but
also in the neighbouring lands of Eastern Europe. Especially in Poland
many new localities were founded under the aegis of Germanic law (*jus
theutonicum*), something which has less to do with German settlers than
with the application of a Western European legal model. However, the
kings and feudal lords of Poland, Bohemia and Hungary vigorously sought
to attract peasants from the West in order to accelerate the exploitation of
their underdeveloped territories.

German colonization of the east was an extremely complex phenomenon
with regard to both the course of events and the historical sequel. The
process transpired over a long period of time, during which various German legal, economic and cultural institutions were exported to the regions
east of the Elbe and the Saale. The step-by-step expansion of the border
marches along the Elbe and the Saale in the tenth century laid the foundations for later eastward movement. However, actual settlement by peasants
began only in the twelfth century when territorial rulers, noblemen and
ecclesiastical seigniors systematically recruited persons willing to sign up
as colonizers in return for advantageous conditions upon their arrival in the

new lands. The purpose of opening up new terrain was to enhance and extend the power of the different lords in question. There was not the slightest hint of ethnic political calculation. Proof of this is the fact that Slavic princes made special efforts to lure experienced peasants from the long-settled regions of Germany and the Netherlands. Many colonists therefore trekked from densely populated areas of Flanders, Holland and Westphalia to the country between the central Elbe, the Erzgebirge and Lower Lusatia. Using techniques of swamp drainage and forest clearance that they had learned back on their native turf, they laid a solid basis for a remunerative agrarian economy in the newly founded settlements. In the contractual agreements which territorial rulers and manorial lords concluded with prospective colonists the most prominent figure is the so-called 'locator', an entrepreneur whose job it was to enlist settlers, negotiate with the relevant seignior, parcel out the assigned terrain and supervise the building of farms. The locator was often recompensed with a larger, rent-free, hide type of farmstead, as well as certain special rights, especially the lucrative office of justice of the peace. The new settlers were enticed with offers of favourable terms of landholding, exemption from all sorts of territorial imposts and numerous legal concessions appropriate to local circumstances.

In the territory east of the Saale and in the central Elbe region peasant colonization picked up speed from the twelfth century onward. Hollanders and Lowland Dutchmen peopled the northern zones, Hessians and Thuringians settled farther to the south, and stately farms and villages soon dotted the countryside. The peasant farming unit of one Frankish hide (*c.* 25 hectares) which became the norm, spread across Upper Saxony and Silesia and penetrated deeply into Poland. One can tell from place names and the physical characteristics of localities that Slavs continued to exercise some influence during the period of German dominion. Still, the large, regularly laid-out, single-street villages are generally of German provenance; the agrarian land of these places often consists of three big fields subdivided into hides. German colonization of what became the trans-Elbian March of Brandenburg got under way mainly after the Wendish Crusade of 1147. The organizers were the Margraves of Brandenburg and the Archbishops of Magdeburg, as well as other clerical and secular feudal lords: the peasant settlers came mostly from the neighbouring eastern part of Lower Saxony, but others arrived on the scene from Flanders and Holland. The native Slavic inhabitants were co-opted for the work of enlarging the cultivated area at an early stage and their fields adapted to the requirements of the new agrarian structure. Thus there was an intermingling of German and Slavic elements, which can also be seen in other settlement districts east of the Elbe.

Apart from Silesia, where colonization started at an early date, the mass immigration of German peasants to Poland started only in the thirteenth century; it especially affected the western regions of the Slavic realm. The German ploughmen were encouraged to come by princes, monastic lords and noblemen who wanted them to make uninhabited or thinly populated tracts of land arable and thereby increase agricultural productivity. The Bishop of Poznań (Posen) received authorization in 1246 from the Prince of Greater Poland to substitute German for Slavic law in villages on diocesan territory and to transfer lower-level jurisdiction to episcopally appointed local magistrates. Numerous special privileges granted to locators in the Poznań area and in other parts of Poland bear witness to the initiatives of many manorial lords in refounding villages according to the principles of German law. These documents contain the following provisions: nomination of the locator, assignment of land according to hides, use of the three-field system and hereditary attachment of peasants to their farms. The German settlers made their way from Silesia into much of Little Poland and even got as far as the high-lying valleys of the Beskids.

In the adjacent territories of Bohemia and Moravia, which had been parts of the Holy Roman Empire since the tenth century, intensive colonization started in the twelfth century. Initially, both native and foreign countrymen were settled upon manors belonging to the nobility and religious orders. German immigration hardly affected the already well-populated Bohemian heartland. However, the forested heights which encircled it and which up to then had been largely deserted were cleared and resettled: the Bohemian Forest, the southern slopes of the Krušné hory (Erzgebirge/Ore Mountains), and the southern margin of the Sudetes now became staple features of Europe's cultural landscape. In neighbouring Moravia the extension of cultivation carried out with the help of German colonists was likewise deliberately fostered by secular and clerical seigniors. Here the goal was not only to found new farming villages but also to attract miners in order to exploit the region's mineral riches. The far-reaching transformation of so much European countryside that has just been outlined must be seen in the context of the overall expansion of Europe in the High Middle Ages. After the tenth century the Continent was free of alien invaders; no external foe threatened its pacific development. The regions occupied by the Northmen and the Hungarians were incorporated into the Western Christian world. Poles, Czechs, Croats and other Slavic peoples had been converted to the Latin Church, and the heathens of Scandinavia were about to be. Without any doubt, by the end of the first millennium, the continuity of Western civilization was assured. In the future the Occident would not be subject to the kind of danger and aggression faced by Russia during the centuries of Tartar rule or by India after the Muslims had come upon the scene. Indeed, the opposite was true. A strenghtened Europe itself engaged in conquest and *reconquista*, extended the scope of its power beyond its traditional frontiers and enlarged the realm in which its version of lordship, its type of economy and its civilization prevailed. New regions were added to Europe when the Moors were pushed back towards the southern part of the Iberian peninsula; the Normans recovered territory in Sicily for the Christian world. In Eastern Europe and in the Baltic, where the borders were still fluid, Latin Catholics confronted Greek Ortho-dox-influenced peoples or still pagan tribal societies, who in the course of the thirteenth century were persuaded to accept the true faith by means of swords wielded by Teutonic knights. The most potent manifestation of European expansionism was the Crusades, which began in 1096 and amounted to an Occidental counterattack against Islam; between 1204 and 1216 there was even a Latin Empire on the soil of Byzantium.

The High Medieval extension of settlement and Europe's economic boom were facilitated by significant progress in the methods of farm management and in agrarian technology. Peasants now had more modern implements, more effective hitching devices for draft animals and improved ways of tilling the soil. The result was a major increase in agricultural productivity, which in turn meant enough food for a growing population. The nutritional advances were so impressive that Jacques Le Goff has been able to argue that 'the spread of the three-field system and bigger yields of protein-rich vegetables were the factors responsible for the diffusion of Christianity, land clearance, the rise of the cities, the construction of cathedrals, and the Crusades.'[26]

As far as technology is concerned, the most important innovation was the two-handled garden plough. It dug deeper furrows, broke up the earth better, and was more much effective with heavier soil than the old stick plough had been. Improved working of the soil promoted metabolism within its uppermost layer and led to higher yields. Because of the en-hanced pulling power of beasts, ploughs, harrows and other field imple-ments could now be employed more effectively; new harnesses in the form of leather horse-collars and head-yokes for oxen led to an increase in the performance of draught animals. Horses could transport burdens over greater distances than before, and peasants were able to get their work done much faster. At the same time the introduction of new wagons, linked to

2　　*Women sowing and harvesting corn, illustrated in a twelfth-century manu-*
script of A Mirror for Maidens (Speculum virginis)

improved drawing capacity, allowed teamsters to carry heavier loads: at the
beginning of the twelfth century the large, four-wheeled wagon came into
use and supplemented the older, simple, two-wheeled cart.

　　The use of iron in the manufacture of work tools became more common.
Important parts of ploughs, spades and cutting implements now tended to
be made from it. The scythe was used for harvesting grain, but there was
still a role for the smaller sickle, which required less iron and damaged ripe
stalks less. Also of no small importance was the spread of water-mills,

3 A beam harrow and a team of horses. The peasant sowing drives away rooks
with a catapult (Luttrell Psalter, made in East Anglia about 1340)

though they were found primarily on estates belonging to great manorial
lords. With the extension of cultivation during the twelfth and thirteenth
centuries the number of mills grew steadily; in the water-rich regions of
Western and Central Europe practically every village ended up by having
one. The mills made it possible to grind grain much more rapidly and
effectively than had been the case with old-fashioned hand models.

Written and archaeological evidence indicates that modern agrarian
technology gradually extended over all of Europe in conjunction with
internal colonization and that the peasants who executed the work of
clearance were already equipped with improved tools when they moved
into virgin territory. The employment of garden ploughs hitched to
wheeled frames was obviously so well-known by the mid-thirteenth century that the Crusades chronicler, Jean de Joinville (1224–1317), noted
with astonishment that Egyptian fellahin were still using the primitive
kind without wheels. Taken as a whole the advances in the agrarian
economy of the High Middle Ages were not based so much upon technological innovation as upon the application of expedients and work methods
that had existed for a long time.

Among the progressive cultivation techniques was, of course, the three-
field tactic. Although it had been known since Carolingian times, only now
did it become the rule. In the past it had been used chiefly on demesne
lands, whereas the peasant plots had been tilled according to the two-field
and grassland systems with longer periods of fallow. As cultivated land

devoted to the growing of grain expanded during the High Middle Ages, so too was the period of fallow increasingly limited to the third year; at the same time the village's arable land was divided into three large fields, in which all local peasants shared equally. At the height of the Middle Ages the three-field economy with winter grain, summer grain and fallow was Europe's dominant form of agriculture; it had augmented harvest yields significantly. Compared to the epoch of the two-field system, productivity was a third greater. The improvement in the area of human nutrition was considerable.

The three-field system, which continued to prevail in most European countries until the end of the eighteenth and the beginning of the nineteenth centuries, was unquestionably one of the main reasons for the progress in the agrarian economy of the High Middle Ages. Along with the extension of grain cultivation, the creation of new arable land in clearance districts and the improvement of work tools, it provided the basis for the immense flourishing of High Mediaeval agriculture. Famines, which in the past occurred regularly, no longer assailed the main countries of Europe; only in certain smaller areas were there still bottlenecks in the food supply. This phenomenon was due on one hand to the liveliness of the grain trade and on the other to the increase in yields and the extension of cultivation resulting from continuing peasant colonization. The greater productivity achieved by use of the three-field system made it possible to reduce the proportion of land devoted to growing grain in favour of specialized crops. Among the latter were dyestuff plants (madder and woad), others for spinning yarn (flax and hemp), legumes, and various kinds of fruits and berries. Grapes spread mightily in areas suited to their cultivation and became significant, not only in the plains and hills of the Mediterranean countries, where viticulture had a long tradition, but also in Central Europe. As a consequence of these shifts, pasturage declined in many places; cattle-raising shrank in importance in relationship to planted crops. Where nature allowed it and where grass grew well, specialized stock-raising put in an appearance. Among such regions were both the marshlands along the maritime coasts of north-western Europe and the elevated zones of the Pyrenees and the Alps, where peasants established cattle farms and proceeded to breed animals intensively.

The fundamental changes that occurred in the Europe of the High Middle Ages were caused in particular by the fact that city life developed vigorously in a reciprocal relationship with demographic growth, internal colonization and the expansion of the agrarian economy; another factor was the enhanced importance of transport and trade, economic activities that were characterized by a sharp division of labour. With the rise of cities as centres of commerce and handicrafts, there emerged a market-determined division of labour between town and country in keeping with which peasants supplied foodstuffs and city-dwellers were responsible for producing industrial goods. Cities developed with particular force north of the Alps and were so dynamic that feudal society was profoundly altered and the peasant way of life powerfully influenced. In the Mediterranean, where cities could be built upon vestiges of antiquity, urban revival began before the eleventh century. However, in Western and Central Europe north of the Alps most cities and market towns were founded during the great period of growth in the twelfth and thirteenth centuries. A new spirit,

4 *Task-master and peasant in a woodcut from Petrus de Crescentiis,* Vom Nutz der Dinge *(Peter Drach, Speyer, 1483)*

a new attitude towards business, and a clear predilection for rational patterns of thought and behaviour were the forces that inspired the denizens of these urban centres. The result was profound: social, economic and political change.

The average urban share of the total population at the end of the High Middle Ages was 10 per cent. Thus, even after the rise of the cities, Europe remained a predominantly agrarian cultural environment in which – apart from urbanized landscapes such as Flanders and Lombardy, where the shift from country to town had taken place more quickly – peasants constituted the great bulk of mankind. Although many cities owed their prosperity to the revival of trade, they must still be viewed in the context of an overwhelmingly agrarian economy. The wave of colonization and demographic growth was just as crucial to urban renewal as the development of commerce and handicrafts. The lustre and the importance of trade over long distances, which Henri Pirenne portrayed so vividly,[27] should not blind us to the fact that city and country were part and parcel of the same edifice. Indeed, these two simultaneously expanding worlds cannot be separated at all: the city is nourished by the country and vice versa. No matter how great the influence of long-distance trade upon the revival of towns may have been, it must be stated unequivocally that demographic and economic growth took place in both the rural and urban sectors and that technological change simultaneously affected both the agricultural and the urban realms of material endeavour.

The forces at work in towns and all the many-faceted processes of change that operated in the High Middle Ages did not leave manorial lordship unscathed. The servile labour farm, which up to then had determined the nature of peasant life in the core regions of Europe, disintegrated. Its decay and dissolution occurred over a longer period of time and proceeded at speeds that differed from one place to another. In some parts of France and Italy the decline of the villatic system had already started in the tenth and eleventh centuries; in Central Europe it was well under way in the twelfth century; and by the end of the thirteenth century *villae* had ceased to exist. The outcome of this process was by no means the disappearance of manorial lordship and complete 'peasant emancipation' but rather the formation of new seigniorial structures and more liberal forms of parcelling out land. Thus there were alterations in the nature of relationships between manorial lords and peasants which bore witness to a loosening of the Early Medieval order of society. This transformation took place in the main countries of Europe with significant variations, and it is therefore obvious that individual agrarian systems had unique features.

In southern Europe the old order was replaced by relationships based upon a status of personal freedom and contracts of a private legal character; in Western and Central Europe the rental income manor predominated. The evolution of the Eastern European landed estate based upon various new methods of turning peasants into bondsmen belongs to the Late Middle Ages and Early Modern times and will concern us later in this book.

The flourishing urban economy had vastly changed the overall cadre and the basic conditions in which agrarian activities were pursued. The consequence of the revival of trade and the prevalence of monetary transactions was to tear down the solid walls that had surrounded autarkic servile labour farms. The incipient division of labour between town and country also penetrated into the *villae* and intensified the exchange of goods. With the increase in the population of cities there was on one hand a greater demand for foodstuffs and on the other a rural market for the rich offerings of an urban industrial economy. This new situation motivated countrymen to augment the production of agricultural commodities, limit their own processing of industrial raw materials and buy their requisites ready-made in town. Peasants were mainly responsible for supplying towns with victuals, while manorial lords sharply reduced demesne farming with servile labour and, for the most part, now demanded from bondsmen payments in money and kind instead of compulsory services. Wearisome conflicts between seigniors and estate administrators and the costly supervision that servile labour farms required encouraged many of the lords to change tactics and exploit their possessions on a rental basis.

Northern Italy, with its prospering cities and trade centres, was the place where the old system of manorial lordship changed first and most radically. While outright bondage did not disappear entirely from Italian soil and many kinds of manorial dependency persisted on the landed estates of secular and clerical lords, nevertheless, as a whole, there did evolve a new system of holdings more or less exempt from feudal encumbrances and based upon contractual agreements between the landowners and the rustic population. The prevailing legal devices were leases and *métayage* (*mezzeria*) or sharecropping, as it was known in the southern United States. The peasant leaseholder was certainly not independent: he had a lord above him, either a big rural landholder or a rich urban merchant. State regulations served the purpose of ensuring that burghers were supplied with food. Likewise, landowners were protected by law from breach of contract, something that hampered the leaseholder's liberty of movement. Furthermore, the sale of land parcels was subject to certain limitations.

In some regions of countries to the north of the Alps there was a considerable loosening of the ties of peasant dependency. However, in contrast to Italy, manorial lords still called the tune throughout the countryside. Two main substitutes for the vanishing servile labour farm are often found. In one instance the lord ceased altogether to farm the demesne: the *terra salica* was then either split up entirely into individual plots or else subdivided among the servile labourers. In the other the core of the former seigniorial farm was handed over to a single rustic who worked it in return for a hard and fast division of payments. The farmsteads of hide peasants were normally detached from the economic cadre of the servile labour estate and passed out to peasants as autonomous, individual units. Compulsory service, now largely superfluous as the lord no longer farmed for himself, were replaced with monetary dues or were limited to only a few days in the year.

In some cases manorial lords granted the peasantry newly created premises and old farmsteads in return for a set monetary rent. This turned out later to be the most satisfactory arrangement for peasants since debasement of coinage meant that the real value of such payments was constantly dropping. The position of the manorial lord was safer if he insisted upon payments in kind, whether as fixed quantities or as a share of the crop. From the twelfth century onward the temporary lease, which had been known in Italy for quite some time, likewise came to be used more frequently in Western Europe. This looser form of land grant, at first often tied to *métayage*, spread widely, above all in northern France, the Netherlands and north-western Germany in the proximity of towns. Temporary leases were granted for relatively short periods; the normal rule was the length of time needed for a crop or a sequence of crops to be planted and harvested.

By the end of the High Middle Ages the legal status of peasants in many European countries had improved greatly. The disappearance of the villatic system often meant that compulsory peasant services were virtually meaningless, while the personal subordination of peasants to manorial lords was much less than before. For the right to farm their plots rustics paid rents that often sank in real value, or else they held a lease, the cost of which was basically determined by market forces. In some areas well-to-do peasants were even able to convert their farms into freeholds. This was now easier to accomplish because the real-estate market had become very fluid and many a thirteenth-century manorial lord was prepared to sell off a portion of his holdings. Rustics in many sections of Eastern and Central Europe were in a better legal position than before and enjoyed greater liberty of movement, as well as more autonomy in the way they farmed. The favourable agrarian economic circumstances of the High Middle Ages and high prices for grain also had a positive effect upon peasant farming, inasmuch as it was more closely linked to markets. The situation is best summarized by citing Friedrich Lütge's judgement that 'the pristine personal legal status of the peasant *vis-à-vis* the reality of his obligations' became ever less important. There was, almost everywhere, no lack of personal liberty as there had been in earlier times. The unfree rustic – or the serf as he was long called by historians – had passed from view. All that remained of his former subordination were certain well-defined payments and services.

A phenomenon that ran parallel to the loosening of manorial lordship was the strengthening of social cohesion and personal bonds between peasants. The autochthonous rural population of the High Middle Ages was firmly anchored in the village community, although the degree of its importance varied somewhat from one region to another. With the dissolution of the servile labour farm the centre of economic gravity shifted to the village, where peasants now collaborated freely in working the arable land. Upon what bases did this new type of village arise? For how long has Central Europe had villages characterized by cooperative utilization of fields and commons? The irregularly planned or conglomerate village with its three-field arrangements and jointly worked arable land – the open field system – cannot be traced back to the Germanic epoch, as many standard historical works were wont to maintain a few decades ago. The fully developed village with its collectively farmed acreage and communal institutions is rather the product of a long evolution. It was born in the early part of the High Middle Ages after peasant farming intensified and it became necessary to establish generally recognized rules for the agrarian exploitation of village precincts. According to Fossier, the Western European village came into being – *la naissance du village* as he puts it – between AD 930 and 1080 in the context of tensions engendered by a variety of forces.[28] Léopold Genicot takes a similar stance: 'From the tenth century, on the Continent, people gathered together in villages and hamlets because of economic progress, demographic expansion, the need for new fields and more food, and the search for security.'[29]

The emergence of the village is the expression of a profound change that took place during the High Middle Ages, above all in the structure of rural settlement, the agrarian economy, the social order and lordship. Recent scholarly investigation has convincingly demonstrated that zones with a predominantly village form of settlement and those in which isolated farmsteads prevailed evolved only in the course of the High Middle Ages, whereas one must speak of a greatly fluctuating pattern of colonization characterized by hamlets and scattered groups of farms in the preceding period. At the very least, the study of settlement patterns has shown that the conglomerate village is more a High Medieval phenomenon. Archaeology, for its part, has made it clear that that small and medium-sized localities were the rule in the Early Middle Ages. The transformation of settlement structure in the High Middle Ages was also accompanied by important changes in the way houses were constructed. Older buildings consisting of poles stuck into the ground gave way to others with uprights resting upon stone bases. This must surely be taken as a sign that the rural population had become more sedentary. The concentration of settlements into the form of villages obviously goes hand in hand with the establishment of permanent dwellings. Moreover, at the same time – specifically, the eleventh and twelfth centuries – new parish churches and chapels sprang up within many villages. In this fashion the village and its peasant inhabitants rose above the mere status of a social agglomeration to that of a community of worshippers; from this time onward a church and a cemetery constitute the hard core of settlements.

With respect to economic practices, the High Medieval village shows certain changes that have already been touched upon in several places. Localities lay claim to their own zones of agrarian activity and thus demarcate themselves. Because of continual demographic growth, shrinking reserves of land are more intensively cultivated, and fields encroach upon meadow and forest commons. The process of concentrating agrarian economic effort upon the production of grain has already been mentioned in connection with discussion of the phenomenon of extending cultivated land. The establishment of villages was but one of two means of exploiting the land in the most effective manner possible. The other was more intensive sequences of planting and harvest cycles in conjunction with the utilization of the three-field system, i.e., the division of arable land into three large tracts. Individual peasants could no longer determine these sequences independently. Collaboration needed all local farmers to obey a compulsory arable land ordinance. The dissolution of the villatic system and the transition to forms of manorial lordship based mainly upon payments meant as a matter of course that servile labour farms became ever less important to the agrarian economy. They were no longer the centre of things in the rural world as they had been in Carolingian times. Peasant life was now orientated much more towards the village, a local economy based upon a compulsory system of working commonly held lands and social relationships within the cadre of the immediate rustic community.

Village development, which has been treated here primarily within the context of the Western and Central European heartland, took place in other parts of the Continent during the High Middle Ages in keeping with quite diverse geographic, economic and political presuppositions that cannot be examined in any detail here. The evolution of rural localities depended above all upon divergent natural spatial factors affecting both planned villages and irregularly laid-out settlements, as well as upon whether it was a matter of an older zone or more recently occupied land. In colonization districts of the twelfth and thirteenth centuries new villages were normally built quite systematically; there is much evidence for this approach from eastern regions. The subject of the multifarious forms taken by village communities and their divergent functions will be entered upon later.

Let us now return to the initial question of the social position of peasants in the High Middle Ages. The conditions of rural life undoubtedly improved markedly in many respects during this era; it is quite proper for certain historians to have stressed this fact. Legal and economic amelioration in the countryside was largely fostered by impulses that proceeded from the activities of towns and recently colonized regions. The danger that dissatisfied peasants might emigrate to cities or newly settled places forced manorial lords to make substantial concessions. Normally, peasants who moved to frontier areas were granted more favourable terms of landholding, greater liberty of movement, and exemption from certain manorial and servile obligations. Thus the extension of cultivation, urbanization and the expansion of the overall economy had a positive effect upon the personal status of ploughmen; they benefited from widespread prosperity, progress in the agrarian economy and the rise in the general standard of living.

However, not every group and stratum of peasant society was able to profit equally from these developments. Some did better than others. The greatest advantages accrued to a kind of peasant elite that emerged in many villages and regions in the course of the thirteenth century. The least affected were persons on the lower rungs of the rustic social ladder, and the numbers of such individuals had grown mightily everywhere. The standard of life of the great mass of the peasant population was still shockingly depressed towards the end of the thirteenth century, something that was at least partly related to the burden of feudal payments. A conservative analysis of incomes makes it clear that, after many peasant farmers had paid off their numerous manorial obligations, they had only enough left to support themselves at a subsistence level. Most peasant farms were so

heavily burdened with feudal rents during the good economic times of the
High Middle Ages that they produced little in the way of surplus even in
normal years; failed harvests amounted to disaster. When different misfortunes such as storms, cattle disease and failed harvests coincided, the bulk
of the peasantry suffered the most bitter deprivation. This led to huge
famines, as the events of the fourteenth century demonstrated.

5

Crisis in the Late Middle Ages

If the High Middle Ages had been a time of prosperity and economic, social and cultural growth in every European country, the fourteenth and fifteenth centuries were a period of stagnation, separation and crisis. Henri Pirenne characterized the Late Middle Ages as follows:

> We may regard the beginning of the fourteenth century as the conclusion of medieval economic expansion. Up to that point we can recognize uniform progress in every realm. Emancipation of the rural population, clearance, drainage, settlement, German colonization beyond the Elbe – all of these things happen at the same time. The increase in the volume of manufactures and commerce profoundly altered the appearance and the essence of society. The Mediterranean and the Black Sea and, on the other margin, the North Sea and the Baltic become avenues for the conduct of trade. More and more harbours and commercial centres spring up along coasts and on islands while the Continent itself is strewn with cities . . . This development ceases at the start of the fourteenth century although without the onset of decline *per se*.[30]

František Graus has underlined the crisis-like features of the Late Middle Ages in Europe and pointed especially to social conflicts: 'a certain restlessness' is visible among many segments of the population.[31] The era was replete with minor struggles, revolts and uprisings in villages and cities; a strange kind of excitability is obvious in them.

Whereas historical investigators used to concentrate upon the central event of the mid-fourteenth century – the Black Death of 1347–51 – and its outcome as if they were bewitched, more recently the tendency has been to examine earlier manifestations of crisis, i.e., circumstances during the preceding five decades. Because of the increase in population and a shortage of land there was a distinct trend in many densely settled regions to establish smaller units and to splinter the arable area. Many farms had been so subdivided by heirs that they were dwarf-sized and could no longer assure their occupants a sufficient livelihood. Alongside the petty peasant farmers were land-poor day workers and cottagers, who in some instances barely had access to a garden and were allowed to use the commons only to a limited extent. As the result of the formation of this broad rural substratum, peasants with farms of their own became a minority within many villages.

In south-western Germany the splintering of holdings on intensively tilled, older settlement terrain and in the vicinity of towns had reached such a stage that many peasant farms now encompassed only a modicum of cultivable land; only with difficulty could they be made to produce yields sufficient to sustain families. Many parcels of common fields had been broken up into tiny pieces and sometimes they were no more than minute fragments of a rod. Cottagers supported themselves by working on larger farms or found employment in rural trades such as the linen industry. In many villages a vast social divide had led to the appearance of two economic classes. On one hand there was a narrow stratum of rich peasants, individuals disposing of really good incomes, and on the other a large substratum of small peasants, day labourers and craftsmen, whose circumstances of life were at best modest and at worst marginal.

Similar conditions could be found at the beginning of the fourteenth century in other regions of Europe as well. In what is now Belgium and the Netherlands the process of breaking up fields was far advanced and had generated a large number of small peasant farms. In many densely inhabited villages 50 to 75 per cent of the agricultural units comprised only three to five hectares; that was the minimum a family required in order to get by. This also meant that more than half of the rural population had to make up what it lacked in income by working for bigger leaseholders or by labouring at home for the wool and textile industry that had sprouted in Flanders, Brabant and Hainault in the second half of the thirteenth century. Many individuals lived precariously and were gravely endangered in times of need. The agrarian growth that had taken place in England for over 200 years also reached its limits and showed similar signs of crisis. Increasing subdivision of farms, exhaustion of land reserves, stagnating yields and the rise of a huge peasant underclass now characterized life in many an English village. Incessant population growth had brought about the splintering of land parcels and spawned a large number of small operations which even in good years could scarcely support a family. New villages were established on terrain incapable of producing adequate harvests for very long.

Generally speaking, at the beginning of the fourteenth century there were signs of serious crisis everywhere in Europe. Subdivision of land, shrinkage of farm size, poor crops and steep price rises were unmistakable symptoms of the fact that the basis for adequately supplying the population's nutritional needs was sharply reduced. Was Europe already overpopulated, as some demographers and economic historians have argued? The thesis of overpopulation is frequently based upon the theories of the Englishman, Thomas Malthus, who postulated cycles of population development and demographic growth linked to the stock of food at a given instance in time. There are some indications that the number of Europe's inhabitants around AD 1300 was in fact approaching a critical limit and reaching a stage like that of many Third World countries in the twentieth century. It was no longer possible to increase the Continent's arable land to any meaningful extent, harvests were meagre and nutritional conditions for large segments of the population miserable. Under such circumstances, failed harvests, murrain and natural catastrophes could prove to be absolutely devastating. This was apparent on the occasion of the great famine of 1315–17 which afflicted a large part of Europe and caused starvation and death on a massive scale. Even before this time inclement weather conditions – over-long winters, wet summers and heavy flooding – had led to bad harvests and supply bottlenecks in some Western European countries. These misfortunes were mild compared to the unusually long and grave famine which spread from England, France and Germany across the Baltic deep into Scandinavia, hitting Eastern Europe as well. Harvests were uncommonly poor, grain prices rose to astronomical levels and the starving masses ate unhealthy substitute foods. People resorted to consuming the meat of infected animals. The result was epidemics and an even greater number of deaths from sickness, debilitation and malnutrition. The annalists of this era speak of relentless contagion and huge population losses. In some places the cemeteries had to be extended; whole villages were depopulated. An after-effect of the 1315–17 failed harvests was the outbreak in England during 1318 of a terrible animal disease that caused further losses.

Far worse for the people of Europe than the famine of the early part of the century was the Great Plague three decades later. The Black Death, which was somehow dragged into Europe from the Orient in 1347, spread like a wave from the coasts of the Mediterranean across France, Spain, England, Germany and Scandinavia (see map 3). Only a few regions were spared or less affected; they included parts of the Netherlands and larger sections of Bohemia and Poland. For some countries it is hard to estimate the exact direction taken by the disease, since no written evidence has survived. Moreover, there is no way of substantiating the belief that there were fewer deaths in the countryside than in the densely inhabited towns. Notations of chroniclers to the effect that there were no shepherds to tend flocks or reapers of grain suggest very high mortality in rural areas. According to older calculations, the population of England dropped by a third to a half as a result of the 1348–9 plague, although it must be granted that there were great differences between individual localities. In France – a country that is thought to have contained 20 million souls before the Black Death struck – the death rate during the main years in question was probably also a third. The rural population, which in some areas had been even denser prior to the Great Plague than it was in the nineteenth century, was very badly hit. Statistics and the comments of annalists confirm the supposition that Germany was as badly affected as

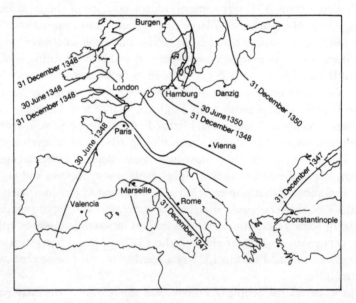

Map 3   The course of the Black Death, 1347–1351 (after Abel, Agrarkrisen, *page 51, figure 6)*

neighbouring countries and that from a quarter to a third of its inhabitants were swept away. Further waves of pestilence washed across the Continent in the following decades and inexorably claimed additional victims (see map 3)

If we glance at the figures that illustrate population development in all of Europe we can get a good picture of the contrast between the demographic circumstances of the High Middle Ages and those of the Late Middle Ages. To cite Russell's calculations, if Europe had reached the level of about 73 million inhabitants altogether at the height of its population growth in 1340, the number fell by the mid-fifteenth century to about 50 million.[32] It follows from this that the Great Plague and succeeding epidemics caused human losses of one-third; the effect was to decimate Europe. To be sure, there are notable differences between individual regions and countries. Whereas England, which dropped from 5 to 3 million inhabitants, was shorn of one-third of its people, Poland and Hungary were deprived of only a quarter of theirs. The immediate consequence of the Great Plague was a kind of collective trauma, which expressed itself in reactions that ranged all the way from extreme religiosity to orgiastic festivals and massive dissipation. Within a short time, the redistribution of possessions among the survivors of the disaster brought them more money than they had ever had before. The fact that large numbers of people weakened by age had passed away meant, initially, a younger, more vigorous work-force and enhanced productivity. However, later outbreaks of pestilence reduced the number of persons in their active years and wiped out countless children as well.

Climate – the favourable character of which had encouraged the population increase and economic growth of the High Middle Ages – seems to have changed for the worse and turned into a negative factor. After a longer period of warmth, conditions became colder in the late thirteenth century. Thus began an era of generally low temperatures, the so-called 'Little Ice Age', which stretched into the Early Modern epoch. The advance of glaciers, pollen analyses and references to frozen lakes provide the neccesary corroborating evidence. The effects were especially noticeable in northern Europe and in elevated regions; the result was a decrease in agricultural yields. The deterioration of the climate had an especially deleterious effect upon the cultivation of grain at higher altitudes, as has been demonstrated in the cases of England and Norway. Quite independent of the great demographic decline, Late Medieval Europe remained a predominantly agrarian society, even if there were some fundamentally urban landscapes such as Flanders, Tuscany and the Paris basin. More than 90 per cent of the population still lived on the land and from the fruits of agriculture. However, the density of rural settlement differed markedly from one region to another; the north of France was more heavily populated than the plains of Eastern Europe.

To a considerable degree, the picture presented by the Late Medieval European countryside was that of derelict, once-inhabited places, abandoned villages and fields – surely something linked to the drop in population. Deserted settlements had been known even in the Early Middle Ages, but their numbers and the historical significance of the phenomenon are especially striking in the Late Middle Ages. In order to comprehend the extent of the Late Medieval process of localities reverting to wasteland, we must turn to existing studies of settlement development in the various regions and countries of Europe. If the number of vanished villages is seen in relationship to the total of inhabited ones, we obtain what may be called the 'desertion quotient'. If we apply this mathematical technique to Germany, we find that 26 per cent of the settlements that had existed at the end of the High Middle Ages were gone two centuries later, i.e., a quarter of them disappeared. A map of wastelands shows that the frequency of the phenomenon varied greatly from region to region. There were many tenantless settlements in Hessia, southern Lower Saxony, some parts of Thuringia and the March of Brandenburg. The quotient was much less in north-western Germany (where the irregularly laid-out or scattered type of village predominated), along the lower Rhine and in the Bavarian heartland south of the Danube.

Late Medieval England resembled Germany with respect to the abandonment of inhabited localities. For this we may cite the work of English investigators. Some counties lost up to 20 per cent of the places listed in the tax rolls of 1334. In other counties the drop was merely 5 to 10 per cent, and in some districts there appears to have been virtually no decline. According to Maurice Beresford[33] and other students of the subject, the remarkably scattered character of wastelands was due fundamentally to the divergent suitability of land for grain cultivation and pasturage: zones of meadowland suffered the fewest losses, those where grain fields predominated the most. Thus the lowest number of deserted villages is found in the marshy terrain of southern and western England, but they are quite common in the Midlands, where soil conditions allowed peasants to choose more freely between growing crops and raising cattle. It can be said that in the case of England all the factors that affected grain cultivation negatively in the Late Middle Ages operated with particular force and enabled pasturage to expand at the expense of tilled fields. It follows that villages that were built in the High Middle Ages on unsuitable soils were the most threatened in their existence. In addition, there was in many places a striking decrease in the number of small peasant farms. On many estates around AD 1300 there were more smallholders and cottagers than there were ploughmen with full-sized farms. During the fourteenth and fifteenth centuries the number of rustics occupying tiny parcels of land fell sharply.

5 *Peasants gathering the harvest: the month of August from a Flemish manuscript calendar illustrated by Simon Bening about 1500*

For some parts of France, especially the Alpine regions and Languedoc, scholars have likewise been able to ascertain that there were many deserted villages and farms. However, generally speaking, only a few such places remained uninhabited for the whole of the Late Middle Ages. Many empty villages were later repopulated and overgrown fields restored to cultivation. The picture differs from Germany and England, for there many of the losses were never made good. It is also obvious that historians must make discriminating judgements when they study this subject. In present-day Belgium and the Netherlands the number of permanently and totally derelict localities also seems to have been minimal. This is obviously related to the fact that these countries were not as badly affected by the waves of pestilence in the fourteenth and fifteenth centuries.

Unlike the Lowlands, Norway, Sweden and Denmark contained many a desolate village and field. Vast tracts of Danish soil – places that were flourishing at the end of the thirteenth century – were unoccupied. The high point of the crisis appears to have been the first decades of the fifteenth century. The proportion of abandoned farms belonging to the Bishop of Roskilde rose from 10 per cent to 26 per cent between 1361 and 1420 but dropped thereafter.[34] As far as Norway is concerned, a district north of Oslo is so far the best investigated: almost 40 per cent of the units listed in the episcopal cadastre (or register) around AD 1400 were vacant. In other parts of the country the situation does not appear to have been as bad. Nevertheless, the number of tenantless farms and villages, especially at higher elevations, was considerable. In the case of Sweden there is an obvious relationship between wastelands and population losses caused by the plague. Villages were left with only a handful of inhabitants who managed to struggle on for a few years but ultimately had to give up because of the decline in the agrarian economy.

This survey of some of the main countries of Late Medieval Europe has demonstrated that there were empty villages and desolate fields everywhere in Europe. The most recent investigations of the subject have been carried out in individual countries with varying degrees of intensity and have focused above all upon temporary and partial abandonment which, along with the permanent kind, provides especially good evidence for the overall diminution of settlement in the fourteenth and fifteenth centuries. Leaving aside regional disparities and uneven distribution within individual zones, the decline in settlement throughout the whole of Europe was astonishingly large. The causes of these events and their relationship with peasant life in the Late Middle Ages is a question that cannot be ignored. What were the reasons that induced countrymen to forsake so many villages, farms and fields?

Since the sources are rarely specific about the background to the abandonment of settlements, there has been plenty of room for speculation. Scholars have advanced all sorts of explanations: wars and feuds, conflagrations and banditry, contagion and disease, floods and natural catastrophes, poor soils, unfavourable climatic conditions, as well as pressure to establish larger localities. Undoubtedly, many of these theories provide partial answers to the problem. However, they do not resolve existing contradictions, and they fail to account for the phenomenon as a whole. Advocates of the war hypothesis are correct in emphasizing that the Late Middle Ages were an especially bellicose period and that many villages were destroyed in the course of military operations, but they cannot tell us why settlements in remote and sheltered places also declined. Proponents of the failed colonization thesis point to the inadequacy of soils in many cleared districts, the consequence of which was the depopulation of the localities in question. Some geographers stress the tendency towards concentration of settlement: small villages were foresaken so that their inhabitants could move to larger, better protected ones, the fields of which could then be cultivated more intensively.

Notwithstanding certain objections, it seems that the agrarian crisis argument of Wilhelm Abel[35] and certain other scholars offers the most persuasive explanation for wasteland phenomena and associated Late Medieval economic processes. Its point of departure is the assumption that the long-term development of prices and wages depends upon demographic shifts. If population increases, there is less leeway in the food supply and grain becomes more expensive; if there are fewer people, bread does not cost as much. As a result of the tremendous drop in population caused by the Black Death, there was a free fall in grain prices; the impact upon the agrarian sector was negative. At the same time fewer human beings meant labour shortages, and the real value of wages rose. Inasmuch as the prices for manufactures remained stable in comparison to agricultural products, producers were caught in the bind between the amounts of money they received for selling basic foodstuffs and what they had to pay for things made by others. Declining yields and rising outlay provoked an enduring crisis in the agrarian economy, which affected both peasants and manorial lords. Rustics and seigniors who had to rely upon hired hands to perform farm chores and who were closely tied to developments in the market-place were the chief victims of the crisis, which in the last analysis was simply one of a grain-based economy.

It follows from Abel's interpretation that among the causes of Late Medieval village abandonment must be included not only the immediate drop in population caused by the plague, but also worse economic conditions for agriculture as a whole; this was the reason why peasants left poorly located settlements. On one hand, the destinations of departing rustics were towns which had also suffered sharp demographic losses owing to the plague and which relied upon immigration from the countryside for the salaried workers required by an expanding economy. On the other hand, peasants moved to villages and neighbourhoods that were better situated and offered more in the way of personal opportunity. Thus it can be seen that an especially large number of the villages founded in Germany's central mountains during the late part of the High Middle Ages were abandoned by their inhabitants. Hessia and Thuringia – in particular, forested areas – stand out in this respect. In other regions too, it seems clear that among the category of the oldest settlements there were only a few deserted places, whereas there was a surprisingly large number of them in hilly country, on poor soil and sites far from transport arteries. The Austrian Alps reveal a similar pattern: villages and farms in open valley terrain were far less affected by abandonment than zones that lay higher up and were harder to exploit agriculturally. One must assume that, after the plague had passed through, peasants decided to leave the mountains for the valleys.

The altered circumstances of the Late Mediaeval agrarian economy not only led to the formation of vast tracts of wasteland: they were also associated with changes in the way natural resources were utilized. One side of the coin was an expansion of economic exploitation in the form of enhanced forestation and more pasturage. The other was more intense cultivation of good soils and favourably situated farmland. The process of broadening the scope of economic utilization is especially evident in the case of wastelands. They were turned into meadows or – though less often – cropped. The fields of abandoned villages were often jointly worked by adjacent villages, in so far as manorial lords agreed to the practice; the usual method was to graze beef cattle and sheep. In certain regions special sheep farms were established on derelict land. They were located in the centres of such places and took advantage of the fallow that lay within the premises. If the soil was totally unsuitable, abandoned fields were allowed to revert to woodland. Residual cultivated terraces long served to remind posterity of a one-time agrarian function.

In the proximity of cities and in pastoral landscapes this development could result in an intensive form of stock-raising. Specialized farms supplied townsmen with milk, butter and meat. The high purchasing power of city-dwellers during the Late Middle Ages created a vigorous demand for mutton, beef, pork, poultry and meat by-products. Low prices for grain – which could be used for fattening stock – fostered this trend. A phenomenon that accompanied the shrinking cereal acreage was an emphasis upon previously less usual crops. Vegetables and fruit became more important, as did fields devoted to the production of textile fibres and dyes. Another expanding branch of the agrarian economy was viticulture. Vineyards dotted many a landscape in France, Spain, Italy and Germany and offered consumers a wide variety of wines. In spite of the difficulties caused by higher elevations and the vagaries of climate, the grape grew virtually everywhere, even on the soil of northern Germany and England where, to be sure, it later disappeared. The taste that the upper strata of urban society had developed for fine vintages stimulated trade with far distant regions. In northern Italy there was an increased demand for select wines from the southern part of the country. Englishmen and Lowlanders insisted upon drinking claret. It is also well recognized that the new consumer markets encouraged the extension of viticulture in the valleys of the Rhône, the Seine, the Moselle and the Rhine. Vineyards quickly became the hallmarks of these regions.

How did the transformation of the Late Mediaeval economy affect the lives of peasants? the answer is that their social situation depended in large measure upon the reaction of feudal lords to changing circumstances. It thus seems appropriate to look first at new forces that were impinging upon Late Medieval manors and the various ways in which seigniors sought to adjust to them: this is a necessary preliminary to discussing the impact of the agrarian depression upon Europe's peasants. The secular and clerical potentates of this era often squeezed their tenants hard in an attempt to make up for lost revenue. From the early fourteenth century onward the economic position of many seigniors was deteriorating. The value of the monetary rents that had replaced compulsory service in the High Middle Ages continued to fall because of coinage debasement, while payments in kind at best guaranteed a stagnating cash flow. The demographic downturn after 1350 exacerbated matters. The plague deprived manorial lords of many of their peasants and hence also of rustic payments and services. The countrymen emigrated *en masse* to cities emptied of inhabitants by pestilence.

In so far as manorial lords were still farming themselves, they were hard hit by the decline in the price of cereals and the mounting expense of their work-force. From about 1375 they began to receive less and less money for their grain – a trend that lasted for a long time and indeed continued until the very end of the fifteenth century. Since there was a severe labour shortage, they had to pay salaries well above the level of the years before the plague. Attempts to impose wage controls were largely unsuccessful; repeated ordinances of this kind bear witness to their ineffectiveness in practice. The logical consequence of this economic development was for seigniors to reduce the scale of their direct involvement in farming. At the same time they resorted to more extensive forms of agrarian activity. By shifting their focus and raising beef and mutton instead of grain, they could lower wage costs and earn more by selling meat products to the lucrative urban consumer market.

In the worst case scenario the agrarian crisis could lead to a dramatic drop in a lord's standard of living. Yet not all seigniors were affected equally by the new economic forces. Those who suffered most were the petty feudatories, persons who belonged to the knightly estate. Studies of the economic status of the lower nobilility in various regions have shown that there was a pronounced drop in income and loss of wealth. Burdened by debt and suffering from arrears in payments due to them, many knights could no longer bear the growing costs of the lifestyle that their position in society seemed to require. They were forced to look for new sources of revenue. If they did not succeed in obtaining remunerative posts in the bureaucracies of nearby territories or making money as mercenaries, they often concluded that their sole recourse was to increase the pressure upon their peasant tenants and raise rents. Another rather common financial escape route for petty noblemen of the Late Middle Ages was to become a robber baron. Knights began to incite feuds mischievously, to attack rich merchants or embark on martial expeditions in order to acquire the means with which to maintain their position on the social ladder. The principal victims of such behaviour were peasants; almost inevitably, they were the ones who bore the brunt of seigniorial feuds.

We can obtain an idea of the difficulties faced by minor noble families from questionnaires sent out by the Elector of Saxony in 1474 for the purpose of determining knightly income and expenditure in his territory.[36] Some of the persons in question had large holdings, possessed several villages with rent-paying peasants and operated farms of their own. They complained bitterly that profits from agrarian enterprise barely covered administrative costs and interest on loans. The reports which the knights forwarded to their overlord are so replete with statistics that it is possible to gain a clear picture of the level and structure of receipts and disbursements of individual households. Wages normally constituted the biggest expense: they were paid to workmen and field hands as well as to domestic servants and business employees. Disbursements for capital equipment were small in relation to salary expenses, but the costs of clothing and other consumer goods were high. Compared with modest manorial income, the outlay for certain items necessary to maintain noble social status was extremely high. Special occasions such as weddings and funerals put a tremendous strain upon a family's financial reserves.

The position of the most powerful feudal lords, suzerains of emergent territorial states, was quite different. Since they did not have to rely mainly upon rustic dues but had large incomes from taxes and tolls – some of which were paid by the prosperous burgher estate – they were less affected by the consequences of the agrarian crisis. Moreover, Late Medieval territories were growing in importance, and this did not leave the peasantry untouched. The suzerain's judicial and administrative organs were beginning to extend their reach. On one hand, intermediate manorial entities lost some of their functions, and on the other, traditional village prerogatives of self-government and autonomy were reduced. In their search for new sources of revenue – i.e., a larger reservoir of taxpayers – and regardless of peasants' divergent legal status, the territorial rulers placed as many peasants as possible under the authority of a single uniform governmental structure: the more subjects they had under their direct aegis, the better off they were fiscally. They imposed additional monetary burdens upon countrymen and restricted the rights of peasant communities to exploit common lands by issuing new woodland and pasturage regulations.

Territorial rulers were likewise in a better position to enforce their demands upon the rural population. They sought to counter the impending threat of emigration by insisting upon high departure taxes or formal oaths of fidelity. In some districts – for example, the Allgäu and Upper Swabia – personal bondage was not only tightened but utilized as a means of enhancing state income: the bureaucracy sharply hiked charges such as death duties and wedding fees. However, these attempts to burden the peasants further and to diminish their legal rights generally ceased after the agrarian crisis was overcome during the fifteenth century. In most parts of western Germany, as well as in France and England, the tendency was to ease servile ties.

How did French manorial lords react to the difficult situation that developed in the countryside as the result of population losses and the changing structure of prices and wages? Research currently available leaves no doubt that seigniorial income dropped perceptibly in many regions of Late Medieval France. The revenues of secular and clerical magnates sank

rapidly and remained on a low level for a long time. There were many
reasons for this development. They included a cut-back in agriculturally
exploited terrain, a decrease in the number of peasants, falling rents and a
surplus of tilled fields, which in turn brought about a decline in interest
rates. Greater running costs of management were caused by sharply rising
wages, which made it harder for Gallic seigneurs to farm for themselves
and which increased both their domestic outlay and business expenses. It
is clear that they gradually recognized the grave threat to their economic
equilibrium and took the necessary countermeasures. One of the more
commonly employed means of financial survival was to limit seigniorial
farming, subdivide the demesne and lease the parcels to peasants in return
for hard cash.

Guy Bois has carried out a detailed study of Late Medieval French social
and economic development and has specifically chosen a region in eastern
Normandy for this purpose.[37] Unlike Abel, who spoke of an agrarian crisis,
Bois maintains that overall social evolution amounted to a 'crisis of feudalism'. Changes in the social position of feudal lords and peasants should be
seen in relation to the economic transformation of the Late Middle Ages in
general. He describes the well-known phenomena and tendencies of the
fourteenth and fifteenth centuries as they revealed themselves in Normandy: declining population, falling grain prices and rising wages in real
terms. The income of Norman feudatories, which had greatly increased
during the High Middle Ages as the result of the extension of cultivation,
now shrank noticeably and put the lords in a difficult position. If they
wished to improve revenues, they had to demand more from ploughmen:
this had a negative impact upon peasant farming and provoked bitter
struggles over the division of wealth. Fundamental conflicts of this kind
intensified during the Hundred Years War (1339–1453) which led to
drastic tax rises and afforded seigneurs an opportunity to supplement their
income with plunder. Many peasant farms experienced great difficulties in
the face of these new burdens, which were only heightened by the demographic effects of pestilence. Thus agrarian productivity fell off. Growing
manorial pressure exacerbated the struggle for the division of wealth and
worsened the crisis altogether. Only when the war ended did things change
for the better, and they did so quickly. There were no longer any oppressive
military burdens, and, as the population had shrunk, more land was
available for cultivation. While, taken as a whole, Bois's study provides
much that enhances our understanding of Late Medieval socio-economic
development, his insights cannot be applied to other parts of Europe
without exercising considerable caution. At all events, the response of

feudal lords to the economic difficulties of the Late Middle Ages varied greatly from country to country and region to region.

A pronounced decline in feudal rents may be observed throughout much of fourteenth- and fifteenth-century England. Detailed studies by English economic historians demonstrate clearly that long-term grain prices fell and that the income of manorial lords dropped sharply. Since wages were related to the prices for which products could be sold on the market, seigniors often had to reduce rents. If we accept Genicot's figures, after 1350 the value of landed estates in the Belgian county of Namur plummeted by a quarter to a half.[38] Seigniorial rental income normally shrank by a third to a half. These were unmistakable signs of an enduring crisis. In the heavily urbanized territories of northern Italy such as Lombardy the situation does not appear to have been quite as bad. Burghers invested some of their assets in agriculture; this led to extensive crop specialization. Agrarian progress was based upon a sophisticated irrigation system fed by canals, the Po river and its tributaries. However, conditions in Tuscany were not as favourable because manorial yields were less. Records from the Pistoia region indicate that rents decreased by a third during the fourteenth century; unquestionably, seigniors were confronted with a revenue crisis. Thus it is fair to say that Italian agriculture was profitable only in Lombardy, where the predominance of towns created a unique set of circumstances.

How then may we assess the situation of Late Medieval peasants who were closely linked to manorial lords and strongly affected by changes in the agrarian economy? The conclusions of an older school of historical thought regarding this basic question are strikingly contradictory. Some scholars argued that the conditions of peasant existence were worse, while others, pointing to various signs of well-being, perceived a marked improvement in the rural standard of living. More recently the international fraternity of reseachers – profiting from a vast accumulation of economic-historical primary sources – has issued more precise, though by no means clear-cut verdicts. Attention has often been directed to the drop in feudal rents, the phenomenon of large-scale abandonment of terrain and the oversupply of land, from which facts the possibly overhasty conclusion has been drawn that manorial lords were worse off than peasants. In any case, considering the great diversity of rural circumstances throughout the many individual countries of Late Medieval Europe, it is difficult to arrive at a balanced, overall judgement about the quality of peasant life.

Peasants were affected by the crisis in the agrarian economy of the Late Middle Ages to the extent that individual farms were subject to market forces. Peasants who could get by without paid help and sold little of their grain to dealers were naturally more or less immune to outside influences. The market share of the peasantry depended upon the size of farms, the development of a monetary economy and the intensity of market relationships in the regions in question. The big peasant farmer who relied upon hired hands and sold larger quantities of grain unquestionably felt the impact of changes in the wage and price structure more than his small-time colleague. A further trend can be seen among petty farmers, namely, a concentration of holdings. This type of rustic now had an opportunity to join the ranks of his wealthier neighbours by purchasing newly available plots of land.

It is thus certain that many small peasant farmers – they represented a high proportion of villagers at the end of the High Medieval colonization wave – benefited from the crisis in agriculture. There was a demand for their labour in so far as they were underemployed at home and, as indicated, they had the chance to enlarge their own acreage. Cultivable land could now be bought on terms, a state of affairs that had not obtained for a long time. Moreover, the abandonment of marginal terrain had brought about an increase in the fruits of rustic endeavour, and the ratio of the population to the available, agriculturally exploitable land had developed favourably through demographic decline.

Medium-sized peasant farmers – who accounted for the great bulk of rustic agrarian activity – were not totally exempt from dependency upon an extraneous work-force, but they did not feel the effects of higher wages as much as bigger peasants did. Prices also did not matter much, since middling ploughmen had but little contact with markets. What did count were manorial services and payments. The multiple character of dues, the varying dimensions of individual peasant holdings and divergent yields often make it difficult to calculate the exact extent of seigniorially imposed burdens. Detailed statistical analyses carried out by agrarian historians do suggest that overall they were quite heavy. After many a peasant had fulfilled his numerous obligations to the local lord and the Church, there was barely enough left for him and his family to survive. It seems that most farms were so encumbered that even in good years they produced little in the way of surplus; in bad times their very existence was threatened. Exposed to the perils of the elements, famine, animal disease and warfare, a large number of Late Medieval peasants lived at the edge of an abyss; their lot was anything but easy. On the ladder of the 'old corporate society' the peasant occupied the lowest rung. He was the principal pillar of the economy, but his labour enjoyed the least esteem.

If one surveys the legal status of Western and Central European plough-men at the end of the Middle Ages, it becomes clear that the manifold attempts of feudal lords to heighten rustic dependency were largely unsuc-cessful. The opportunities peasants had to emigrate, the role of towns and various other factors impinged upon the manor and frequently brought about a liberalization of the laws that applied to them. Rights of tenancy improved in many parts of the long-settled regions of Germany. A peasant could transform temporally limited possession of land into a hereditary fief or other forms of tenancy which, for all practical purposes, guaranteed continuity of occupation. In Bavaria, notwithstanding seigniorial resist-ance, hereditary fiefs spread although there was still much precarious tenure. In Franconia there was less opposition to a shift in the direction of transferable possession liable to payment of fees: it became the pre-dominant form of tenure. Along the lower Rhine – under the influ-ence of circumstances in the neighbouring Netherlands – there developed straightfoward lease relationships and loose forms of rustic dependency.

In eastern Germany as well as Eastern Europe as a whole the patterns of agrarian development were entirely different: the foundations for the landed estate of Early Modern times, which we shall examine later, were laid in the Late Middle Ages. This led to agrarian dualism, i.e., a di-chotomy between east and west. In the course of a process of re-feudalization, eastern manorial lords managed to broaden the scope of the force they could bring to bear upon the peasant population. By resorting to their local judicial powers, seigniors succeeded in imposing extensive rustic service obligations and used the resultant compulsory labour to farm their own enlarged estates. Thus the crisis of the Late Middle Ages led to a fundamental alteration of the Eastern European agrarian system at the expense of the ploughman and put an end to the preferential legal and social status that many East Elbian peasants had wrung from the ruling elite during the colonization wave of the High Middle Ages. The knightly nobility exploited the political weakness of territorial states and arrogated to itself judicial authority over rustics, by means of which it was able to restrict peasants' liberty of movement and create a situation of hereditary personal subjection.

Conversely, in Western Europe the late Middle Ages witnessed a relaxa-tion of the ties of peasant dependency. Indeed, with the passage of time, the law accorded ploughmen a remarkable degree of personal liberty. The concomitant of this development was a series of rustic uprisings and revolts, now more frequent than ever. In northern France bondage had by no means disappeared during the Middle Ages, but there were drastic differences between one region and another. In Hainault there was hardly any serfdom. However, this extreme variety of villeinage was more commonly encountered in Champagne and Lorraine, where peasants still had to pay the head tax or *chevage* and an arbitrarily determined tribute called the *taille*. Bondage also still existed in Burgundy and around Dijon. All the same, bodily ownership of peasants was well on its way to extinction as the consequence of individual manumission or wholesale communal emancipation. The breakdown of the old manorial system and the oversupply of land in Late Medieval England likewise led to a lasting improvement in the legal status of countrymen. Despite their defeat in the Great Rebellion of 1381 English peasants continued to benefit from a loosening of servile ties. New economic circumstances led to the alteration of bondage into a form of dependency known as the copyhold. The copyholder was relieved of many payments by an agreement concluded in the manorial court. His legal status and tenure were recorded in a duplicate of the seigniorial registry of land parcels or manorial court roll. From the fifteenth century onward the last vestiges of serfdom vanished from English soil. By the beginning of Early Modern times England's peasants were unquestionably the freest, legally speaking, in the whole of Europe.

6

Uprisings and Resistance

In the Late Middle Ages different parts of Europe experienced a series of spectacular rural uprisings, a subject that has long fascinated students of history. A wave of peasant revolts spread like an epidemic across countries such as Flanders, Italy, France and England during the fourteenth and fifteenth centuries; the high point was the German Peasant War of 1525. The succeeding epoch – the period from the sixteenth to the eighteenth centuries – also witnessed a cycle of rustic insurrections and mass revolts which only concluded with the demise of the 'old corporate society' in the aftermath of the French Revolution. While these disturbances had divergent roots, dimensions and objectives, they still constitute, taken as a whole, an impressive manifestation of the peasantry's determination to ward off the exploitation by higher social strata that was their fate in much of Europe.

Opposition to seigniorial abuse was not a brand-new, Late Medieval phenomenon. In both the Early and the High Middle Ages various forms of peasant resistance are seen within the context of the tensions engendered by incipient feudalism. To be sure, resistance was less sensational and not as broadly based as in the Late Middle Ages. In Carolingian times ploughmen often sought to withstand the exactions of nascent manorial lordship by simply refusing to render the services required of them and by protesting against excessive payment demands. Among the most significant peasant insurrections of the Early Middle Ages was unquestionably the Stellinga Revolt of 861, which involved a very large number of Saxon peasants. As far the High Middle Ages are concerned, the mass uprising of a rural people known as the Stedinger is especially noteworthy. The countrymen who inhabited the lower reaches of the Weser fought the Archbishops of Bremen and the Counts of Oldenburg for many years and were overcome by the might of their foes and the aggressive actions of a crusading army only in the Battle of Altenesch (1234). The recalcitrance of High Medieval peasants towards feudal lords was rarely expressed in a flashy display of weapons but rather in a variety of more subtle quotidian forms of contumacy such as refusing to work or make payments, emigration to new settlements or flight to a nearby town. Inasmuch as the great bulk of the rural populace was subject to the villatic system, with its manifold legal and economic restrictions, it follows that the most significant acts of resistance occurred on servile labour farms and within the context of local manorial dominion.

If one wishes to understand the peculiar character and the significance of peasant uprisings in the Europe of the *ancien régime*, certain basic facts of that epoch must be borne in mind. As far as violent resistance is concerned, it is essential to discard the commonly held view that the peasant was peaceful and unarmed. In reality peasants were equipped with a whole arsenal of simple but for the most part regularly employed weapons, not merely with cudgels. If the carrying of arms was restricted to knights and mercenary troops in most countries, peasants nevertheless used weapons until well into the eighteenth century. In the mountainous region of Central Europe and in Scandinavia, where free peasants were long the rule rather than the exception, the right to bear arms was commonly exercised. It is apparent that stockmen honed their combat skills more than arable farmers did and that they kept their lethal implements for much longer. Likewise, many rustics had either served for years as soldiers or had participated in at least one campaign. When they were discharged, they even took home certain weapons such as halberds and pikes and stashed them away; these devices could be dug out of the barn and used again as necessity dictated.

The need to own weapons and the ability to use them was all the greater, inasmuch as the rural populace was particularly exposed to the unpredictable forces of nature and incidents of war. Peasants were in fact confronted with all kinds of threats to their personal security. For centuries the main characteristics of rural life had been incessant danger, emergencies, and violence; it followed as a matter of course that self-defence was an elementary precaution. Peasants had to fend off attacks by quarrelsome neighbours; they had to safeguard their herds against marauding dogs and ravenous predators. Wolf packs could emerge from nearby woods and become a genuine peril; they devoured sheep and goats and could even pounce on human beings during the hard winter months. When peasants made their way to remote fields, they often carried nail-studded stakes order to repel a sudden assault from some quarter.

Because they were under constant threat, peasant communities and neighbourhoods evinced a powerful sense of cohesion. Notwithstanding the diversity of settlement patterns and differing socio-economic conditions in the various countries of Europe, the rustic community was a fundamental entity within the pre-1789 social edifice. It was the focal point of country life, the basic unit for the payment of manorial and governmental dues, the cadre of economic activity and, last but not least, a natural self-defence collectivity. There was no lack of occasions for a call to arms: attacks by brigands, raids by undisciplined mercenaries and incursions from neighbouring communities. One could hear from afar alarms sounded from the bell-towers of parish churches or other warning signals. The village inhabitants gathered in the main street and barricaded it with overturned wagons or construction materials and locked themselves into the church, which was explicitly constructed for defence in many places. Women and children, along with the most valuable supplies, were placed in a safe location in the centre of the structure, while the men took up their posts along the windows and tower. The walls of the building were often equipped with loopholes for firing missiles. Thus the village church and its surroundings were turned into a stronghold capable of withstanding a hostile troop of mercenaries or a band of robbers at least for a while.

The justification – in fact, the obligation – for resorting to whatever means of self-defence were available resulted from the fact that pre-industrial society had no institutions like a modern police force to fall back on for protection. Maintenance of order in the countryside depended in large measure upon the involvement of the rural population, whether it was a case of repelling invaders or apprehending criminals. Villagers were thus required to grab their weapons and use them to turn back assailants and miscreants. In the light of the military potential of peasant communities and their defensive responsibilities, it is hardly surprising that many peasants spontaneously took up arms and considered such behaviour legitimate because they believed that their rights had been violated. Thus mobilization of the village home guard could easily become a revolt if countrymen felt that they were being oppressed by high manorial dues or taxes imposed by the state.

What were the tactics employed by peasants to fend off demands which they regarded as violations of their ancient rights? What were the forms of

rustic opposition to the encroachments of manorial lords and state authorities, and where did the borders lie between everyday resistance and outright defiance, bow, sword or gun in hand? Investigation of the various
manifestations of peasant insurrection has been greatly stimulated by the
work of the Russian historian, Boris Porshnev,[39] who drew a distinction
between minor and major types of resistance. His studies of rural uprisings
in Early Modern France led him to propose three basic categories of peasant
protest. The first is partial opposition, which Porshnev understands as
personal or collective rejection of specific demands or regulations, as well
as legal contests between peasants and manorial lords over individual
rights and obligations. Departure or flight is the second form of opposition: ploughmen do not rise up against the specific demands of feudal lords
but break with them completely and move to other places in the hope of
securing better conditions of life. The third stage of recalcitrance is reached
when rustics rebel openly and resort to collective violence in an attempt to
overturn existing relationships with their masters. Porshnev linked his
threefold typology of rural revolts to the unfolding of the Early Modern
French state and argued that peasant resistance fostered the growth of
centralized, national monarchies. In his view, absolutism – the most
evolved form of monarchical rule – was the necessary outcome of the
peasant battle for justice.

Critics of the Porshnev thesis objected that a purported peasant class
struggle had been elevated, unjustifiably, to the status of a general law
governing the development of feudal society. Moreover, the suggestion
that every rustic activity focused upon an increase of productivity should
be seen as an indirect expression of the 'class struggle' produced widespread
dissent. Notwithstanding many such objections in principle, it is fair to
say that Porshnev's typology fructified both Marxian and Western European research on the subject of peasant uprisings and has had a powerful
impact upon later generations of scholars. Other writers have preferred
to differentiate between latent and open manifestations of resistance.
This type of distinction is persuasive because it takes into account the
various levels of conflict and the overall social context. The stage of
underlying opposition is significant in so far as it engenders dissatisfaction
and leads to the point where recalcitrance passes into the phase of outright
violence.

Marxian-orientated investigations in Eastern European countries continued along the path of a differentiated analysis of the forms of peasant
resistance laid out by Porshnev; his approach to the topic was the basis for
intensive study of individual rural revolts. At the same time there was a

conscious attempt to integrate the history of rustic disturbances into that of some of the national states in question. This tendency was especially noticeable in the 1970s and 1980s on many occasions commemorating different peasant uprisings. The festivities extended all the way from Hungarian celebrations of the 1514 revolt, Yugoslav observances of the four hundredth anniversary of the Windish (Slovene) Rebellion of 1573, the jubilee of the 1775 Bohemian insurrection, down to a whole series of ceremonies in 1975 recalling the German Peasant War of 1525. In every instance it was obvious that scholarly research was being made to serve the purposes of promoting a patriotically coloured, Marxian image of history. The leadership of the German Democratic Republic was at particular pains to stress the national character of the German Peasant War. It seemed pertinent to invoke the hoary authority of Friedrich Engels, who had called the events of 1525 the 'most magnificent revolutionary effort ever of the German people'. This venerated oracle had already written in 1870:

> The Germans have a revolutionary tradition too. There was a time when Germany produced men of stature who could take their place alongside the revolutionaries of other countries, when the German people could develop the endurance and the energy that would have produced the most sublime results in the case of a centralized nation, when German peasants and plebeians were bursting with ideas and plans which often enough caused later generations, looking back upon these events, to recoil in horror.[40]

Western European studies of peasant uprisings have been strongly influenced by the French school of research. After Porshnev had presented his Marxian synoptic account of rural revolts in France, the ideological paradigm which had previously held sway seemed open to question; it no longer appeared certain that the disturbances of the sixteenth and seventeenth centuries were mainly regional challenges to the fiscal policies of a centralizing state. It was above all the controversy between Porshnev and Roland Mousnier[41] that led to enhanced interest in Early Modern insurrections, rural social structure and social transformation altogether in Western European countries. A number of special questions captured the attention of French and English scholars. The single most important problem was to understand better the various organizational features of protest movements. The result was to underline the strong attachment of rebellious peasants to their own community as the basis of attempts at resistance.

Further studies were concerned with the substance of peasant uprisings and how peasants envisaged their objectives. Were the revolts against taxation (Mousnier) or anti-feudal (Porshnev)? Were there different kinds of social protest? Still other investigations focused upon the issue of social legitimation. This question was important in so far as it tended to identify the causes of peasant resistance and led to a discussion of basic behavioural patterns. Clearly, rustic revolts cannot be considered merely as elementary outbursts of rage resulting from totally irrational impulses. Of course, this was the way Leopold von Ranke viewed such phenomena. The German Peasant War – whose incongruous and destructive traits he underscored – was the 'greatest natural disaster in [the history of] the German state'. If we are prepared to accept the approach of more recent investigators, rural uprisings and revolts have to be seen within the overall context of value systems and behavioural models that determine peasant mentality. We may thus disregard the apparent irrationality of rustic insurrections and explain them in terms of specific paradigms of social conduct, till now barely understood.

German historians have traditionally concentrated upon the 1525 Peasant War and Late Medieval disturbances that have often been depicted as

6   *The laced shoes of a rebellious peasant from the Upper Rhine (1513)*

its matrix. Undoubtedly, the former event was the most radical and widespread rustic conflagration that the country ever experienced – before that time or later. It is hardly surprising that it remains a focal point of scholarly and public attention. For a long while the standard monograph was the volume by Georg Franz. The author believed that the causes of the Peasant War lay not in the economic but in the political realm, namely, in the clash between the older principle of collective social action and its more recent antithesis of princely authority. Peasants fought to preserve local autonomy in the face of an ever more intrusive territorial state determined to have its writ fully obeyed within both the confines of villages and everywhere else; princes would brook no contradiction of their right to dominion. Younger West German historians, who revised the work of their predecessors in a number of important ways, long remained under the methodological and ideological influence of Franz. Historians in the German Democratic Republic naturally treated the Peasant War from a Marxian perspective, labelling the whole affair an 'early bourgeois revolution'. The result was a collection of individual studies that dealt with the multifarious features of a conflict that neatly fits the parameters of a classical Marxian mass uprising. Be this as it may, there was great interest in both parts of Germany on the occasion of the four hundred and fiftieth anniversary of the event in 1975.

Peasant revolts seem to have broken out especially when country folk were convinced that their time-honoured rights were being violated. However, their sense of legality was distinct from the rigid corpus of erudite written law that the Early Modern state was fostering. Peasants invoked ancient, orally transmitted norms and attitudes that reflected their legacy of collective resolution of judicial issues; with the passage of time values corroborated by their actual experience of life took on the binding quality of customary rights. Traditional unwritten rules, regarded as valid in the great majority of rural areas, applied to the most important categories of peasant life, that is, family, village and society. During the sixteenth century legal scholars employed by state bureaucracies collected and codified much of the heritage of customary law. While the influence of this judicial tradition was thereby strengthened, the flexibility and adaptability that had distinguished it for so many centuries were no more.

In view of the extraordinary dimensions of the body of European rustic law, it is difficult to make any generally valid statements about the subject. Nevertheless, one can ascertain a basic conviction that was evidently common to all Early Modern peasant revolts: the peasants were absolutely certain that their venerable rights had been infringed by the innovations of ruthless bureaucrats or greedy manorial lords, who had arrogated to themselves the authority of a fair-minded king. Two other features may be discerned: a strong belief in the force of tradition and the ruler's commitment to justice. The conservative stance of ploughmen – emphasized again and again in the literature on the topic – and their deliberate, unremitting insistence upon respect for traditional values are normally considered to have been manifestations of ignorance and backwardness. This is of course patently wrong. One cannot overlook the basic conditions of rural existence and the unique peasant mentality which results from them. As social anthropologists have recently recognized, the heart of the matter is that peasant society is based upon the power of experience to a degree that no other human collectivity is. The fact that ploughmen hold fast to concrete experience must be seen in the context of the fixed rhythms of country life, the regular sequence of the seasons, command of agrarian skills and well-established patterns of assuring one's livelihood. The changes that occurred in the sixteenth and seventeenth centuries benefited the rural population in some respects but also caused much misfortune and pain. Sixteenth-century agrarian prosperity led to tremendous population growth and an increase in the size of the rural underclass. The Catholic–Protestant Wars were devastating. Years of price inflation followed upon years of pestilence and damaged the agrarian economy. Bureaucratic fiscal pressures engendered hate and bitterness.

When manorial lords sought to raise the level of payments and services, the peasants thought that they could call upon the supreme ruler. The rustic world-view included the image of the king as the protector of his subjects, whose most holy duty was to guarantee peace and justice. The peasant mind could not imagine that the king wished his subjects to be unhappy. He was certainly not responsible; the disastrous innovations merely represented the misdeeds of rapacious bureaucrats. Peasants were totally convinced that the king did not know how bad things were for them because he was being deceived by shameless sycophants at court. Thus uprisings often took place in outlying districts and remote regions, sites that lay at the greatest distance from the seat of government – a milieu in which it was easy for strange rumours to circulate about what was happening at court. The minority of kings and unresolved problems of royal succession likewise tended to encourage misconceptions about the will of the central governmental authority.

What were the factors that ignited peasant rebellions and a resort to the use of violence? The threshold was crossed above all when some innovation was perceived as a provocation and peasant hopes were entirely disappointed. Ploughmen interpreted an innovation as an injury to a system of just and time-tested usages, as upsetting a traditional, firmly grounded equilibrium. The new, Early Modern habit of regular fiscal demands fell under this rubric and was clearly an inequity. It was not so much the actual amount of the levy but rather a matter of the over-exercised rustic imagination.

The introduction of systematic fiscal exactions in the sixteenth and seventeenth centuries was unquestionably one of the most controversial and odious steps taken by governments of the era. The financial difficulties caused by religious wars and military operations abroad forced kingdoms such as France and Spain – where the powers of central administration were growing most rapidly – to seek to enhance revenues with all the means at the state's disposal. These countries chose to impose duties on commodities and thus encumbered the salt, grain and wine trades. Indirect taxation that applied to goods required by everyone became the basis of fiscal policy. The first indignant reaction came from the lower strata of the urban populace. Initially, many peasants seemed to be less affected by the new measures since they were largely self-sufficient. However, as time passed, the bureaucracies in question began to extend the scope of direct taxation; an ever greater proportion of the population was caught up in the fiscal net. Certain individual taxes were raised sharply. Thus it was that direct levies became a hard and fast institution – the rule, so to speak – even though they had been explained away at first as temporary and unique. In France the head tax became the chief source of state income. It hit the peasants hardest because they constituted the bulk of the country's inhabitants. Between 1630 and 1640 the government collected the poll tax so frequently that it became for all practical purposes a regular form of assessment. It can hardly have been by chance that this was the decade which witnessed the most violent peasant uprisings.

Peasants were provoked not only by state fiscal measures but also in many instances by hikes in payments they owed to manorial lords. Long extant fees – those sanctioned by tradition – were rarely the object of protest; ploughmen believed that they were inescapable burdens because of their antiquity. On the other hand, new demands were regarded as not in conformity with custom. When peasants rebelled, they generally did not question manorial lordship as such but limited themselves to rejecting new levies. Conflicts and tensions could also develop when there was a change of seigniors. The appearance of a new lord or administrator represented a breach of a traditional relationship of fidelity and mutual solidarity, which

7   *Rebellious peasants in Allgäu during the Peasant War, shown on the title-page*
of the Menninger Bundesordnung *(1525)*

in many instances had been based upon long association with a particular
noble family. New, more onerous obligations could not be justified either
in terms of generally recognized customary law or according to the peasant's own perception of right and wrong.

In some Central and Eastern European countries in which the state's
right to levy taxes was not crystal clear, as it was in France, rulers were
forced to fall back upon others means of siphoning off rural resources.
Soldiers were trained and equipped at the expense of local communities;
they were dispatched into the open countryside to be quartered and fed by
the inhabitants. These much feared practices often turned into officially
tolerated larceny. Rustics particularly hated subsidizing the armed forces
because the soldiers behaved in villages and on farms as if they were in a
conquered land. The incessant quartering and foraging that took place in
Germany during the Thirty Years War plunged the rural populace into the
most extreme form of poverty. The great Catalan Rebellion of 1640 began
because mountain villages refused to quarter soldiers who had been ordered

to march to France. Battles between predatory soldiers and enraged peasants valiantly defending their farms and laying ambushes for the marauders were a frequent and totally realistic motif of seventeenth-century illustrative art.

When anger and bitterness had reached a peak and the threshold of violence had been crossed, the now thoroughly determined peasants grabbed their weapons. Equipped with pitchforks and spades, nail-studded stakes and razor-sharp scythes, they arrayed themselves in martial order. Whoever did not want to join them was threatened with dire reprisals. After troops from different villages had met at a pre-arranged site, they elected an overall commander. Every community normally kept together within the assembled army and would only follow its own leaders. Rustic hosts that mobilized in this manner could quickly encompass several thousand men. The commanders tried to discipline the disorderly swarms of combatants and organize them as regiments that could function as proper squares on the battlefield; the unfit were sent home. In the German Peasant War of 1525 the so-called 'Baltringer Horde' rapidly turned into an army of 7000–10,000 ploughmen from the most diverse areas of Upper Swabia. Threatening letters were sent to villages that had delayed sending their contingents and proved effective in forcing them to participate in the campaign. It would appear that the largest hosts of all were formed in Russia: when the famous rebel chieftain, Emelian Pugachev, went to war, he had at least 20,000 men under his command. Such forces were, however, only the hard military core of rural uprisings. The people who directly supported or at least sanctioned a rebellion certainly numbered several hundred thousand souls. In most cases peasant troops were extremely wayward and subject to great numerical fluctuation. As the host advanced in the direction of the enemy, there was constant change and substitution. Peasants from one village would accompany the army for a while and then take French leave, either because they feared that they were too far from home or had prematurely concluded that the objectives of the revolt had already been attained.

Commanders of peasant hosts were often not of rural origin themselves but stemmed rather from other segments of the population. Götz von Berlichingen, the prominent leader of the German Peasant War (who was later immortalized by Geothe), was the scion of a Franconian knightly dynasty; he had much previous military experience and was in fact pressed into service by the peasants. Other peasant armies of that age were headed not so much by fellow rustics as by burghers, craftsmen, noblemen and clerics. When peasants held a council of war or when their forces were relatively small, well-to-do and influential countrymen – people such as village magistrates, local judges and jurors – stood out. The lowest stratum of the rural populace was evidently never part of the leadership; field hands and paid labourers rarely became commanders. In France, Hungary and other countries, members of non-rustic social stata were also frequently to be found in positions of authority. Petty nobles were often talked into collaborating and assuming leadership roles by their peasant subjects and neighbours: the object was to exploit their social prestige, personal abilities and military talent. Battle-tested, already retired soldiers were likewise persuaded to take up arms again and use their skills to guide rural folk in combat.

The situation in Eastern Europe was similar. The chieftains were frequently men who had served or held higher posts in the armies that fought against the Turks. György Dósza, who led the Hungarian peasants during the 1514 uprising, had been in charge of a fortress on the Ottoman border. He had been responsible for protecting the frontier region and had conducted military operations personally. Mitija Gubec, the Croatian commander in 1572, had distinguished himself in the struggle against the Sublime Porte as well. Cossacks, the legally free cavalrymen of the southern Russian steppes, played a major role in revolts on their home territory. On one hand, they were closely associated with the rulers of Poland and Russia and manned the outposts that fended off Turkish raiders; on the other, they were on intimate terms with servile peasants who flocked to their ranks. The military proficiency of Cossack hetmans Bohdan Khmelnitsky (1648) and Pugachev (1773–4), who commanded truly formidable forces, was of great benefit to contemporary peasant insurgents. Stenka Razin, another Cossack rebel, was the head of a movement which spread like wildfire across the broad plains of the lower Volga between 1661 and 1671 and became a genuine threat to the power of the nascent central government in Moscow.

The most important point of reference for many peasant revolts was the village. When the perception of external threat increased, social tensions within the community abated; hatred of a new lord or pillaging troops relieved internal stresses. When faced by danger from outside, local rustics formed a solid front and demonstrated such cohesion, particularly during the first days of an uprising. Social strains between autochthonous peasants, landless newcomers, rich farmers, poor cottagers, leaseholders and hired hands existed in every village, but they subsided as the external peril increased and solidarity in the face of the enemy was called for. The individual peasant's strong identification with his village certainly derived from its long-established structure. It consisted of an easily surveyed group of households, each of which was to some extent autonomous but all of which had to collaborate in everday matters. Village autonomy in Western and Central Europe had grown considerably since the High Middle Ages, in conjunction with the tendency of manorial lords to withdraw from farming on their own and to leave the work of cultivation to a more or less independent peasantry.

The degree of rustic identification with the village was especially evident in specific cases of rebellion. In the Twelve Articles of the 1525 German Peasant War the key to understanding rustic demands is the community perceived as a collectively organized locus of power. It should be accorded far-reaching rights: it should appoint parish priests, collect tithes, regulate hunting and fishing, and control access to common woods and fields. Here we can see clearly how the south German village of the sixteenth century was the centre of the rustic spiritual world. However, it was not just in Upper Swabia but elsewhere in Europe as well that villages sought to settle their affairs as they deemed best, monitoring activities within their own precincts and resolving conflicts by themselves.

If we turn our attention to individual peasant uprisings of the Early Modern Era, we find that the Hungarian revolt of 1514 is significant because of its primordial savagery and the sheer numbers of ploughmen who participated in it. There are both similarities and differences between it and other great European peasant rebellions. In the decades prior to 1514 there had been scattered disturbances within the kingdom of Hungary, but they had not had a supra-regional character. The unifying factor – the reason why a number of local protests grew into a general insurrection – was a plan for a crusade.

The papal legate had proclaimed a crusade against the infidel Turk and had secured the consent of royal advisors for his scheme. The counsellors were hoping that the Ottomans could be defeated by a rustic host that would not cost the government very much. However, episcopal selfishness and seigniorial repressive measures had recently caused immense dissatisfaction among the populace at large; all that was needed for an outbreak of violence was a tiny spark. The nobility forbade the peasants to join the crusaders and even dragged some of them back home. Pressured by the nobles, the king prohibited further recruitment and ordered his troops to return. It was at this point that the main army, led by Dósza, reversed its route of march and fell upon the nobility. In late May of 1514 the rustic warriors collided with an army of noblemen near Nagylak and routed it; several aristocrats and a number of high churchmen were captured and executed. In the meantime peasant forces that had gathered on the Big Alföld and in marginal areas had begun to battle against the nobility. In mid-July there was a decisive engagement near Timişoara in which the peasants suffered a bloody defeat. Dósza and his comrades were dispatched in an exceedingly brutal manner.

No Hungarian peasant political agenda has survived the events of 1514; only a few recorded remarks of the movement's chieftains give us an idea of the insurrection's objectives. The rebels clearly wanted a strong monarchy from which the intermediate feudal authorities – the magnates and the high clergy – would be excluded. The nobility should be exterminated, and clerics should all have the same rank. However, the goal was not a republican or democratic order but rather a return to a patriarchal form of government which, the peasants imagined, had existed once before. There should be a free peasantry under a strong king, who would put an end to the arbitrary actions of the all too numerous petty nobility and judicial lordlings. The leaders of the uprising stemmed above all from two social strata. On one hand, there were a few representatives of the gentry like Dósza. The more important leadership element, by far, was sacerdotal – an equal mixture of priests from village parishes and market towns. Among them were many Franciscans, the same friars who had read out the crusading bull and had recruited the peasants. Like the leaders, the participants in the rebellion came mainly from market towns and larger localities in the Big Alföld. This was obviously the focal point of the uprising. The leading elements within this stratum were socially mobile peasants from the market towns. Since the insurrection came as something of a surprise, the political programme did not attain the same degree of significance that it had in other European peasant rebellions.

How did the uprising affect the lot of Hungary's rustic population? After the rebels had been vanquished the king convoked a diet or assembly, which approved an edict that authorized reprisals and compensation. The movement's leaders and persons who had agitated in favour of it were to be executed. The peasants were made adscript to the glebe and hereditary bondage introduced – measures that fulfilled a long-standing wish of the nobility. Peasants were forbidden to carry weapons and had to pay for the damage they had wreaked. However, crucial parts of the law were later rescinded, and so the failure of the rebellion did not lead to a permanent worsening of the situation in the Hungarian countryside.

The German Peasant War, which began a decade later, was certainly among the biggest rural uprisings of European history. It involved several different factors, namely, the influence of the Protesant Reformation and an inherent rustic predilection for rebellion. Once combined, they produced a mass movement of enormous proportions. A latent restlessness among the peasantry took on the character of a collective fever after Lutheran clergy began to roam the land, preaching the Evangelical faith and assailing the doctrines of the old Church. Protestant propaganda only reinforced many demands for rustic liberty and self-determination that had been circulating for decades and had already led to a series of uprisings. The numerous disturbances that can be pinpointed in southern Germany from the late fifteenth century to the threshold of the Reformation had different causes. Because material and legal circumstances varied considerably from one place to another, it is difficult to find a common denominator in them. However, one can discern among partly divergent, partly identical rebel objectives certain basic tendencies: a common front in countering the efforts of ruling princes to impose uniform legal routines upon all their subjects; rejection of restrictions upon communal autonomy; and finally, refusal to accept increased dues and services. Peasants insisted upon the maintenance of tradition – 'the old law' – *vis-à-vis* the pretensions of the emergent territorial state.

In addition to general political causes, socio-economic factors should also be considered, in so far as these may be appropriate. It is evident that, by the time the Peasant War began, material conditions in the German countryside were much worse than they had been for quite a while. While it is true that agriculture had done remarkably well at the start of the sixteenth century, the structure of agrarian society was weak and prone to crises. Sharp population growth in long-settled regions had produced a huge village underclass, people who had to work on the side in order to get by. The right to use the commons was absolutely crucial to land-poor rustics; new regulations issued by locals lords, restricting access to woods, meadows and waterways, hit them especially hard. Increased payments, the burden of tithes, poor harvests and the novel fiscal demands of the territorial state drove large segments of the population to the limits of their endurance. Moreover, in the heavily fragmented political regions of Germany, knights and monastic orders sought to solve their financial problems at the expense of the peasants and the collective rights of villages, which only heightened existing social tensions. The nobility's fiscal privileges aroused envy and resentment everywhere while, on their part, petty feudal lords were confronted by challenges to the legitimacy of their rule. The Church too was suffering from a decline in its authority; clergymen and monks were increasingly the objects of derision. When Lutheran preachers turned up to proclaim the teachings of the Gospel, using 'divine law' as an argument in support of the Reformation and lending a new validity to peasant complaints, the result was rebellion.

The German Peasant War, the details of which cannot be related here, affected most of southern, western and central Germany. Whereas earlier revolts had been limited mainly to the Alps, their foothills and the Upper Rhine, the great 1525 uprising reached deep into Thuringia. Only the duchy of Bavaria, the kingdom of Bohemia and the north German low-lands were spared. The general insurrection began in certain villages on the south-eastern edge of the Black Forest and then spread across Upper Swabia towards the north. Other nuclei were in Alsace, the Upper Rhine, Württemberg and Franconia. In early March the famous Twelve Articles, the movement's most influential and indicative document, were promul-gated in Upper Swabia. They were simultaneously 'gravamina, a reform programme, and a political manifesto' (Peter Blickle) and more or less the cement that linked individual rebel actions.[42]

What was the peculiar attraction of the Twelve Articles which, after they were printed in Augsburg, were rapidly distributed over all of Ger-many? The answer is that they registered the insurgent peasants' major concerns and condensed their many specific complaints into a few main points, which lent a sharp cutting edge and great power of conviction to the rustic line of argument. Precise demands were cleverly associated with the overall principle of God's word as revealed by the Holy Gospel. The document's rationale is impressive: it proceeds at a steady, measured and harmonious pace. The introduction attempts to allay indignation over the illegality of rebellion: since the principal rustic grievances are in accord with Scripture, peasants cannot be considered guilty of sedition. The Lord's precepts are simple and involve nothing other than love, peace and spiritual unity.

The first eleven articles prove conclusively that peasant demands are in conformity with the word of the Almighty. They constitute a systematic programme and encompass the following main points. Communities have the right to pick their own pastors. The small tithe must be rescinded, and there must be a more equitable division of the large one. Above all else, bondage must be abolished. Everybody must be allowed to hunt and fish freely and have unlimited access to village common lands. Servile labour should be reduced to manageable proportions. Death duties should be done away with entirely since they represent a particularly unfair burden upon peasants. The final twelfth article revives the introductory theme, stressing once again the peasants' basic concern for justifying their actions. The

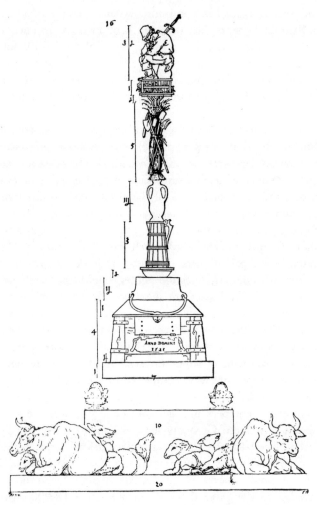

8   *Albrecht Dürer's sketch for a statue in memory of the failure of the German peasant revolt in 1525. The sheep and cattle on the base seem to take part in the peasant's dejection. His simple belongings (a wooden chest for clothes and valuables, with a milk can and a butter churn, a tied sheaf of corn and a basket with a chicken) are stacked into an unsteady tower, with the weary peasant mounted on it, dressed in rags, with torn shoes and an old sword, the symbol of his unsuccessful rebellion.*

document thus succeeded in combining what up to then had been scattered, individual laments and linking them in each instance with the
Word of God, which was held up as the only valid principle for dealing
with rural affairs. Except for the insistence upon free election of pastors, the
demands were not fundamentally new. However, the fact that they had
been packaged so adroitly guaranteed that they would have an explosive
impact.

The rebels assailed the old Church with a particular passion. Monastic
establishments and churches were plundered everywhere; priests and members of religious orders were personally assaulted. The peasants maintained
that clerics, instead of leading mankind onto the path of evangelical
righteousness and truth, had ruthlessly harassed God's children; monasteries and nunneries were places of treachery and oppression. The goal of the
insurgents was to be rid of the clergy as a property-owning and privileged
social estate. The pillar of the new Church should be a minister chosen and
remunerated by his parishioners. The rebel attitude towards the nobility
was less clear. Without any question nobles should lose their special legal
and economic rights and associate themselves more closely with the life
of local communities. The abolition of bondage, reduced payments and
services, and the elimination of their special legal status would have
permanently crippled noblemen. Castles and châteaux were attacked
and plundered everywhere; when ancestral residences were not actually
wrecked, their inhabitants were compelled by threats to life and limb to
abandon the premises.

After the insurgent peasants had controlled political events in much
of southern and western Germany for some months, the princes struck
back. Troops hired by the territorial rulers defeated the peasants in a
number of battles in the summer of 1525. Duke Antoine of Lorraine
routed the massed squares of the Alsatian ploughmen near Saverne
and proceeded to slaughter them wholesale: some 18,000 rustics were
cut down. The Thuringian peasants led by Thomas Müntzer suffered a
similar disaster near Frankenhausen. They were massacred by the thousands; surviving participants were subjected to stringent criminal prosecu-
tion. It has been estimated that the total number of deaths in the Peasant
War amounted to more than 70,000. Material destruction is very difficult
to calculate, inasmuch as the high penalty payments imposed upon the
peasantry do not provide precise data concerning the damages inflicted
upon castles, châteaux and monastic foundations. Even if the venerable
thesis of a peasant 'political disenfranchisement' resulting from the
events of 1525 can now be regarded as superseded, it is still not possible

to formulate definitive judgements about the long-term effects of the uprising.

Unquestionably the peasants' defeat represented a victory of territorial princes, who were now able to extend their authority and restrict rustic self-government. The Reformation, seen as a movement of the people at large, was surely less significant and suffered some loss of credibility. Although his initial reaction was benevolent, Martin Luther soon decisively distanced himself from the rural struggle for liberty. His polemic 'Against the Larcenous and Murderous Peasants' served to legitimize the territorial rulers' brutal repression of the insurgency.

If, after this detailed analysis of the German Peasant War, we shift our attention to other significant rural uprisings of Early Modern times, we must look towards the east and mention sixteenth- and seventeenth-century revolts of Russian peasants, which stand in close causal relationship to the expansion and exacerbation of serfdom. In the case of these popular insurrections rustics reduced to the status of bondage united with certain oppressed ethnic groups in southern Russia and, under Cossack leadership, fought doggedly against domination by owners of landed estates and tsarist autocracy. During the seventeenth century the violent outbreaks of rural unrest associated with the names of Khmelnitsky and, to an even greater extent, Razin shook the foundations of the Muscovite state for years on end. The massive rebellion of Pugachev a hundred years later was only the most spectacular in a long series of peasant upheavals in imperial Russia. Prompted by the intrepid cavalry chieftain, peasants, non-Russian peoples and Pugachev's fellow Cossacks streamed together to form a mighty popular army that was able to withstand the tsar's forces for an extended period of time. However, after capturing Kazan in 1774, the rebellion's leader could not prevent the gradual dissolution of his host, the military backbone of resistance to the Kremlin.

As has already been indicated, many rural disturbances in western Europe were caused above all by fiscal pressures which the Early Modern state exerted with all the means at its disposal. The 1548 Aquitaine uprising, provoked by the *gabelle* or tax on salt, was one of the most serious peasant protests against the new taxation machinery. The Croquants and the Tard Avisés were rustic rebels in southern France whose geographic reach was about the same as the opponents of the salt levy. They hoisted the banner of revolt in 1594 towards the end of the Wars of Religion and again in 1637, when France entered the struggle against Spain and the anti-imperial coalition in Germany. The 1640 Catalan insurgency erupted in connection with taxes which the King of Spain attempted to collect

9   *The Cossack leader Pugachev, who unleashed a major peasant rebellion in Russia in 1713. He was finally captured and taken to Moscow in an iron cage to be executed*

from the rural population when he was embarking on hostilities with France. In 1705, during the War of the Spanish Succession (1701–14), large numbers of peasants again rebelled in Catalonia, Valencia and Aragon.

Among later peasant revolts in Germany we may single out the Bavarian uprising of 1705. Austrian troops had occupied the Electorate and were systematically looting the country, something that greatly embittered the population. When the Austrians proceeded to press young rustics for service in the Imperial Army, the result was a general insurrection, especially by the peasants of Upper and Lower Bavaria. The rebels organized themselves militarily according to the existing home-guard system but they were very badly equipped, mainly with iron-tipped spears, forks and morning stars (spiked clubs). The result of the peasants' defeat on Christmas Day of 1705 was a hecatomb: some 3000 of them were butchered after they had already laid down their weapons and asked for quarter.

What did the many European peasant revolts actually achieve? The balance, viewed in tangible terms, is certainly very negative: almost all the uprisings ended in sanguinary routs – the Hungarian insurrection of 1514, the German Peasant War of 1525 and Pugachev's 1774 Russian rebellion. Stout-hearted leaders, men such as Dósza and Müntzer, were executed in the most gruesome fashion after they had surrendered, in order to deter any future popular opposition. Were the many rustic sacrifices in vain? Did they serve no purpose at all? Were the disturbances merely irrational outbreaks of raw violence, as the ploughmen's opponents maintained? Of course, one can point to certain partial successes of rural resistance movements, for example, the cancellation of new payments and imposts, tax reductions and the abolition of restrictions upon liberty of movement. Within the context of the evolution of the Early Modern state, peasant uprisings certainly contributed to the process of public expression of rustic political will, demonstrating to the authorities the limits of bureaucratic power. Therefore, rural revolts were by no means outbursts of senseless bestiality. Rather, they reflected the widely held view that 'there are bounds to lordship and it is dependent upon at least the passive consent of the subject population' (Walter Schulze).[43] Payments and taxes could not exceed a certain level, that is, surpass the point at which the subsistence of rural families and communities was threatened. Josef Blum has emphasized that many eighteenth-century disturbances may have ended with only partial triumph or total failure, but the events in question made a deep impression upon the minds of the ruling estates: 'the excesses [that accompanied the uprisings] caused them to fear for their own lives, families and property.'[44] Thus, on the eve of the French Revolution, peasant insurgency encouraged the nobility and the princes to consider agrarian reforms and to think again about their corporate privileges. Peasant emancipation in the late eighteenth and nineteenth centuries was not something that happened all on its own, but in the last analysis a process that was profoundly influenced by the centuries-old rustic struggle for justice.

7

The Western Manor and the Eastern Estate

When the chief countries of Europe carried out so-called 'peasant emancipation' during the first half of the nineteenth century, there was a fundamental difference between the agrarian systems of east and west. The geographical border between them was roughly the course of the Elbe river: to the east the landed estate prevailed, to the west the manor. The main feature of the west was the small peasant farm which for the most part paid the lord in money and kind; in the east large farms of noble landowners predominated, and peasants were compelled to render heavy labour services. While seigniories in the west did encompass some arable land that was worked from the manor on behalf of the lord, such farms were not very common. In the east this type of seigniory was the rule rather than the exception. There were also differences in the function and significance of rural communities. East of the Elbe they were closely linked to the estate owner, as many of them had only one lord. The estate owner also exercised police authority and served as the local justice of the peace; the peasants were his hereditary subjects. In the villages west of the great river lordship was greatly fragmented since several seigniors simultaneously exercised rights and held lands within individual localities. The rural population was normally much more autonomous and enjoyed greater leeway than in the east.

On the far side of the Elbe the landed estates stretched from Holstein across Mecklenburg, Pomerania and East Prussia into Poland and Russia, and across the March of Brandenburg, Lusatia, Bohemia and Moravia into Romania. To the west of the Elbe manorial lordship existed in a variety of guises in Germany, France and other occidental countries. Thus two zones with divergent farming systems were clearly marked off from each other in Early Modern times. This fundamental division – agrarian dualism – not only characterized relationships between the ruling strata and the subject population before the rural reforms of the nineteenth century, but also determined the social and economic circumstances of peasant life in both of the great geographic realms in question. The contrast between the situations east and west of the Elbe is well illustrated in travel books written by contemporaries. When a visitor from the kingdom of Hannover – where most peasants lived quite comfortably – spent several days in Mecklenburg – a region in which the landed estate and serfdom were especially prevalent – he recorded his experiences with a sense of horror:

> Whoever passes a day upon a landed estate in Mecklenburg is bound to see outrageous things, enough to make one's heart bleed, even when the lord happens to be a decent person; only if one is accustomed to such abominations can feelings of common humanity be repressed. I went there, and the first thing I saw when I entered the house was a big, thick whip hanging on the wall. The superintendent used it to requite whatever misdemeanours had been committed, and certainly took it with him when he rode into the fields to observe a serf who was ploughing and lashed either the horses or the man depending upon which of them had done something wrong. What an awful spectacle this was for me![45]

At what point in time did agrarian dualism arise in Europe? When did the trans-Elbian landed estate, which had such a long-lasting and negative impact upon the peasantry of the eastern half of the Continent, originate? This variety of lordship certainly does not go back to the High Middle Ages, when the districts beyond the river were intensively colonized and totally transformed by Germans from the west. New villages were founded, peasants paid rent for inheritable farms, the three-field system spread and yields increased. Within the broad framework of extending arable land, German peasants often managed to secure economic, social and legal conditions better than those that applied to fellow rustics who had remained behind on long-settled territory. The Slavic population, at least in part, was also able to benefit from more advantageous terms, especially in villages that were reorganized according to German law codes. Most newcomers paid rent for their inheritable holdings, and their obligations consisted mainly of payments and only to a lesser extent of services. Alongside the peasant farms – the characteristic feature of east German villages – were those of the secular and ecclesiastical lords. Their plots did not exceed by much the size of neighbouring rustic ones and therefore required but little in the way of servile labour. While the biggest seigniors were the German and Slavic territorial princes, most land was controlled by an internally very stratified nobility. Further development was greatly influenced by the fact that the holdings of the territorial rulers passed increasingly into the hands of knightly dynasts. The income of ruling princes, nobles and prelates was derived mostly from payments in money and kind; hide rentals were the principal source.

The Late Middle Ages were a crucial turning-point and led to divergent agrarian development in east and west. In the fourteenth and fifteenth centuries – as we have already seen – all of Europe was engulfed by a tidal wave of immensely complex economic and social problems that may be interpreted partly as a crisis of the feudal system and partly as an agrarian one. Pestilence, population decline, abandoned villages and fields, falling grain prices, a shortage of rustic tenants, civil wars, knightly feuds and invasions like those of the fearsome Hussites and the Turks created a situation of general disorder. In order to cope with the difficult economic circumstances with which they were confronted, eastern European seigniors resorted, in part, to the means used by their compeers in the west. In order to keep wage costs down, they set upper limits to the salaries of household servants and tried, as far as it was feasible, to extract higher payments from peasants. However, above and beyond this and unlike western manorial lords, the easterners implemented measures which in the course of time would turn their peasants into bondsmen. Instead of mitigating feudal obligations as the English nobility did, seigniors in many eastern European countries demanded higher payments from peasants, restricted rustic mobility and enlarged their own estates at the expense of ploughmen. In the course of the fifteenth century a series of laws steadily reduced liberty of movement throughout the eastern European countryside; the result was the conversion of rural folk into genuine serfs.

The profound economic, social, political and cultural changes of the sixteenth century also had an enduring impact upon agrarian relationships. Accelerated demographic growth created a growing demand for agricultural commodities and led to an expansion of market opportunities. However, the greatest progress in Europe's economy was in the non-agrarian sector. It was the townsmen who profited most from overall economic development, overseas exploration, and flourishing, worldwide trading activities. The great harbour cities on the western seaboard – primarily in England and the Lowlands – became the focuses of European commerce. The Baltic turned into a marginal body of water after the Hanseatic League was forced to yield economic and political hegemony to its competitors along the North Sea and the Channel; the power of the vacuum engendered by the Atlantic maritime states was almost irresistible. The structural differences between Western Europe – with its dense network of towns, broadly based craft industries and lively exchange of goods – and the east, poor in cities, manufactures and population, became ever more pronounced. In both parts of Europe manorial lords faced the problem of how they should cope with these changes and what means they might employ to maintain their position in society. For the east this meant a fateful turn in the road, a new epoch that would give rise to the landed estate and its concomitant of full-fledged bondage. The tendency for peasants to become attached to the soil was linked to a growth in seigniorial farming and the compulsory labour services it required. By the end of the sixteenth century the standard agrarian institution in the east was the landed estate based upon serfdom, increased seigniorial farming activities, a much heavier burden of compulsory service and domestic servitude. If manorial farms in the fifteenth century were on the average three times larger than peasant plots, the lords were able to double their holdings in the sixteenth century; their estates now amounted to about two-fifths of the hide area of villages.

If we subdivide Eastern Europe for explanatory purposes and direct our attention to the German regions east of the Elbe, we find that seigniors resolved their economic problems in a variety of ways and increased their political power by exploiting their position as representatives of the noble estate. Territorial rulers were especially weak wherever the lords managed to upgrade their corporate functions and achieve autonomy, as was the case in Schleswig-Holstein, certain parts of Lusatia and East Prussia. Eastern Holstein and Brandenburg were evidently the leading regions in the process of subjecting peasants to manorial rule and extending the scope of seigniorial farming. In Silesia the destruction that occurred during the Hussite Wars and a number of epidemics made it easier for the lords to enlarge their estates; the weakness of the ducal government fostered the development of a system of noble rule characterized by the exercise of judicial authority and advowsons to govern ecclesiastical patronage. In Pomerania of the sixteenth century the nobility succeeded in acquiring wide-ranging privileges which it used to expand its farming activities at the expense of the peasantry.

When east German lords first extended their estates, they were able to fall back upon a large reservoir of land that had been abandoned in the late Middle Ages; it was either added to existing manors or served as the basis for establishing knightly domiciles. Initially, wasteland had little value and was only lightly worked by the seigniors. However, as prices for agrarian commodities rose during the sixteenth century and marvellous sales opportunities for east German grain presented themselves in north-western Europe, the eastern landed estates rapidly expanded in order to profit from the new market. The weakness of territorial government led to the transfer of judicial lordship and fiscal authority to the knightly estates, which of course greatly enhanced manorial power. At the same time rustic rights of tenancy were restricted; unfavourable terms of occupancy became much more common. This allowed the lords to absorb peasant plots; such dispossession enabled them vastly to expand their own tracts of land. Detailed studies of the increase in the amount of land farmed by seigniors in the March of Brandenburg have shown that manorial fields grew very considerably, especially in the sixteenth century. The estates were first enlarged by taking control of wastelands and thereafter by seizing peasant holdings and driving the inhabitants from their farms. Not only were the rustics expelled from their hides but there was now also a need for a seigniorial work-force. Thus, at the beginning of the Early Modern Era, peasant liberty of movement was further restricted, soil bondage tight-ened and servile labour obligations extended. Runaway ploughmen were severely punished when they were caught. They and their children had become mere estate accessories. Now their only function in life was mano-rial subservience.

In Poland and Lithuania – both countries belonged to the core zone of the eastern European landed estate in Early Modern times (see map 4) – the personal legal status of rustics degenerated into serfdom. The Polish diets of the 1500s proceeded to strengthen the legal and political powers of the nobility *vis-à-vis* the peasantry and townsmen; seigniorial predominance was firmly grounded for centuries to come. The magnates and gentry fully controlled the Sejm (parliament) and could impose any measures they wished. The Polish monarchy was so weak domestically that, for the most part, it had to give free reign to a nobility that had become virtually omnipotent, thanks to the growing grain trade and the expansion of the landed estate.

Enlarged manors, more land farmed by seigniorial landowners, in-creased rustic labour services and enhanced feudal rule were not only characteristic of eastern Germany and Poland but also of Bohemia, Moravia, Hungary and Romania. In all of these countries the process of refeudalization may be seen, in some cases engendering peasant resistance. Peasants came to be regarded more and more as the personal property of feudal lords, who claimed the right to sell either plots without tenants or villeins without land. Serfdom sometimes had outright legal sanction

Map 4 The eighteenth-century landed estate (after Kaak, Gutherrschaft, page 474)

as, for example, in 1595, when Michael the Brave of Romania issued an strict ordinance, according to which ploughmen became adscript to the glebe.

Large parts of Belorus (White Russia) and the Ukraine were subject to Poland and Lithuania in the sixteenth century and consequently also belonged to the zone of an agrarian system based upon landed estates. However, to the east of these countries, the sixteenth century witnessed the domestic growth and expansion abroad of the Muscovite state – a process that was marked by a hard internal power struggle involving the tsars as the champions of central authority and the nobility as the defenders of local rule. The nobles succeeded in their effort to ratify the 1497 law which deprived peasant tenants of the unlimited right to leave their farms; they could do so in the future only under specific conditions and only after all issues in dispute had been resolved. Landowners now devoted more and more of their time to administering their estates and sought to exploit the rustic work-force more intensively. Payments in money and kind were replaced increasingly by labour services, and the previous equilibrium between material reimbursement and compulsory work was changed to the peasants' disadvantage. In the course of the sixteenth century the amount of time in which Russian peasants had to slave for their lords doubled in many places; peasants ended up by spending as many days on the seigniorial estate as they did on their own plots of land. The fact that Muscovy had no access to the Baltic was evidently the reason why farming by Russian noblemen evolved more slowly than it did in neighbouring Poland and Russia, and why the tsarist state long remained economically backward in comparison to the countries of Western and Central Europe. In his study of the international economy of the Early Modern era Immanuel Wallerstein quite correctly points out that Russia did not form a part of the western commercial world until the accession of Peter the Great in 1689.[46]

What caused most eastern European peasants to fall under the yoke of serfdom in the sixteenth century, a time when feudal ties in the west were clearly being relaxed? The explanation for the striking discrepancy between peasant fortunes in the two halves of Europe lies in differing patterns of historical evolution. In western European states such as France and England kings managed to establish their predominance over the nobility during the sixteenth century, whereas in eastern European countries like Poland and Hungary noblemen dominated politics. The princes and kings of the east, weakened by wars, succession struggles and shrinking revenues, desperately needed the support of the nobility in order to be able to exercise even a modicum of power. All sorts of concessions were made to manorial lords, especially in regard to their relationships with the rural population. In this context it is clear that there is every reason to label the kingdom of Poland a 'noble republic'. The nobility's corporate representatives made all important political decisions and reinforced their privileged socio-economic position. In 1518 King Sigismund even had to pledge that he would not accept any appeals from peasants against their masters.

The dwindling of towns and the urban bourgeoisie in Eastern Europe certainly fostered the growth of noble political control. The prosperous cities of the fourteenth and fifteenth centuries had had a considerable impact upon the economic and political life of the east, but then decline set in. Its causes were manifold: the collapse of the Hanseatic League, which had included a number of Baltic towns; a downturn in business as the consequence of a drop in population; wars and domestic power struggles; and finally increasing competition from English and Dutch merchants in the exchange of goods between the east and the west. The economic crisis faced by the towns gave the nobility, helped by its close links to the monarchy, the chance to break the bourgeois monopoly of foreign and domestic trade, to prohibit cities from granting asylum to runaway serfs, to outwit the burghers in commercial transactions and to secure price advantages for its own products by virtue of tariff reductions.

Weakened by the measures rammed through diets by princes and noblemen, many eastern European cities began to stagnate. At the same time western European towns entered upon a growth phase that led to great economic progress, above all in England and the Lowlands. The differences in the development of town life between east and west were of importance not only for the development of relationships between manorial lords and peasants but for European history altogether. The special character of events and trends in Eastern Europe meant that there was no challenge to the claim of the nobility to determine the course of social, economic and political life. Conversely, the west experienced the rise of an energetic bourgeoisie that played a leading role in the process of imposing European hegemony upon the world at large. The weakness of its cities evidently had much to do with the fact that Eastern Europe remained predominantly agrarian and backward.

Eastern Europe's function in the international economic order of Early Modern times has recently been discussed anew in the context of the controversy engendered by Wallerstein's thesis of the modern world system.[47] The American scholar distinguishes the following zones according to their role within a sixteenth-century world economy characterized by a division of labour: (1) the nucleus – and most advanced individual component – of north-western Europe, a region including England, the Netherlands and parts of France; (2) the semi-periphery that included southern France, Spain and western Germany; (3) the periphery of which the first zone was the centre and which embraced on one hand Spain's American colonies and on the other the grain-producing countries of the Baltic (see map 5); and (4) a vast outer ring of lands running from Russia across Turkey as far as China – all countries that, unlike the periphery, were not directly orientated to the European world economy. As far as Eastern Europe is concerned, Wallerstein has been criticized – and correctly so – for not having differentiated sufficiently between specific regions and for not having paid adequate attention to divergent patterns of development.

Since eastern European rulers had little contact with the rural population, the latter was primarily under the thumb of the nobility. Manorial

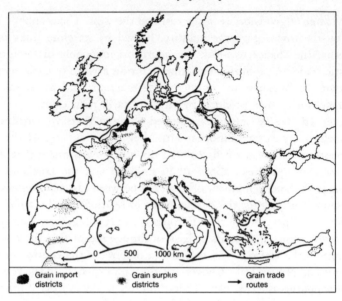

*Map 5   Cereal cultivation and the grain trade in the seventeenth century
(after N.J.G. Pounds,* An Historical Geography of Europe, 1500–1840,
Cambridge, 1979, page 62)

lords utilized the patrimonial powers over peasants that they had arrogated
to themselves in order to restrict liberty of movement further, increase
feudal burdens and impair tenant rights. The seigniors thus became village
autocrats and enforced the strictest kind of bondage. This development was
accompanied by a remarkable increase in the production of grain on their
estates for the export market. If the eastern European ruling stratum had
previously sold few commodities on the open market, it now undertook to
extend its direct role in farming on a very broad scale. This frequently
occurred at the expense of the peasantry: those who used to work their own
hides became cottagers and day labourers. At the same time the level of
compulsory services was raised to several days a week; for all practical
purposes, this meant that rustic farming activity was totally orientated to
the nobleman's land.

Several phases may be distinguished in the evolution of the eastern
European landed estate from the sixteenth to the eighteenth centuries.
Excellent market conditions up to the end of the sixteenth century enabled
it to mature fully; a concomitant was the successful imposition of serfdom.

With a new period of crisis looming on the horizon in the early seventeenth century, manorial lords sought to reinforce the institution of hereditary subjection and issued additional ordinances adversely affecting the life of peasants. The effects of the Thirty Years War and the Swedish–Polish War contributed in a fundamental way to the further expansion and strengthening of the landed estate during the latter half of the seventeenth century. As a consequence of population losses and of people having been driven from their homes, many East Elbian peasants had to give up their rights of hereditary rental occupancy and their ancestral farms; poor terms of tenancy became more common than ever. Peasant legislation of this period perpetuated subjection to the landed estate, compulsory service within the seigniorial household and very broad servile labour requirements.

It was during the eighteenth century that the country estate reached its highest stage of development. Noble landowners were now independent lords in their own bailiwicks and – some of them at any rate – ruthlessly exploited their monopoly of power to implement their objectives: forced labour often amounted to six days in the week. The shrinking peasant estate – in the corporate sense of the word – and the remaining rural population became so much a part of the manorial farm that rustics came to be regarded as mere appurtenances of landed property. This trend was accompanied by stagnating and in some instances declining productivity. Under such conditions peasant farming made little progress or even fell behind. The problematic evolution of the agrarian world caused certain German territorial princes to attempt social reforms designed to protect the interests of the ploughman.

During the last decades of the eighteenth century the skeins of agrarian development within the various individual regions became ever more complex and diverse. As far as east Central Europe is concerned, Prussia and Austria were the only countries that sought to bring about real change in the rural world by introducing new policies. Emperor Joseph II implemented a form of peasant emancipation in Bohemia, Moravia and Galicia, which preceded by a few years the steps taken by revolutionary France, but which did not go as far. In other places, especially in Poland and Russia, peasant subjection turned into the most stringent variety of serfdom imaginable. Reforms of a social and a technological character were generally carried out separately and only rarely complemented one another – as, for example, they did in Holstein, where concentration of scattered holdings, changes in personal relationships between lord and peasant and rationalization of arrangements within subdivided common fields began to be effected. The extension of arable land in the eighteenth century led to an increased number of better-off peasants but did little to improve the lot of the rustics who lived on the landed estates of the nobility and who constituted the great bulk of the servile population. The very worst case was that of Mecklenburg. After the massive dispossession of peasants in favour of manorial lordships, servile day labourers became the rule everywhere; independent peasant farmers were in effect decimated.

What did the everyday world of the rural population within the context of the Early Modern landed estate actually look like? Taken together, peasant ordinances, contemporary descriptions and recent scholarly research enable us to obtain a fairly clear picture of the kind of life led by peasants subjected to manorial rule in the territories east of the Elbe. Among the many burdens imposed upon the peasant within the cadre of the landed estate, the foremost were work requirements: they encompassed miscellaneous manual labour, carting, threshing grain, running errands, planting and the like. Usually, corvée did not need to be performed in person; peasants were at liberty to send their domestic help or neighbours to substitute for them. The extent and the nature of compulsory services varied considerably in accordance with local agreements and custom. Cartage was provided by a peasant who had a plot large enough to maintain a team of draught animals. In regions where the landed estate was most developed daily services were required of the peasant who occupied a whole hide. As a general rule, service obligations of the rural population were calculated on the basis of the size of peasant farms and divergent terms of tenancy.

Compulsory labour provoked constant rustic complaints about massive waste of time and energy. Peasants had to come from afar and could only begin to toil later in the morning; they had to stop early if they lived in remote villages. Penalties imposed upon dilatory ploughmen did little good and only increased tensions. Moreover, obligatory work had to be scheduled the night before; in the meantime the weather might have changed, resulting in cancellation of the seigniorial command. This was bad enough for the estate owner but how much worse for peasants who needed their teams for their own farms! Corvée led to numerous disputes and litigation, since peasants made a point of doing no more than they absolutely had to, whereas the lord and even more, someone who had leased an estate, were constantly seeking to derive as much benefit as they could from the sweat of servile brows.

In view of the extreme hardship caused by service obligations and payments, the economic lot of many manorially subject peasants was anything but enviable. A perceptive mid-eighteenth-century observer rendered the following judgement about the fate of peasants in the March of Brandenburg:

> It is well known that country folk live from hand to mouth and can reckon themselves lucky if they are able to perform their seigniorial and public duties properly. In the best of circumstances their own farms produce just enough for them to get by. It is impossible for a peasant to lay anything aside for the following year. If there is but the slightest mishap – an inadequate or even a failed harvest, the loss of one head of cattle or an epidemic resulting in many animal deaths, damage caused by fire, hailstorms or the like – then both the estate owner and the government must remit his obligations.[48]

In Upper Silesia, where the landed estate had proliferated, a commission of 1786 concluded that a dependent peasant farm that had fulfilled all its obligations had an annual profit of only five thalers. Daily experience, the report goes on, demonstrates that a meagre harvest or the lost of a single draught animal immediately stops some peasants from farming since they are unable to obtain credit. 'Above and beyond this, a subject peasant who has suffered a misfortune through no fault of his own is consoled with a shower of blows from pitiless magistrates, and because he can no longer discharge whatever *robot* services [corvée] he owes his lord, he is expelled from his farm and must then look around to see how he can best support himself and his family.'[49] The experienced agrarian economist, Albrecht Thaer, expressed a similar judgement about the peasants of the Electoral March in 1806:

> The yield of their farms is so paltry that there is nothing left to sell. Such misery is cause for astonishment when one recollects that monarchs have always recognized the importance of the peasant estate and have taken pains to ensure its survival. The nature of the evil lies in the present system which makes the peasant increasingly indigent, stupid and lethargic.[50]

If one probes the dimensions of the eastern European zone characterized by the predominance of the landed estate, the following boundaries seem to apply (see map 4). The demarcation is relatively clear in the west and the south. Beginning in Holstein the frontier runs roughly along the course of the Elbe towards the south-east, although the parts of Electoral Saxony that lie beyond the river must be excluded. Galicia, the Ukraine and some neighbouring districts likewise fell within the range of the landed estate. Other peripheral areas were attached to the larger zone: in the south-west Bohemia and Moravia and, farther to the south, Hungary, Wallachia and Moldavia. With respect to central Russia the border is less clear, but it seems that the line between the realm of the landed estate and peripheral territory to its east ran from the Finnish Gulf in the north to the Crimea in the south.

The western boundary was the zone of the occidental manor which reached from the Elbe across Germany, France and several adjacent lands. Let us try to define the chief traits of the variety of manorial lordship that prevailed within the western European agrarian world. What were the differences in the lives of peasants between east and west? Since the disappearance of the servile labour farm in the High Middle Ages diverse types of manorial rule had evolved: in all of them most land was handed over to dependent peasants in return for payments in money and kind. While seigniors did farm a portion of their domains themselves, such activities were never even remotely as extensive as they were in the case of the eastern European landed estate.

Important impulses affecting the evolution of the western German agrarian system during the Early Modern Era came from the territorial princes. It was not the knights but the rulers of the states within the Holy Roman Empire who must be seen as the victors of the German Peasant War; it was they who exercised a powerful influence upon the evolution of country life from that time onward. Inasmuch as mercantilistically orien-tated princes were very interested in fostering commerce, it is only natural that they would also concern themselves with agrarian problems. The mere fact that a productive peasantry was essential from fiscal and military perspectives caused them to intervene in the affairs of the rural world. At the same time they sought to support the peasants in warding off fresh seigniorial demands, particularly when the pressure came from lords who were farming for themselves. However, one must be careful to distinguish this variety of territorial princely agrarian policy from measures that the rulers took on their own domains; after all, they too were manorial lords, though their revenues served to finance the workings of the state.

In order to preserve the productive capacity of peasant farms, the territorial princes issued ordinances prohibiting their subdivision; other decrees were designed to ensure that such plots were large enough to remain economically viable. Although subdivision was implemented in much of south-western and western Germany, the territorial governments fought as hard as they could against it, indeed against the breakup of peasant farms altogether. In other regions, especially north-western Germany, such intervention was more successful and assisted greatly in confirming the principle of the indivisibility of rustic holdings, also known as the 'rule of heirs apparent'; occasionally it was put into effect for the first time. In Bavaria such edicts may be traced back to the mid-fifteenth century when the authorities began to devise an entity called the 'core farm'. The same institution is found later on in other parts of Germany and Austria. The hide ceases to be primarily a farmstead and is turned into a fiscal concept, a basis for assessment; it is used to calculate payments – especially taxation rates – and services due to the territorial prince. Any subdivison, splintering or reduction adversely affects the material interests of bureaucratic government which consequently opposes changes of this kind.

Let us next direct our attention to the terms of peasant tenancy on the western European manor of Early Modern times. The principal milestone on the path of continuing evolution and amelioration was that formerly heterogeneous arrangements gave way to relatively uniform ones: now only a few basic categories of land tenure remained. The first was outright ownership, for which, however, rent still had to be paid. Next came the very widespread hereditary leasehold. Finally, from the early seventeenth century onward, north-west Germany's hereditary 'steward tenancy'* took its place alongside the hereditary leasehold. In addition to these especially favourable legal arrangements, there were two other types of tenure that were much less so: one limited tenancy to the lifetime of the peasant in question, and the other allowed him to be dispossessed without prior notice. However, both became less important in the seventeenth and eighteenth centuries, since the legal status of farms was overshadowed by the basic tendency for them to become hereditary in practice. Finally, yet another trend should be pointed out: payments and services were frozen once and for all in the form of monetary rents. Compulsory labour was increasingly reckoned in monetary terms and then converted into a fixed rental.

The burdens which peasants had to bear as the result of their manorial obligations varied considerably throughout Western and Central Europe.

---

* Translator's note: the *Meierhof* was originally an outlying farm turned over to a seigniorial peasant administrator or steward; it has an etymological relationship of sorts with 'major-domo'. It was ultimately so common a phenomenon as to give rise to what is perhaps the most often encountered German patronym, i.e., 'Meyer'.

They ranged all the way from a slight encumbrance to an oppressive handicap. The payments were either set arbitrarily by the seignior or negotiated bilaterally; local custom played an important role in this respect. The result was that the scope of duties and services differed greatly from one place to another, not only from country to country but within regions. Many peasants fulfilled their obligations exclusively in one way or another, but most of them did so in mixed fashion, namely, by paying in money and kind as well as by providing labour services. As time passed, a manorial lord might permit individual peasants to commute certain obligations into a monetary sum. The uniformity of feudal burdens was often upset when a manor or parts of it passed into the hands of another lord as the result of sale or inheritance; the peasants of each of the seignior's manors continued to pay what they owed in the traditional form.

A peasant's feudal burdens by no means corresponded only to the dimensions of the land he cultivated. The quality of the soil, proximity to market towns and the economic interests of the manorial lord also had a powerful impact upon the extent and the character of the rustic's obligations. If the seignior farmed little himself and was not especially concerned with production for the market, it was natural for him to demand the fulfilment of peasant obligations in money and kind. Compulsory labour had long constituted an important category of feudal dues, but in Early Modern times it declined further. Normally, corvée took the form of working the lord's fields, processing agrarian commodities, cartage or beating the bushes for him when he engaged in hunting. Since relatively few central and western European manorial lords farmed for themselves, compulsory services tended to be limited to just a few days each year. If seigniors did produce for the market, corvée could amount to as much as forty to fifty days annually. However, this burden was not nearly as onerous as the one borne by the peasant who inhabited an eastern European landed estate.

The tithe was another of the major payments that the western European ploughman had to worry about. All land, even that in the hands of the nobility, townsmen and ecclesiastical bodies, was subject to it. Originally the tithe had been imposed in order to support the Church and to provide for the poor, but with the passage of the centuries it changed its character, and the beneficiaries were mainly secular persons, especially noblemen. The care of the needy and the requirements of the local parish were often totally neglected, and it is not surprising that tithe reform was one of the principal demands in the German Peasant War. The introduction of new crops or the planting of previously uncultivated land could easily lead to violent disagreements between the people who were supposed to pay the tithe and those who had the right to collect it: the question was whether new produce came under old definitions or not. It is clear that the tithe was an institution that posed an obstacle to the advancement of the agrarian economy.

The payments and services which ploughmen owed manorial lords were but one part of the total material burden they had to bear. The Early Modern state derived the great bulk of its tax revenues from the rural population. The complete or at least partial fiscal immunity of the nobility and the clergy meant that peasants had to pay the largest share of government levies. Because of the great heterogeneity of payments, services and taxes owed by the peasantry, it is difficult to estimate how much of their income was encumbered. It is probably fair to say that in eighteenth-century western Germany they had to hand over 25 to 40 per cent of their gross earnings. In Württemberg the amount of the 'feudal quota' varied between 28 and 34 per cent: it was made up primarily of grain duties, tithes and taxes.[51] However, such statistics conceal great differences between individual peasant farms.

The diverse types of feudal tenure described above were accompanied by yet other forms of tenancy in France and Germany, namely, various kinds of temporally limited leases and sharecropping. The principal differences between these two broad categories had to do with stipulations regarding animal stock and agricultural implements. In the case of a term lease the cattle and the equipment were provided by the tenant, a peasant who farmed on his own behalf and paid the landowner in money and kind. In the case of *métayage* the animals and the tools belonged at least in part to the proprietor who, while taking upon himself a portion of the risk, also shared in the harvest. Both lease types were very popular in certain parts of Western Europe, such as the Paris basin and the Rhineland, because they left room for a periodic adjustment of payments in money and kind to market conditions. The duration of these leases was normally rather short: they were signed for three, six or, at the very most, nine years.

Sharecropping was also extremely common in Mediterranean countries, especially Italy and Spain. Indeed, southern Europe was marked altogether by highly disparate agrarian relationships and great variation in the circumstances of rural life. Many states of the Apennine peninsula encompassed a wide range of farming methods, land tenure and living standards. In Piedmont the tendency was for farms to be split into ever smaller units and turned over to sharecroppers. Far to the south, in Sicily, agriculture was still ensnared in a web of feudal ties; by the seventeenth century there was hardly a peasant who was not caught up in it. A specially hated figure was the overseer, who functioned as the link between the latifundary and the indigent leaseholder. In the *mezzogiorno* there was a crass contrast between the enormous possessions of the Church and the nobility in interior regions and the small peasant sharecroppers along the coast. In the Papal States there were both ecclesiastical manors and seigniories of Roman patrician dynasties. In Tuscany it was common for the land to be farmed by both the proprietor and the leaseholder; this proved advantageous to both parties in the heartland of the *mezzadria*, the hilly northwestern sector of the grand duchy. In the fertile Po valley small peasant farms, the tenancy of which could take the form of either a hereditary fief or a term lease, predominated.

In sixteenth-century Spain both secular and ecclesiastical seigniories became firmly established. Manorial lords sought to extend their holdings in order to take advantage of favourable market conditions, the result of which was increased pressure upon peasant farms. The seigniors contrived a fixed system of fees for the right to farm land by reviving many feudal dues that had lapsed into merely symbolic payments during the Late Middle Ages. However, in the seventeenth century the period of relative rural prosperity, based on high prices for agricultural products, came to an end and rustics were faced by a crisis of debt. The landowners, who tended to be urban residents, often withdrew the capital they had invested in the countryside or else engaged in real-estate speculation, the result of which was heavy mortgaging of peasant farms. The economic situation of the rural population deteriorated significantly at that time, and there was a simultaneous concentration of landed property in the hands of a tiny group of individuals. Agrarian relationships developed most positively in seventeenth-century Andalusia, where there were no harmful changes in the patterns of land tenure and the social position of the peasantry.

England and the Netherlands were the two western European countries in which early capitalist forms of agriculture developed most strongly. Agrarian conditions in the southern Netherlands were still very much like those in western Germany. However, in the north, which declared its independence from Spain in 1581, there were amazing innovations. While large noble and ecclesiastical landholdings were by no means a rarity in the eastern provinces, small and medium-sized properties became increasingly common phenomena. In addition to agreements of three to twelve years and long-term contracts which obliged the tenant to improve land that had been turned over to him, there were hereditary leases. Farming of large estates by their owners was quite unusual. In the western provinces –

especially Zeeland, Holland and Frisia – the social and political transformation which accompanied the Reformation and the struggle for independence led to a general abrogation of manorial rights and to large-scale subdivision and redistribution of land, most of which fell into the hands of burghers. This fostered the introduction of modern, more efficient farming techniques on peasant holdings, most of which were let for short periods of time. It thus became possible for agriculture to adjust to new economic circumstances. At the same time huge sums were invested in land reclamation and the draining of marshland.

England, like the Netherlands, was a country that was much more developed prior to the agrarian revolution of the eighteenth century than the rest of Europe. The English rural world had already begun to evolve noticeably in the 1300s, when the manors of great lords and village communities embarked upon a process of change that extended into the early seventeenth century. After the dissolution of feudal ties, land frequently changed hands and agricultural productivity was greatly enhanced. This development was accelerated by more intensive market relationships, an increase in regional and supra-regional trade, the strengthening of monetary exchange and the emergence of a stratum of urban entrepreneurs, i.e., burghers who were prepared to risk their capital assets. Although enclosures were limited mainly to the counties of central England, appropriation of common land was a phenomenon which, along with King Henry VIII's secularization of the immense stock of monastic property, led to an expansion of large estates and a transformation of relationships between manorial lords and country folk. By the end of the Middle Ages, but especially during the sixteenth and the seventeenth centuries, the English agrarian world was moving steadily in the direction of a threefold social stratification. The top layer consisted of the manorial lords, the owners of the land; next came the tenants, who worked their farms on the basis of a lease; and finally, there were the rural labourers who possessed nothing at all. The disappearance of the English peasantry cannot be ascribed solely to enclosures; the fact that land was widely bought and sold had much to do with changes in the structure of English agriculture and rural society.

In the fifteenth and sixteenth centuries only those peasant families that occupied a farm for a limited period of time or for life risked losing it. This applied to about one-third of the country population; the remaining peasants worked their land under better terms of tenancy. Also crucial were frequent sales and purchases of peasant farms; market conditions encouraged the old nobility to sell rather than buy land. Thus there was an expansion of the lowest stratum of the nobility, the so-called gentry, which was made up on one hand of wealthy townsmen and on the other of top-rank peasants, freeholders who had managed to increase the size of their holdings. Up to the mid-seventeenth century the number of small farms does not seem to have declined – something which occurred only in the succeeding era. The political crisis of 1640 and the ensuing years of civil war led to a drastic increase in taxation, the effect of which was a drop in agrarian income and migration from rural districts to the cities. Taken together, these factors provoked radical change in rural socio-economic conditions and landholding patterns. Small proprietors moved in grow-ing numbers to England's towns and put administrators in charge of their farms. The lower nobility and the yeomanry were likewise inclined to liquefy their capital and invest it in other profitable ventures. Con-versely, manorial lords began once again to enlarge their estates by buying up small farms.

The financial advantages of leasing large tracts of land were obviously the reason why landowners purchased many small farms and turned them over to managers; the latter were also granted credit on a broad scale in order to increase profits. As time passed, the small farms became heavily mortgaged; more and more credit was extended to 'administrator lease-holders'. The net result of these developments was the disappearance of the English peasantry. This trend reached its peak in the second half of the eighteenth century, when the enclosures that brought about the destruc-tion of traditional village structures and age-old patterns of rustic life were legally sanctioned.

The totally unfettered peasant society of Scandinavia provides a sharp contrast to the capitalist patterns of the English and Dutch agrarian world. This was especially true of Norway, where there was no Continental-style manorial dependency at all, but rather a broad stratum of free peasants. It was only during the seventeenth century that the nobility attempted to emulate the practices that prevailed to the south and exploit the rural population for its own benefit. While it proved impossible to dispossess the ploughman, the terms of tenure deteriorated and there were more leaseholders than before. Although absolute numbers of free peasants grew because of land clearance and subdivision, two-thirds of the rustics were tenants by 1625. The government long made a point of supporting the peasantry, since they constituted the bulk of taxpayers and provided the manpower for Norway's militia. An edict of 1687 stated that a person who owned one estate could not have a farm above and beyond the one he worked himself. The ordinance meant that large-scale landholding could no longer be made to turn a profit, and so manorial lords preferred to sell tenant farms to their occupants.

Sixteenth and seventeenth-century Sweden witnessed a great expansion of the nobility in the context of the country's involvement in power politics and the opportunities this offered to ambitious persons. Although the peasantry, which had played an important role in the country's life since the Middle Ages, suffered a set-back, it was still able to maintain its pivotal position. Even if the objective of government policy was to concentrate trade and business activities in the cities, the old principle of commercial freedom remained in effect. In certain regions peasants continued to trade vigorously and to transport their goods in boats. An important rural stratum was made up of the superintendents and inspectors of large industrial and agricultural enterprises; some of them entered the ranks of the nobility. As in Norway, crown peasants were able to become independent farmers from about 1700 onward. In neighbouring Denmark there was little change in rural social stratification during Early Modern times, although the nobility was in a stronger position than in the northern regions of Scandinavia. Free allodial peasants represented only a small proportion of the country population. Some 90 per cent of small and medium-sized peasant farms paid rent either to the nobility or to the Church. However, there were relatively few cottagers and landless labourers. Extremely favourable conditions in the international grain and cattle markets caused Danish noblemen to exploit their privileged position and enlarge their estates in certain parts of the country at the expense of the peasantry.

This survey of agrarian systems in Early Modern Europe has demonstrated the existence of a pronounced dualism; the line of demarcation ran roughly along the Elbe river. Eastern Europe was characterized by the landed estate whereas other forms of manorial lordship prevailed in the west. Between these two vast realms there were several mixed zones, of which early capitalist England and the Netherlands, the free peasant regions of Scandinavia and the Mediterranean world should be singled out. If we ask to what extent the institutions we have discussed had an impact upon later times, we must point above all to the landed estate, the legacy of which was a crucial factor in the economic, social and political fortunes of nineteenth- and twentieth-century Eastern Europe. The gigantic territory east of the Elbe that reached all the way from the Finnish Gulf in the north-east down to the shores of the Black Sea lagged far behind the rest of Europe in terms of socio-economic evolution and can be regarded as the zone of the very worst oppression of the rural population. Might the backwardness of Eastern Europe – once again the subject of debate, owing to the spectacular collapse of Communism and endemic economic crises – be linked to its peculiar agrarian constitution? We can do little more than broach the question here.

The landed estate was both a manifestation of Eastern Europe's retardation and a factor that exaccerbated it. Nevertheless, this variety of manorial lordship cannot be equated with Europe's quondam exploitation of overseas colonies or compared to its relationship with the developing countries of the Third World. Eastern Europe evolved autonomously. Its seigniors pursued policies that were entirely their own and were orientated solely to their corporate interests. Without a strong central authority – Russia is the exception to the rule – the lords were incapable of creating a stable feudal order. No fundamental social reform could have been expected from a nobility that was totally averse to change. Thus the movement to do away with the landed estate in the nineteenth century was led not by aristocrats but mainly by persons who came from a non-rural setting. The landed estate with its rigid dependence upon servile labour was not in a position to cope with new economic and political challenges. The abrogation of feudal relationships led to fundamental social transformation within the ex-domain of the landed estate, especially in Prussia and Russia. However, noble properties retained considerable importance as economic units until the upheavals of 1917 and 1945.

8

Population, Settlement and Agrarian Zones in Early Modern Times

From the sixteenth to the late eighteenth centuries Europe experienced profound economic, social, political and cultural changes which of course also affected agriculture and the rural populace. The effect of these upheavals, brought about by a combination of factors, was clearly evident in many realms of human life and activity. Geographic discoveries directed Europe's attention to other continents and led to the establishment of new trade routes. The seafaring nations competed with one another in a race to open up and exploit foreign lands and previously unknown parts of the world, while Russia set about conquering and settling the gigantic territory of Siberia. Having concentrated upon the Baltic and the Mediterranean during the Late Middle Ages, Europe now focused its gaze primarily upon the Atlantic. The countries and cities of its western littoral grew in size and wealth after they began to trade with the Americas. All of this becomes obvious when one compares the fate of Lisbon, Antwerp, Amsterdam or London with that of old Mediterranean towns such as Genoa and Venice.

The rapid development of urban centres was due in large measure to the emergence of pristine forms of government. Early Modern Europe gave birth to new states and nations, which proved to be remarkably dynamic. Their flowering was accompanied by the rise of capitals – residences of kings and princes – which came to overshadow the older towns. Madrid, which had long been something of a provincial backwater, took its place at the head of prosperous Spain's impressive array of cities. In the Spanish Netherlands Brussels solidified its position *vis-à-vis* its rivals, and Amsterdam became the dominant metropolis of the United Provinces. In France Paris was more the nucleus of the kingdom than it had ever been. Because of the expansion of business and trade new regional, commercial and financial centres sprang up.

The rise of the cities is undeniably a manifestation of Early Modern Europe's strong demographic growth. If we accept the figures worked out by Roger Mols and André Armengaud,[52] Europe's population grew from 80 to 187 million between 1500 and 1800. This amounts to a 250 per cent increase, though there were variations from country to country and from one era to another. Italy's population grew relatively little during these three centuries, from 10 to 18 million, whereas England's expanded from 4 to 11 million. The crisis-ridden seventeenth century produced a negative balance for Spain and Central Europe. Spain fell from 10 to 9 million inhabitants; Germany, which suffered terrible destruction during the Thirty Years War, dropped from 16 to 15 million. The greatest overall growth was during the sixteenth century and again in the period after 1740; the seventeenth century was marked by stagnation in a number of countries.

What were the reasons for this huge increase, especially during the latter half of the eighteenth century? As far as the urban milieu is concerned, there were surely improvements in the layout of houses, in the water supply and the control of public health: they can only have had a positive demographic impact. In the countryside it is obvious that changes in nutrition played an important role in providing a steadier flow of foodstuffs and new varieties of edible plants. One can also discern progress in personal hygiene and medical care. The main causes of stagnation were epidemics, other outbreaks of disease, shortages of food due to poor harvests and, on a longer-term basis, the deterioration of the climate. Weather conditions, which worsened in the Late Middle Ages and began to improve only gradually during the eighteenth century, seem to have been responsible in part for a series of nutritional crises during the epoch in question.

Climatic factors did not have as harmful an effect as did the numerous wars and devastating diseases, which in certain years led to an enormous rise in mortality. Epidemics such as the plague, cholera and dysentery, endemic common illnesses such as tuberculosis and leprosy caused many deaths: the inadequate sanitation of tightly built-up cities and of densely inhabited, conglomerate villages greatly helped contagion. The often poorly fed rural and urban underclass suffered more from sickness and famine than physically stronger, wealthier families. The latter could more readily obtain the food they needed in order to survive; they had better homes and a higher standard of living altogether.

When the population of Europe began to expand mightily in the sixteenth century, after a long period of stagnation, the effect on settlement patterns was remarkable. Demographic growth was reflected not only in the expansion of villages and towns but also in the extension of cultivated areas and land clearance. A process that had stalled got under way again. The starting-point was in localities and on terrain that had been abandoned and reverted to wilderness. Overgrown fields in the vicinity of existing villages were ploughed and planted anew. Frequently, old and new arable lands were fully integrated, so much so that it was virtually impossible to tell them apart. However, wasteland recovery did not suffice for the needs of the growing population, in part because some of the desolate areas now had mature tree cover that was protected by forest ordinances. Demographic pressures forced Europeans to begin exploiting totally virgin territory in woods, mountains and marshes, next to rivers and the sea. South-western Germany's Zimmern Chronicle of about 1550 comments on conditions as follows: 'thus they began to clear the land and to cultivate ancient fields and meadows where many years ago there had been a village, and, forsooth, a new one arose.'[53] Similar things happened in many other places; even in inclement regions hardly any land remained unsettled.

It is likely that by 1560 Germany was as thickly populated as it had been before the time of the Black Death, that is, prior to 1340. However, since neither wars nor disease were blocking demographic growth in the later sixteenth century, it was necessary to break the ground in areas that had never been ploughed; only thus would there be enough food for everybody. Wherever it was possible, moors and primevally barren soil were cultivated, meadows turned into arable fields, and woodland destroyed. Deforestation was so extensive that in many territories the princes had to prohibit further clearance and limit the practice of transhumance. It is difficult to determine how successful they were in enforcing such rules. Peasants were under great pressure and had to find new sources of food for themselves and their families. They had no choice but to resort to agriculturally marginal terrain.

The bogs along the coast of the North Sea continued to be drained and protected by the construction of dikes. In the Netherlands between 1565 and 1615 some 44,000 hectares of marshland were wrested from the waters – a total that was more than that achieved in the following two centuries. A similar process occurred along the north-western German littoral. In the fourteenth and fifteenth centuries, adjacent to the Bay of Heligoland, much land had been lost and many villages and fields inundated: a new phase of drainage and dike-building began in the sixteenth century. In Jeverland, on the coast near Harle and in other places, 40,000 hectares of wetlands were reclaimed during the sixteenth and early seventeenth centuries. That was more than two-thirds of the territory in Lower Saxony which we know to have been drained between the thirteenth and sixteenth centuries. In neighbouring Schleswig-Holstein vast areas of marshland were also made arable.

During the sixteenth century the eastern parts of Central Europe also experienced a new wave of land clearance and colonization. It was a process characterized by a variety of individual developments, each independent of the others (see map 6). Lithuanian peasants moved into northern East Prussia. Dutch marsh farmers – Mennonites who left their home country for religious reasons – emigrated to the region at the mouth of the Vistula. They began to settle in the Vistula–Nogat delta about 1550 and were so successful in draining it that the value of the land increased many times over within a very short period. Polish manorial lords were quick to draw upon the services of the expert Dutch colonists: villages founded by them could be found everywhere in the low country of the Vistula. German

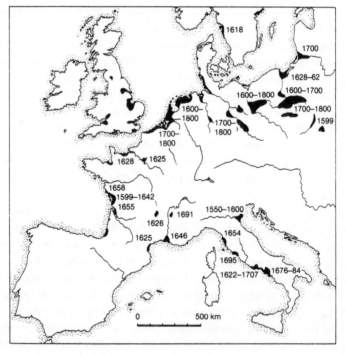

Map 6   The drainage of wetlands, 1600–1800 (after N.J.G. Pounds, An
Historical Geography of Europe, 1500–1840, *Cambridge, 1979, page 198)*

peasants from eastern Pomerania penetrated into virgin areas in the south of the province. Other settlers from Brandenburg's New March and Lower Silesia pressed into the belt of woodland that still separated Germans from Poles. The outlying spurs of these various individual population movements, resulting from the powerful demographic growth to the west, extended across West Prussia and Poznań as far as central Poland and Volhynia.

In France the great crises of the fourteenth and fifteenth centuries had led to a damaging reversal of settlement patterns and to grave set-backs in agriculture: contagious disease and warfare had depopulated vast tracts of land in both the northern and southern parts of the country. In the early sixteenth century the movement to extend arable land began anew, and within a few decades many French villages had grown to the point where further expansion was virtually impossible. Wastelands were cultivated once again. Arable farmers and cattlemen penetrated into woodlands and brush-covered country, and it became necessary to take measures to protect the forests that remained. The Wars of Religion interrupted the process for a while, but by the end of the century clearance was once more in full swing. As far as England is concerned, it is clear that the conversion of abandoned land and pasturage into cultivated fields was delayed by the favourable market conditions for wool that had developed in the Late Middle Ages; enclosures were also a factor. Conditions in Scandinavia resembled those on the Continent: the consequence of population growth was an increase in agriculturally exploited land.

In some regions land clearance and the extension of cultivated areas led to sharp social differentiation between the older rural population and recently arrived people. The work, carried out jointly by indigenous peasants and newcomers, frequently took place on the margins of existing fields and overlapped into the commons. Social gradations between peasants who enjoyed the full range of communal rights and disadvantaged petty rustics increased greatly, especially in those areas where the law mandated indivisible inheritance. From the late fifteenth century onward, in both northern Germany and in the eastern zone of German settlement, 'mark cottagers' and other small-time farmers – so-called *Kötter* who were also known as *Kätner*, *Kossäten* and *Gärtner* – appeared beside long-settled ploughmen, so-called *Meier* and *Erben*. The late arrivals were distinguished from their predecessors not so much by the smaller size of their farms as by limited communal rights. Legal discrimination expressed itself above all in restrictions upon access to the mark, i.e., to demarcated village commons.

Since the farms of 'mark cottagers' were usually tiny, they were forced to seek employment outside agriculture. This was especially true of the 'brink-sitters' or 'brink cottagers', who may be dated to the second half of the sixteenth century and who worked largely outside forming. For the most part all they possessed was a house and a garden; they lived on the edge or the brink – as the word was used in Middle English – of farms belonging to the long-settled inhabitants of villages. A similar, contemporary group were the 'hirelings' who were specially common in north-western Germany. Since they did not have enough land of their own, they leased smaller plots from well-established settlers and paid the rent by working on the farms of their better situated fellow peasants. The hirelings lived in buildings alongside the holdings of their social superiors and were thus also a factor in the ever increasing density of village populations. The manorial lords encouraged the settlement of such people for two reasons. First, inasmuch as cottagers also owed payments and services, they enhanced seigniorial revenues; second, they served to maintain the economic productivity of the older farms. However, their regional distribution was by no means uniform. The mark variety could be found only to a limited extent in long-settled loess districts since larger marks – the most crucial prerequisite for immigrants – were the exception. Conversely, territory that had just been demarcated for clearance and cultivation was ideal for settling cottagers and provided the sites where the classical forms of this socio-economic phenomenon evolved.

After the end of the Thirty Years War (1616–48) a new phase of internal colonization began. The damage and population losses caused by the fighting made government intervention in the agrarian economy necessary; only thus could the direct and indirect impact of the endemic warfare of three decades be overcome. In many regions the problem was less the physical destruction resulting from combat than demographic decline owing to disease and famine. Most deserted fields and villages were quickly reoccupied after 1648, and there was little change in the total amount of cultivated land. The initial focus of reconstruction efforts was straightforwardly demographic. The mercantilist-orientated authorities strove to increase human numbers as fast as possible; their immediate goal was to attain once again pre-war levels of population. However, estate owners profited from the situation: they incorporated abandoned peasant fields into the land they farmed for themselves and imposed more rigorous legal terms upon the ploughmen. Newcomers were often settled on disadvantageous, non-hereditary terms and could be deprived of their farms with little notice. The estate owner could now dispossess peasants in a variety of ways and establish special settlements for his personal work-force.

Both contemporaries and historians were fascinated most of all by large-scale land reclamation projects like the draining of lakes, the cultivation of entire moors, and dike construction on river flood plains and in coastal lowlands. The kingdom of Prussia stood out in this respect. In the swamps of Oder near Frankfurt, an area which is said to have encompassed only 56 square kilometres before the mid-eighteenth century, some 56,000 hectares emerged from the slime between 1747 and 1753; another 30,000 hectares were opened to cultivation in the fens of the Warta by 1786. Before he died, King Frederick the Great also oversaw the conversion of 22,500 hectares of marshland near Drömling in the Old March into pasture, forest and arable fields. Among the people who emigrated to Prussia the most important were the 20,000 Salzburgers, who were driven from their homeland because of their Protestant faith and settled as a compact group in East Prussia. To implant these mountain farmers successfully in a completely strange environment – the flat terrain of East Prussia – was a genuinely magnificent achievement. The Salzburgers were granted extensive rights of self-government; every magistrate and family elder received a whole hide exempt from dues.

Frederick also systematically promoted the extension of cultivated land throughout all his realms. The settlers generally arrived from adjacent territories – Saxony, Thuringia and Mecklenburg – but also from more remote places such as Württemberg, which provided large numbers of immigrants for West Prussia. Most new arrivals were anything but poor, and many of them possessed very respectable capital sums. The 300,000 colonists whom the king attracted to Prussia brought with them large amounts of money, as well as huge stocks of horses, beef cattle and sheep. The immigrants were settled mostly on state land, although the nobility was also involved in certain areas. Roughly 400,000 hectares came into production in the bogs of the Oder and the Warta, and Frederick had every right to claim that he had added a whole province to the kingdom in the midst of peace.

Prussia was not the only state in which large-scale settlement projects were carried out: other Central and Eastern European countries were also the scene of similar schemes. The struggle to expel the Turks from Hungary – Buda was reconquered by the Austrians in 1686 – had left large sections of the Pannonian basin depopulated. At first German peasants began to occupy marginal districts in a disorderly fashion; however, owners of large estates thereupon assumed control of resettlement efforts. Thus

German ethnic enclaves were established in the Bakony Forest, in the hilly country near Buda and in the Baranya. Only after the Treaty of Passarowitz (Požarevac) in 1718, according to which the Banat became a Habsburg crown domain, did a major wave of colonization begin; it reached its peak under Empress Maria Theresa a few decades later. It was not just Germans who arrived. Other nationalities were also persuaded to settle in what would turn into the bread basket of the Balkans. The object was not to Germanize but to populate the territories in question; in frontier zones military considerations likewise played an important role. The immigrants came from Swabia, the Palatinate and even from as far away as Lorraine. They were personally free and given their farms on a hereditary basis. The same strategy was applied in Galicia and Bukovina. At almost the same time – the end of the Seven Years War (1763) – Tsarina Catherine the Great issued an invitation to participate in the resettlement of Russia. Newcomers would receive their farms free of dues for thirty years; they could continue to practise their own religion; and they would enjoy full rights of self-government. The imperial proclamation evoked a powerful response, particularly in certain German territorial states. The result was the establishment a few years later of large new settlements centred upon the lower Volga near Saratov. This was the historical background to the Soviet Union's Volga German Republic, which disappeared in the aftermath of the catastrophic events of World War II.

The extension of cultivated land in Early Modern times was orientated in each of the various zones of settlement to the particular traits and economic potential of the land itself (see map 7). Agriculture and the circumstances of peasant life were strongly influenced in pre-industrial Europe by geographical peculiarities and structural differences between individual agrarian zones – not to mention the impact of widely varying regional political, social and cultural conditions or the effect of the transitory state of Europe's overall economy. What were the supra-regional agrarian zones of the Early Modern era and how did agriculture develop in specific countries and landscapes? The four great agrarian realms were distinguished earlier in this book: the nucleus of Central and Western Europe, Scandinavia, Eastern Europe and the Mediterranean.

Let us begin a survey of Early Modern European agricultural development with the core zone of Central and Western Europe. It stretched from the British Isles across France to Germany, where it touched the perimeter of the eastern zone; to the south it bordered on the Mediterranean world, where agrarian and climatic conditions were so different. In the centre of

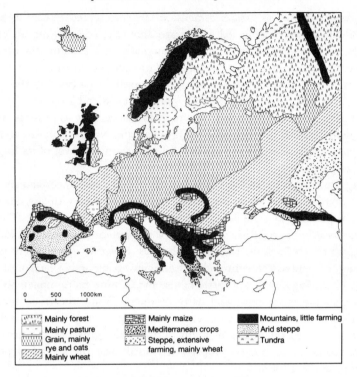

Map 7   The farming zones of Europe

Europe the nucleus encompassed broad plains, such as the basins of the countryside of northern France and the north German lowlands, as well as the extensive central heights that reached down to the Alps and southern Europe. It should be stressed that the agricultural evolution of individual countries and subregions within the core zone varied considerably during the centuries discussed in this chapter.

Agrarian development in the British Isles – which has a damp but, thanks to the Gulf Stream, relatively mild climate – was influenced by changes of a legal, social and technological nature which had taken place since the Late Middle Ages. Scotland and northern England were for the most part isolated and backward; agricultural activity there was concentrated upon growing crops, stock-raising and the exploitation of extensive forests. As time passed and the demand for meat and animal products in the expanding cities of England grew, the cattle trade benefited substantially. The traditional drove from Scotland to the meadows of southern

England took on ever greater dimensions: by the eighteenth century some 40,000 head were being led southward annually for fattening on grasslands, prior to slaughter and sale in urban markets. The main Scottish crop was grain, above all barley. The preferred method was the inner-outer field system. The inner field, which usually amounted to a third of the cultivated area, was continually planted – one season with barley and the next with oats. The outer field was used to grow oats as long as possible; when the yield declined, it was converted into pasture. Notwithstanding certain improvements, Scottish agriculture did not attain the level of its English counterpart.

Agriculture in Ireland was even less developed than in Scotland and was restricted until the beginning of the eighteenth century to stock-raising and the planting of grain, an enterprise only marginally profitable. The life of the socially oppressed Irish peasants was miserable, and they lacked the strength to rebel against their English lords. However, government intervention prevented the ruling class from converting arable land into pasture, increasing the size of cattle herds, and earning more money because of higher prices for meat and dairy products. While the trend towards stock-raising was thus slowed, it was not stopped altogether. Ireland had to import large quantities of grain during the eighteenth century. The Irish people could not be properly fed until after the spread of potato culture in the 1790s.

Agrarian development in England followed an entirely different path. The transformation of agriculture and rural society was linked to changes in planting methods and new approaches to farm management. The interest in agrarian improvements was obvious as early as the sixteenth century, when a truly amazing number of books dealing with individual issues were published. Profit-orientated, commercial techniques were introduced at an early stage. There was a never-ending effort to adjust production to market conditions. Large amounts of money were invested in farming facilities and agricultural implements. The regular planting of feed crops and irrigated pastures were phenomena that could already be found frequently in the sixteenth century; by the latter half of the seventeenth century their importance as progressive measures was taken for granted. By that time too the fall in grain prices, accelerated by the growing demand for wool products, was more pronounced than ever. Another feature was the major effort made to promote a rational sequence of crops and to devise the most suitable technique for achieving this. The so-called Norfolk four-field rotation system proved most successful: clover, wheat, beet and barley followed upon one another. It is therefore hardly surprising that the entrepreneurial spirit of farmers, incessant concern for modernization, and the fortunate conjunction of better methods of planting and stock-raising prepared the way for the 'new agriculture'. This soon attained very high standards and turned out to be a prime factor in the agrarian revolution of the second half of the eighteenth century.

The growing importance of the pastoral economy led to a more logical system of stock-raising. Sheep provided larger quantities of wool, beef cattle became heavier and more numerous and cows produced more milk. At the same time there was a much greater range of plants: farmers preferred feed crops and vegetables which served to protect the quality of the soil. Indeed, even earlier the productivity of the earth had been enhanced by more expeditious crop rotation, increased reliance upon manure and improved agricultural implements. A prelude to new ways of working the soil was the system of multiple fields that was introduced in conjunction with the expansion of legume culture. After 1650 fodder plants were widely grown: the complicated sequence of crops reached its zenith in the Norfolk system already mentioned, the prototype of novel, late eighteenth-century agriculture.

Trends comparable to developments in the English agrarian economy were visible just across the Channel and the adjacent sector of the North Sea, in Flanders and Holland. Since the sixteenth century the Lowlands had belonged to the most fertile agrarian regions of Western Europe and had supported a well-to-do rustic population. Agriculture here, as elsewhere, had been affected by cycles of boom and bust, prosperity and crisis. However, it had evolved practices and features that were all its own. Agriculture in the Lowlands flourished for a remarkably long time during the sixteenth and seventeenth centuries and demonstrated a tremendous growth potential. Unquestionably, there is a close relationship between agrarian progress in Holland and the dominance of the northern Netherlands in the international trade of the seventeenth century.

The importance that Flemish and Dutch peasants attached to stock-raising provides solid evidence of their ability to react rapidly to changes in Europe's overall economy. The farmers of the Lowlands were genuine entrepreneurs who knew how to take maximum advantage of both developments in the world of nature and new sales markets. The most important crops in polder districts were plants suitable for fodder; they were the necessary foundation for the emergence of efficient animal husbandry, in turn the presupposition for a sophisticated dairy economy. In the interior districts of Flanders grain was grown to a limited extent but in a rational manner; feed crops were also planted. As the number of cattle increased, there were greater quantities of manure and hence better fertilization than in other countries. Fibre plants such as hemp and flax, as well as madder and woad, the raw material for the dyes so important to the textile industry, were more commonly encountered. At the same time planting cycles were modernized: now they also included feed crops and legumes, which were grown in the context of a carefully calibrated strategy to preserve the fecundity of the soil.

Without any doubt the Lowlands reached an advanced stage of agrarian economic development at this time. However, there was also substantial economic progress in the neighbouring regions of northern France and western Germany. Dutch influence on northern France was especially evident, for here too stock-raising and feed crops began to take an increasingly important place alongside the grain economy. To be sure, this did not lead peasants to conclude that they must specialize in animal husbandry, despite the fact that Paris and Rouen produced a strong demand for meat and dairy products. Northern French peasants continued to concentrate on grain, and wherever climate and soils favoured such crops, stock-raising was clearly a subsidiary source of income.

On the other hand, in regions less suited to growing grain, stock-raising did constitute the main activity of the rural population. Meat and dairy products became goods that were exchanged in order to satisfy the cereal needs of the communities in question. In hilly country and in mountainous areas, where animal husbandry was more important, there were – in part at least – closer ties to agrarian markets than in the case of lowland peasants who concentrated upon growing grain. This is the reason why in fertile regions such as Picardy and Beauvais the earth was ploughed, according to the rhythm of the three-field system, mainly in order to plant rye and wheat, as well as – in the case of better soils – legumes. Agricultural management also gradually improved in a technological and economic sense. In many places the traditional three-field system was gradually abandoned in favour of more appropriate and varied approaches that included not only grain and other cereals but also legumes, until finally – in the eighteenth century when alfalfa (lucerne) and herbaceous grasses were widely cultivated in Normandy and Brittany – forage plants became a fundamental component of crop rotation. Bigger cattle herds provided larger quantities of manure and thus helped more rapid regeneration of the soil; the result was less and less fallow.

Similar tendencies in the evolution of the agrarian economy may be seen in western Germany. While the three-field system still predominated in many regions, changes of a progressive nature were gradually introduced.

The fallow that was inherent to the three-field system was used increasingly for kitchen vegetables and grazing from about the mid-eighteenth century; the habit of seeding it spread, especially in intensively farmed agrarian regions such as the Rhineland. In the littoral landscapes of the Baltic, in Saxony and a few other places, the farmland was often subdivided on a very broad scale: the multiple field system predominated. In certain areas of north-western Germany the one-field system had survived: grain was planted uninterruptedly on the same acreage, generally only rye but sometimes alternately with oats and buckwheat. This was possible only with the heavy application of manure and clumps of dried peat. In Schleswig-Holstein there was a special kind of crop rotation known as *Koppelwirtschaft*. It involved intensive cultivation of field grasses: the land was used alternately for cereals and pasture.

The new methods of working the soil, which also included very extensive cultivation of plants for the consumer market, legumes and feed crops, and which thus also permitted stock-raising on a larger scale, were found in the eighteenth century chiefly in the Rhine–Main region, the Lower Rhine and on some of the fertile plains of central Germany. However, it is clear that, on the higher elevations of the interior and towards the eastern part of the country, agricultural land was utilized far less intensively. This may be ascribed to poor soil conditions and a less advantageous location with respect to transport arteries. Since there was little pasture, stock-raising was of slight importance. On the other hand, where meadowland was abundant – for example, along the Frisian littoral – cattle played a major role. This was also true of Alpine regions, where the trend in favour of stock-raising already evident at the end of the Middle Ages persisted.

If we turn our attention away from Central Europe to Scandinavia, we are confronted with an agrarian zone, the natural features and climate of which are vastly different. The most striking facet of Europe's northern regions is the sharp contrast between the predominantly forest and cattle-orientated economy of the mountains and the cultivated fields of the valleys and plains. Another result of climatic disparities was a wide range of districts that specialized in particular kinds of crops. In Norway and Sweden the most frequently grown cereal by far was barley, which even managed to thrive far to the north on the shores of the Gulf of Bothnia; on the plains to the south it often coincided with almost equally robust rye. Stock-raising was most widespread in the north, especially on the margins of the gigantic forests that covered so much of the Scandinavian peninsula. The consequence of so dense a cover of vegetation was the emergence of many human enclaves within the woods and above all along the streams

that coursed through them. It was in the vicinity of these village settlements and scattered sylvan hamlets that there were stretches of arable land
laid out in a uniform pattern of fields.

The agrarian landscape of peninsular Scandinavia retained its singular
character during the seventeenth and eighteenth centuries and served as an
example for neighbouring Denmark. From the sixteenth century onward
the Danes had been raising cattle intensively, a state of affairs that was
reflected in high export earnings for meat and dairy products. Peasants
devoted their energies increasingly to fattening cattle, especially when
grain prices fell and this activity became more profitable. In the eighteenth
century enhanced demand for butter caused them to shift their focus
from meat production to dairying; this led to a great increase in the
importation of milch cows from Holland. Scandinavian farmers, with some
exceptions, clung to antiquated methods of cultivation: both irregular and
systematic rotation continued to be practised in the customary form almost
everywhere.

In the enormous agrarian zone of Eastern Europe, which reached from
trans-Elbian Germany deep into Russia, the agricultural landscape resembled that of northern Europe in many respects. The dense forest cover
sometimes forced eastern European peasants to fell trees and create arable
land in areas where soil conditions offered the prospect of good yields. Vast
plains were ideally suited for large-scale cereal production, especially rye.
Apart from certain individual regions where it was actively pursued, stock-
raising was not particularly significant. From the mid-sixteenth century
onward grass culture and natural pasturage became less important in some
places; this was especially true of the territory between the Vistula and the
Bug. Newly arable land was used mainly for growing grain because of
the expansion of international demand and the sometimes very rapid rise in
the profitability of cereals. In Poland prices for agrarian products obviously
increased faster than in the neighbouring regions of Eastern Europe, the
result of which was the deterioration of social conditions mentioned above
– namely, the expansion of noblemen's estates and a return to serfdom.
However, the growth phase of Polish agriculture was interrupted for an
extended period: the war with Sweden between 1665 and 1660 severely
damaged the Polish economy.

In other eastern European lands, such as Bohemia, Moravia, Hungary
and Bulgaria, the effect of the rise in demand and prices for cereals was not
as strongly felt. Hence, landed estates did not become as common an
institution as they were in Poland and the eastern portions of Germany. In
the plains of the Balkans and in the Danube basin, especially Bulgaria and

Wallachia, peasants began to plant maize. 'Corn', the preferred name of North Americans for their primeval native crop, did extremely well in these regions, where it was called *Türken, kukorica* or *kukuruz*. In Russia the land used for cereal culture expanded considerably during the sixteenth century, and much terrain was ploughed anew. While it proved possible to alter Eastern Europe's agrarian economy because of major shifts in the forms of production and the tightening of servile bonds, there were no changes in the manner of cultivation and agricultural methods. Rather, the three-field system and simple approaches to the planting of field grasses remained the predominant farming techniques.

The countries of southern Europe, i.e., the lands that lay on the northern shores of the Mediterranean, differed from one another greatly in terms of vegetation and in the nature of their agrarian economies; the reason was the great variety of climatic conditions and physical geographical traits. A zone so heterogeneous was bound to produce a wide range of agricultural products, and there were certain to be sharp contrasts between landscapes immediately adjacent to one another. Agriculture in mountainous regions gave no sign during Early Modern times of altering its traditional patterns of exploiting forest resources and pasture. In the higher areas of the Alps, the Apennines and the Pyrenees, rustics occupied themselves mainly in raising beef cattle and sheep. However, the possibilities of supporting oneself this way were so limited that many younger mountain denizens were forced to leave their home villages and seek their livelihood down in the valleys.

The extraordinary mobility of mountain-dwellers was also evident in the seasonal migration of herds of beef cattle and sheep from alpine pasture to grassland at lower elevations. Transhumance was so much a feature of certain landscapes in Spain, southern France and Italy that it determined the rhythm of economic life altogether. However, this phenomenon gave rise to many conflicts between sedentary peasants and nomadic herdsmen, who were always on the watch for broad tracts of meadowland. On the mesetas of Old and New Castile, where extensive grain cultivation and sheep grazing coincided, feuds constantly broke out between cereal farmers, who were extending their fields in order to take advantage of rising prices, and shepherds who insisted that traditional browsing rights be respected.

Climatic conditions in hilly country and Mediterranean piedmont regions were generally quite favourable. During the sixteenth and early seventeenth centuries these privileged zones – in which there were many different kinds of agrarian activities – presented a picture of genuine prosperity. The presuppositions for farming within the vast northern Mediterranean arc that stretches from the intensively cultivated hills of Tuscany across the piedmont of southern France into the delicate patchwork of coastal districts in Catalonia were ideal. Against the background of variegated Mediterranean vegetation grapes, olives and many types of fruit throve on sunny slopes all the way from the Iberian peninsula across Italy to the Peloponnese. Where temperatures were high enough, citrus fruits were widely cultivated; on occasion attempts were also made to grow cotton. Fertile surfaces were converted into arable land for cereal production: wheat was the main crop, but other varieties of grain such as rye, barley and millet were also planted.

From about the mid-seventeenth century agriculture in certain Mediterranean countries began to decline quite noticeably. Poor market circumstances led to stagnation and, in some cases, to outright retrogression. Peasants reverted to obsolete methods of planting, the result of which was a gradual contraction of arable land and hence an expansion of uncultivated, less intensely utilized pastoral terrain. This trend was especially evident in the central part of southern Italy, where agriculture had made great progress during the sixteenth century. During the succeeding 200 years unhealthy swamps and malaria-infested flood plains became the predominant features of certain areas, and the scanty soil cover was washed away by erosion. Some of the land that earlier settlers had managed to recover from the forces of nature reverted to a state of desolation.

This survey of the diverse agrarian landscapes of Early Modern Europe has demonstrated that there were many different ways in which the earth could be made to bear fruit and animals raised for human consumption. The heterogeneity of approaches to farming also left its mark upon the rural population; despite common traits there was a rich palette of rustic lifestyles. While changes in the agrarian practices of this epoch were relatively modest compared to those in other branches of Europe's economy, nevertheless they had a decisive impact upon the peasant world. Because peasants were intrinsically conservative, innovation came about only very slowly, and its tempo, extent and effects varied from one place to another. It follows as a matter of course that any attempt to generalize about agricultural evolution at any time in European history is fraught with risk and caution is in order. Regional developmental disparities characterized the Early Modern period as they had earlier eras, notwithstanding the fact that improved transport and communication networks, larger markets and a more sophistcated trading infrastructure facilitated contacts between different zones, peoples and communities.

Such divergences were the result not only of mother nature but also reflected varying patterns of economic and political evolution. From the sixteenth down to the late eighteenth century a host of incongruous factors combined to transform the relationships of individual European countries and economic regions with one another. Certain localities which had previously stood in the forefront of growth suddenly became insignificant. As we have already seen, a severe depression affected certain once flourishing Apennine regions in the seventeenth and eighteenth centuries and ended up by impoverishing them. The retardation of southern Italy is to be traced back to this era and is not to be ascribed, as certain observers would have it, to the malevolent influence of the Mafia in more recent times. In other countries, notably England and the Netherlands, economic development – despite a few set-backs – proceeded in a very positive way. These states succeeded in creating a truly modern agrarian economy. Finally, it should be noted that the obvious differences in the evolution of individual agrarian regions were influenced by political events, such as the French Wars of Religion and the Thirty Years War in Germany.

9

Economic Shifts, Nutritional Problems and Rural Society

The phenomena of mass poverty and widespread social misery, which were particularly acute in some countries during the early nineteenth century, were often blamed upon exploitative capitalism. The terrible conditions under which workers had to live in British industrial towns, the revolts of Silesian weavers and the distress suffered by craftsmen led some contemporaries to conclude that the new age of machines was the root cause of such evils. Friedrich Engels, who published his famous book about the English working class in 1845, also believed that the dire predicament of workmen was a manifestation of spreading industrial capitalism. He contrasted the wretchedness of the factory milieu, which he vividly described, with the lives of rural spinners in pre-industrial times.

> They led a very comfortable existence; they passed their days in an atmosphere of tranquillity, propriety, rightousness, and godliness; they were better off materially than their successors; they did not have to overexert themselves; they worked no more than they wanted to and still earned as much as they required; they had enough spare time for healthy labour in their gardens or fields, really a form of recreation; and they could also play games with neighbouring families.[54]

Does this idyllic image of rural workers' lives in the pre-industrial epoch correspond with reality? Were the tribulations of broad segments of both the rural and urban populace during the first half of the nineteenth century actually a consequence of incipient industrialization? Even during the age in question some scholars and publicists passionately disagreed with Engels's argument that the new factories were responsible for the

anguish of much of the working class. B. Hildebrandt, a respected economist, cited the still entirely agrarian province of Upper Hessia as an
example of social conditions in a pre-industrial society.[55] The region had no
factories or factory workers, modern spinning mills or steam engines; it
was made up of rural communities characterized by traditional agricultural
pursuits and crafts. In spite of these 'normal' circumstances the agonies of
common people in years of economic crisis were almost unbearable. During
the dreadful famine winter of 1847–8 a homeless woman in Marburg bore
two children in the middle of the street at a temperature of 10 degrees
Centigrade. In the district of Hünfeld the authorities divided the poor into
bands of mendicants and gave them permission to beg in different parts of
the town and adjacent villages, according to a fixed schedule. The number
of totally impoverished persons in many comunities amounted to about a
third of the population – a state of affairs comparable to the situation today
in developing countries like India or Ethiopia.

Numerous written sources and social-historical studies leave little
doubt that the conditions that obtained in Upper Hessia in 1846 also
existed in many other regions. They include individual reports and scholarly monographs, simple messages and detailed accounts, documentary
records of local officials, and very extensive data concerning prices and
wages – altogether a rich fund of research material which bears witness to
the harsh life of the underclass in the pre-industrial world. All this evidence makes it quite clear that circumstances in both city and country were
anything but rosy. What is interesting is that the picture drawn by Engels
fails to take into account the awful economic crises that shook old-fashioned agrarian society. One especially misses any reference to the failed
harvests and famines that regularly exacerbated mankind's woes. More
recent investigation in the fields of social and economic history has shown
that mass indigence, undernourishment and starvation were basic components of social life prior to the mid-nineteenth century; indeed, difficulties
in the supply of essential foodstuffs and agrarian crises were quite common
from the Middle Ages onward. Wilhelm Abel has been especially assidu-
ous in examining the relationships between agrarian economics, demographic evolution and crisis phenomena; the conclusions he has reached are
highly significant.

It has been recognized for a long time that agricultural yields vary
considerably. Humanity has known for ages that good harvests are succeeded by bad ones and that record crops are followed by scanty ones.
However, despite strenuous efforts, it has not been possible so far to
establish any periodicity in the oscillation of harvests. Ever since the Bible

spoke about the sequence of seven fat and seven lean years in ancient Egypt, there have been incessant attempts to discover a firm pattern in fluctuating yields. Eighteenth-century scientists thought that they had proved that poor harvests occurred every seven to ten years. Nineteenth-century statisticians sought to demonstrate that there was a link between harvest cycles and the frequency of sunspots. Yet other scholars posit correlations between differences in rainfall, temperature, air pressure, wind force and other influences. The net result of all this theorizing is that harvest rhythms may be explained by a combination of individual factors. This is hardly surprising in view of the manifold effects upon agricultural yields that result from discrepancies within Europe in climate, methods of working the soil and altitude.

The impact of harvest oscillations upon grain prices is unmistakable: bad crops led to rising prices and good yields to a decline. However, these results were also dependent upon both the level of household incomes and the size of farms. A bad harvest could even force the small-time peasant to consume a portion of the next year's seed grain. In times of want cereal prices rose far more rapidly than those for less badly needed agrarian products or industrial goods. The inhabitants of towns, who had no choice but to buy basic food items, had even less room for manoeuvre than they normally did. The market for industrial products shrank and the economic crisis worsened if grain prices escalated. The consequences of poor harvests and inflation were especially grave if the cost of cereals had already reached a high level and wages were relatively low, as was the case during the second half of the eighteenth century. The famine of 1771–2, which was characterized by specially sharp price increases, may serve as an example.

In much of central Europe the crisis of 1771–2 amounted to a full-scale famine catastrophe: large segments of the population were confronted with extreme price rises and suffered terribly as a result. For example, in certain remote parts of the Erzgebirge the cost of rye increased 1000 per cent and bread 600 per cent. People could not feed themselves adequately, disease broke out and there were many deaths from starvation. A doctor from the Thuringian district of Eichsfeld, where the yield of the stony soil was meagre, reported the devastating consequences of famine:

> I cannot look back save with a sense of horror upon the heartache of our region; I shudder when I think of the mournful, dismal, and gruesome condition of so many of our people. My patients lay there without any hope of survival. The first hay crop, the second mow, garden produce, vegetables, fruit from trees – everything was

spoiled. The sweat of the countryman's brow had all been in vain. A tide of misfortune and, worst of all, gnawing hunger, afflicted these unfortunate individuals . . . It is no wonder that, in order to save their miserable lives, these poor devils fell back upon brutish and unnatural nourishment, by which I mean grass, thistles, noxious varieties of weeds, broths concocted from marl, roasted oat chaff, tares, and other kinds of rough vegetation. Indeed, exigence even forced them in the end to resort to the kind of food that foxes devour.[56]

French scholars refer to disasters within the harvest cycle like that of 1771–2 as crises of the *type ancien*. Spiralling inflation, a phenomenon that has been analysed in great detail by Emile Labrousse, certainly had a more powerful impact upon the mass of humanity in the pre-industrial epoch than did the spectacular financial and commercial crises of more recent times, which have monopolized the attention of economic historians. Bad harvests and sky-rocketing prices had a calamitous effect on the lives of vast numbers of village and city dwellers. Especially hard hit were thickly populated, partly industry-orientated agricultural districts such as the Erzgebirge or the Eichsfeld, localities in which farming had become a subsidiary form of livelihood through subdivision of property or did not pay because of the inferior quality of the soil. Regions of this kind were common throughout much of Central and Western Europe. Skimpy profits from working the land had to be supplemented by outside employment. Spinning, weaving, mining, lumbering, haulage, shopkeeping and a variety of craft jobs provided the income required, above and beyond the pittance that peasants could earn by labouring in fields, cattle barns and garden plots.

Old-fashioned European agrarian society was not only influenced by harvest crises but also deeply affected by fluctuations in the longer-term evolution of market conditions which, on its part, was closely tied to the general development of prices, wages and other quantifiable traits of economic activity. After the problems that had marked many decades of agrarian crisis during the Late Middle Ages had been overcome, the sixteenth century produced an upsurge in the agrarian economy that was simultaneously a cause and a result of demographic growth. Despite expansion of the cultivated ground, agricultural production could not keep pace with the increase in the population: the costs of grain and industrial products rose so much that scholars have spoken of a veritable price revolution (see figure 1). By 1600 Frenchmen were paying six and a half times as much for cereals as they had a century earlier. In England,

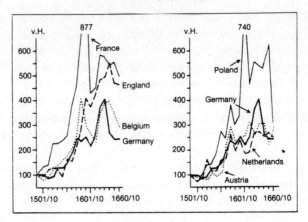

Figure 1   Grain prices in Central Europe, 1500–1670 (after Abel Agrarkrisen,
page 123)

Belgium and Poland the figure was four times as much, in the Netherlands three times and in Austria two and a half. Altogether grain prices
climbed by 386 per cent during this period, or about 4 per cent a year.
Compared with twentieth-century circumstances, this is a relatively
modest rate of inflation, and the term 'price revolution' therefore seems
exaggerated.

However, purchasing power lagged behind. Wages and income did not
rise fast enough to compensate for the higher cost of grain. The masses
were thus forced to change their eating habits and turn to foodstuffs that
provided the most nutrition for the least money. While cereals remained
an important part of their diet, they came to rely on other plant products
as well and limited their consumption of meat. In contrast to grain, the
prices of most industrial goods and wages climbed by slightly more than
50 per cent. For the families of salaried workers whose consumption of food
remained the same as before, these changes meant greater outlays for bread
and substitute victuals and·fewer resources for other necessities of life. The
result was that the living standard of the rural and urban underclass
deteriorated perceptibly. Conversely, husbandmen benefited from higher
grain prices, in so far as their farms were not too small, too remote from
markets or heavily indebted. The profits which could be made in certain
agricultural districts under the favourable market conditions of this era are
reflected in elaborate peasant houses and expensive interior furnishings.
Such evidence allows us to conclude that the rustic population, especially

peasants who farmed on a large scale and had regular access to markets, was increasingly prosperous.

In the early seventeenth century the agricultural boom in the main countries of Europe came to a standstill, and a long phase of depression began. In Germany the economic crisis was exacerbated by the Thirty Years War and the great population losses it entailed. However, in France and England too there were clear signs of crisis in the demographic and economic circumstances of the rural world. Exports of eastern European grain and Danish cattle to Western Europe dropped perceptibly. Prices for agrarian commodities remained at a low level for an extended period and impeded reconstruction in Germany as production costs rose. Cereals were cheap, but wages were high and did not come down for a long time. Economic historians are quite correct when they speak of an age of stagnation and depression, by which they particularly mean conditions in the countryside.

As far as longer-term historical development is concerned, the seventeenth-century depression nevertheless constitutes an intermediate phase. It was little more than a lull in the expansion of the agrarian economy that had begun in the sixteenth century and recommenced in the eighteenth, albeit at a pace that varied from one country to another. In Germany, where the rupture in economic development was more pronounced, owing to the impact of the Thirty Years War, recovery began sooner than elsewhere. If one takes all of Central and Western Europe into account, it would appear that the turn-round in the economy occurred around 1750, when growth in the population is once again obvious. The reliability of data for demographic expansion varies from one European country to another. The population of Prussia, within the kingdom's 1740 frontiers, more than doubled between 1740 and 1805. The number of Frenchmen increased during the same period by 150 per cent, i.e., from just under 20 to 30 million people. England's population grew by 165 per cent, i.e., from roughly 6 to 10 million persons. One result of this solid demographic expansion was a substantial rise in farm prices and a general flourishing of agriculture.

The growth of the agrarian economy caused by demographic trends was helped in part by the extension of arable land and the techniques employed in this process, a subject we have already touched upon. Equally important were improvements in the means of production, i.e., increases in the amount of labour and capital invested in specific tracts of land. We should first mention the ever more common practice during the second half of the eighteenth century of planting sections of fallow terrain and thus enhancing the effectiveness of the three-field system. Clover was the perfect crop for this purpose. It provided more stock feed; more cattle meant larger quantities of manure and hence better grain harvests. Other invaluable plants were cabbages, beetroots, garden peas, lentils and vetch. However, it took a long time for this better method of working the soil to prevail: strict rules for cultivating subdivided fields, traditional patterns of exploiting pasture, rights of tithe beneficiaries and peasant mistrust of novelty were serious obstacles. Various forms of crop rotation spread along the Baltic littoral.

Farmers who were enthusiastic about experiments availed themselves of opportunities to try out new crops. Tobacco, sunflowers, maize and above all, potatoes, should be singled out in this regard. The last-named plant spread rapidly in the late eighteenth century and saved Europe from experiencing a catastrophic shortage of food. The famine of 1771–2 had a great deal to do with the later popularity of this import from America. Contemporaries reckoned that potatoes provided three times the nutritional value of grain grown on a field of the same size. They were also better for the soil, enhanced its fertility and increased grain yields. The greater overall quantities of fodder that resulted from better methods of cultivation were also advantageous for stock-raising. Planted fallow and improved pasture meant that a farmer could keep more cattle and feed them in stalls during the summer. Animal husbandry likewise profited from a greater emphasis on breeding and the systematic use of studs. The eighteenth century was by no means slow with respect to inventions and new agrarian technology. However, innovation was more readily accepted in some countries than in others. Most new or improved farm implements came into general use only in the nineteenth century, especially more efficient ploughs, harrows and threshing devices.

What were the effects of enhanced agricultural productivity and agrarian technological progress on food supply in general? In spite of the advances described above, the nutritional difficulties that arose because of population growth during the latter half of the eighteenth century could not be entirely overcome. The masses had enough to eat only when harvests were good; if the yields were poor, there was still starvation and widespread misery. Europe's peasants lived almost entirely from what they were able to wring from mother nature herself until well into the Modern Era. We know a great deal about the different kinds of food but relatively little about how meals were prepared. Whatever was cooked on rustic hearths stemmed for the most part from crops raised in the immediate vicinity of the villages in question or garnered in field and forest. For a long time grain, which was processed in many different ways, was the main ingredient of the rural diet. In southern Europe wheat was widely cultivated; in Central and Western Europe rye flour was also used to bake bread. In northern Europe the short growing season meant that summer cereals, above all barley and oats, served this purpose. From the sixteenth century onward buckwheat spread into Central Europe and was especially successful on nutrient-poor sandy and clay soils. Until the advent of chemical fertilizers it constituted an important supplementary source of nutrition for many peasant households and was regarded, along with potatoes, as the archetypical food of the rural proletariat.

The everday peasant menu included not only bread and other cereal products but also vegetables, orchard fruits and garden items, as well as dairy products, eggs, fish and meat. Meat was heavily salted or, if it was fresh, cooked in the soup pot and eaten along with bread; it was roasted only on special occasions. In the Late Middle Ages the annual per capita consumption was very high, at least 60 kilos, but the figure dropped between the sixteenth and nineteenth centuries. As a consequence of changes in supply and demand during the 1500s, cattle and meat prices rose dramatically. A large portion of the rural and urban population simply could not afford to eat meat products unless the animals had been raised in their own barns. Hence, as time passed, average consumption fell markedly: by 1800 the figure amounted to only 15 kilos per person per annum. It was only during the second half of the nineteenth century that enhanced levels of personal income in European industrial states led to an increase: around 1900 the average individual ate about 50 kilos of meat a year.

The drop in meat consumption in Early Modern times and the transition to a monotonous diet of plant foods and cereals constitute evidence of the declining living standards of the mass of the population. Because of growing food shortages at the end of the eighteenth century owing to demographic expansion, potatoes were often substituted for bread. As we have seen, the yield of potatoes per square metre was higher than that of grain, and it is hardly surprising that they became a major crop in the gardens of land-poor petty peasant or wage-earning households. No other source of nutrition gained so quickly in importance during the late eighteenth and nineteenth centuries in Europe as the potato. It became a popular food of the first rank, especially in the predominantly industrial countries of England and Germany, a fact that was reflected in vigorous market activity. However, in the Mediterranean it never managed to achieve the same significance in the diet of the average family as it did north of the Alps.

Without any question the rapid spread of the potato was an essential factor in overcoming the alimentary problems that particularly affected the lower strata of the population. In the last great famine of European history, which occurred in 1846–7 and was caused by highly exceptional meteorological conditions, the helplessness of humanity when confronted by the forces of nature manifested itself once again. The failure of the potato crop along with a poor cereal harvest led to a disastrous bottleneck in food supplies. The effects of the famine were worst in Ireland, where small farmers constituted the bulk of the populace and potatoes were almost the only source of nourishment. Every eighth Irishman is said to have died of hunger; other inhabitants of the Emerald Isle managed to survive by emigrating to America.

It is clear from comparison of the differing consumption levels for grain, meat and potatoes that the pattern of European nutrition changed fundamentally during Early Modern times. There can be little doubt how monotonous and inadequate the average person's diet was down to the mid-nineteenth century. Only as a result of industrialization and progress in the agrarian economy after 1850 was there a long-term rise in income and hence also perceptible improvement in the kinds of food available to the masses. Nutritional standards and the general quality of life varied in Europe from one country to another, depending upon the degree of economic development. Within the rustic world, the clearest disparities were those between Eastern and Western Europe. Eastern peasants were much less well off around 1900 than their western counterparts. Travellers drew a sobering picture of conditions in the Russian countryside. In 1891–2 harvest failures caused a horrifying famine, and there were many deaths among the rural populace.

Sebastian Münster, a citizen of Basel, published a book in 1544 entitled *Cosmographie* and graphically portrayed the low living standards of the Western European ploughman of his age. His description of the simplicity of everday rural existence – the primitive nature of food, clothing and housing – applies especially to the husbandmen of southern Germany but is no less valid for many other lands of sixteenth-century Europe:

> The third estate is comprised of country folk; they reside in villages, hamlets, and on farms and are called boors [*Bauern*] because they work the soil [*bebauen*] and prepare the fields for crops. They lead a truly vile and unhappy life. Every one of them dwells in isolation and has as his sole companions domestics and cattle. Peasant houses are very bad, being made of mud and wood and set flat upon the ground

with only straw to cover the bare earth. Their food is dark rye bread, oatmeal gruel or boiled peas and lentils. Their sole beverages are water and milk. Their dress consists of a jacket cut from ticking, a pair of laced sandals [*Bundschuhe*] and a felt hat. These people can never relax but must labour from early in the morning until late at night. They take the food that they have grown on the land or produced from their animals into the next town and sell it in order to buy what they need. They must serve their lord throughout much of the year, plough the earth, sow, reap, drag the harvest into their barns, chop firewood and dig ditches. There is absolutely nothing that these poor wretches do not have to do or that can be delayed without incurring loss.[57]

The sandals that Münster mentions – so different from the elegant slip-on footwear of Renaisance townsmen – were quintessentially rustic and served as a rebel symbol in the German Peasant War, the struggle against lords secular and spiritual. The peasant wardrobe contained woollen and linen items, a direct reflection of the available raw materials. Both fleece and flax fibres were hand-spun; the home-made fabric served for blankets and sheets or was cut into articles of dress. The surplus yarn or cloth was sold in the markets of neighbouring towns or to wandering traders. Before the era of mass-production factories, the manufacture of linen goods was an important source of supplementary income for peasant households. This was especially true of regions in which domestic linen weaving was heavily concentrated until the industry was ruined in the early nineteenth century by competition from the new textile mills.

Home-made dresses, trousers and coats largely replaced the earlier standard, crudely worked smocks and animal skins as protection against the cruelty of the elements in Early Modern times. However, rustics in remote regions and Eastern Europe long continued to wear primitive raiment, and this distinguished them from ornately dressed noblemen or burghers. In towns, buckles, leather belts and buttons replaced the ropes and bands of cloth which held together peasant clothing; socks and shoes were substituted for the moccasins of the German Peasant War, leggings and wooden clogs. Leather shoes were well-known in the countryside during the eighteenth century, but they began to be worn for everyday work only in the nineteenth century. Rural folk spent more money on clothing as their incomes increased. This was especially true of the upper-most stratum, where a certain degree of luxury in male outer garments and female dress was a necessary status symbol. The holiday finery of well-to-do prosperous peasants corresponded to the behavioural norms of contemporary corporate society but was hardly representative of the rural masses. Because they were so well-made and the materials of such high quality, these sumptuous vestments have survived and may be viewed today in the glass display cases of many folk-art museums.

Peasant homes were usually quite simple and cramped. We are very well-informed about the dimensions and furnishings of rustic dwellings, thanks to the superb open-air museums that have meanwhile been built in most European countries in order to educate the public about the country world's vanished domestic culture. In such places many different types of houses and farm buildings, with a full inventory of chattels and equipment, have been gathered and carefully reassembled. Because of the favourable development of the agrarian economy in some localities, especially in the Netherlands and Alsace, peasant houses became increasingly luxurious and comfortable. In the case of larger farms, the living space was divided into kitchens, bedrooms and parlours. However, even in the seventeenth and eighteenth centuries there were still many rustic abodes that consisted mainly of a single large chamber.

In so far as farms were made up of several buildings with different functions, peasant dwellings were surrounded by stalls, hay lofts and workrooms. The furniture in living quarters was normally quite minimal. If the house contained only a single room, benches were grouped around the fireplace and the dinner-table: they served as both seats and beds. As time passed and families enjoyed a modicum of prosperity, special sleeping arrangements were devised for married couples and small children. Notwithstanding the gradual differentiation of dwelling space, the hearth remained the focal point of homes. The benches located next to outside walls had to be moved when beds were set up there. Hired hands and maids had to sleep in attics above the animal stalls. When food was served, the whole houshold gathered around a large dining-table; at the hour of the main meal, a large pot of steaming soup was placed in its centre. Everybody dipped his spoon into the pot until the beginning of the nineteenth century.

Rustic living standards, as they have been described here in terms of nutrition, clothing and housing, were the tangible manifestation of disparities between individual families. In most of Europe the country population of Early Modern times was anything but homogeneous; indeed, it was highly stratified. Property assessments from the time of the German Peasant War show clearly that there were vast differences in wealth among south-west German and Thuringian husbandmen. Alongside rich peasants with extensive holdings there were petty ploughmen who were barely able to pay their share of the tax. As the population expanded, highly scattered farming plots became more and more the rule in regions such as Württemberg, which were characterized by partition of land among heirs. However, in districts such as Lower Saxony, where undivided inheritance prevailed, the number and size of farms remained relatively constant throughout the Early Modern era. However, in both of these instances, the proportion of village inhabitants with little land increased greatly between the sixteenth and the eighteenth centuries; in many places the ratio was almost 50 per cent by 1800. The growth of a land-poor or landless underclass and the resultant unequal distribution of income created grave social problems.

In the duchy of Brunswick-Wolfenbüttel, where single heir principles applied, there were 830 large farms (11 per cent), 1200 medium-sized ones (17 per cent), and 5182 small ones in 1656.[58] From this rough categorization of peasant holdings, we may deduce that the proportion of so-called full-time peasants – that is, those who were able to live from the proceeds of agriculture – was relatively small. The full-timers, the half-timers and the cottagers jointly constituted the village community, and all of them were entitled to use the commons. However, as the population grew, there were more and more local inhabitants who did not belong to the community. They included many day workers who had homes of their own, as well as lodgers who paid rent to the householders with whom they lived. Finally, there were the numerous domestics. This village substratum rarely enjoyed any of the rights of community members. Since such persons had little land, they required guaranteed access to meadow and forest commons if they wished to raise even a small number of cattle. As long as there were not too many of them, their presence was tolerated, but with demographic expansion they found themselves increasingly excluded from the communal pastures and woodlands. They were often the non-inheriting sons of farmers. They dwelt on tiny plots and, as they were seeking to make an independent livelihood, they had to supplement their income by working for daily wages on the farms of prosperous peasants or learning a craft. The upsurge in the numbers of these individuals during the eighteenth century upset the equilibrium of village life. In Brunswick-Wolfenbüttel large and medium-sized farms increased by only 40 per cent in the period from 1658 to 1800, but small ones grew by 123 per cent.

Similar developments in village social structure during Early Modern times may also be observed in other regions. From the sixteenth century onward, but especially in the 1700s, the stratification of many German rural communities underwent a fundamental transformation. The full-time peasants often became a minority; however, they remained political-ly dominant, since participation in local government depended upon landholding. The character of rural society thus changed substantially, though one must stress the marked differences between Lower Saxon districts with undivided inheritance, the villages of eastern European estate owners and the densely settled, craft-orientated communities of south-western Germany, which divided their land. A growing portion of countrymen could only survive by working for wages or by making objects fellow villagers would want to buy. Even if such families managed to acquire homes of their own, they generally remained underprivileged and socially disadvantaged.

During the eighteenth century the rustic underclass spread unchecked in most European countries. Most persons with little or no land supported themselves as field labourers, as daily wage-earners or as employees of rural industrial enterprises. This stratum of the population also included domes-tic servants, unmarried individuals who lived with peasant or noble mas-ters. People of this ilk had relatively secure jobs and did not have to worry about board and lodging. However, they lacked basic rights and had no chances of social mobility. They could not establish families of their own, their personal life was subject to the daily rhythm of employers' households and they encountered great difficulties when they sought their fortunes elsewhere. It is usually very hard to catch a glimpse of them in the sources since they were so fully integrated into the domestic world. In Eastern Europe around the year 1800 one can use the large number of landed estates as a statistical basis and deduce that servants comprised between 10 and 15 per cent of rural residents. In the rest of Europe the figure was much lower, owing to the prevalence of small and medium-sized farms.

Because the sources are complete and because so much research has been done, we have an excellent understanding of the French rural world on the eve of the 1789 Revolution. Let us conclude our remarks on rustic social structure by sketching peasant life in France. The uppermost stratum consisted of the owners and tenants of large farms, the dimensions of which generally needed the use of paid labour. The chief characteristic of this group was its economic autonomy: it was largely immune to the ups and downs of the market-place and agrarian crises caused by bad weather. Well-to-do farmers were always able to feed themselves. They were in a position to sell cattle and grain at the most favourable moment and maximize their profits. Their ratio to the rest of the country population varied from region to region. They comprised 2 to 3 per cent of the inhabitants of the *département* of the Nord, but in some parts of western France they amounted to about 20 per cent. The opposite side of the coin was that the economic power of rich peasants made other villagers highly dependent upon them. This was especially true of petty peasants, day workers and domestics. Wealth and social pre-eminence also had a political impact: affluent rustics set the tone in communal assemblies.

The common trait of persons who belonged to the middle stratum of rural society was subsistence farming, for the most part only with the help of family members. The Russian agrarian economist, Alexander Chayanov, has devised a set of criteria for peasant family farms on the basis of a study of historical conditions in his own country, and they would seem to apply equally well to France.[59] The principal objective of peasant family farmers was to produce as much food as they needed to survive, and hence their connections with the market-place were marginal. In order to buy clothing or pay taxes and feudal dues, these peasants did sell a portion of their harvest. In certain districts of western France characterized by relatively minor social differentiation there was a stable peasant social structure that included a large middle stratum. In the *département* of Sarthe intermediate rank farmers accounted for 60 per cent of the total rural population and thus formed the solid core of the peasantry. Another 20 per cent – the *laboureurs* – were wealthy, and a further 20 per cent – the *journaliers* – were workers paid by the day. The middle group also encompassed most of the vintners, a state of affairs that typified many other regions as well.

Small-time peasants constituted an absolute majority of the rural population in many parts of France towards the end of the eighteenth century. Generally home-owners with a tiny plot of arable land, they cultivated relatively unprofitable cereals with poor yields; they also raised vegetables and small animals. All of this sufficed to cover their food requirements for only part of the year. They had no recourse but to work for wages or otherwise earn the cash they needed in order to survive. In the non-agrarian sector petty crafts were a sure way to make a bit of extra money. Pottery, basket-weaving and, above all, the rural textile industry, which grew rapidly during the eighteenth century, provided the answer to the problem of supplementary income. The bottom rung of the social ladder was occupied by the rural proletariat. It was made up mainly of day labourers, who generally had a house and a diminutive garden. This impoverished segment of rustic society – for the most part it subsisted from wages – represented about 60 per cent of the population in certain areas of Normandy in 1789, though the ratios were much lower elsewhere in the province. Domestic servants, employed and fed all year long on big farms, held more secure jobs, although they were hardly better off materially than salaried workers.

The social situation in the French countryside towards the end of the *ancien régime* amounted to polarization. The uppermost stratum was growing stronger. Petty rustics and wage-earners were indigent while the intermediate category of peasants was shrinking. Rural middle-class dropouts entered the ranks of the day labourers or *manouvriers*. The still had land of their own in the eighteenth century, but much of their income came from jobs they performed for others. The greatest growth was among servants employed on large farms; domestics had no personal possessions and were entirely dependent upon their masters. The expansion of this group is an indication of the spread of English-style agrarian capitalism in many parts of France. The emergence of an underclass provided some of the social ingredients for the explosion that occurred in 1789.

10

Neighbours and Village Communities

For a long time it was not thought worthwhile to look in detail at the village community of Early Modern times, although there was a rich fund of source material for studying the subject. Why were scholars so hesitant? After the defeat of the peasant rebels in 1525 it seemed that the village community in the insurgent regions of south-western Germany was not nearly as important as before. The main argument was that the political position and legal status of peasants had changed: they had become subject to their lords. At first rustics were disarmed in many communities, and on occasion village meetings were banned. Rights of local self-government were restricted as far as possible. For example, the peasants of Reichenau had to turn over control of the town hall to the abbot and were no longer permitted to choose their own burgomaster; a new provincial ordinance that largely abolished communal autonomy was promulgated in the Rheingau. On the other hand, Tyrolese country folk – the German Peasant War notwithstanding – continued to constitute an officially recognized estate; this also happened elsewhere in southern Germany. Moreover, peasants were accorded corporate representation for the first time in certain smaller territorial states. From a broader perspective, it is true that the rebellion led to a further extension of princely power and the limitation of rural self-government. Wherever university-trained bureaucrats managed to impose to principles of Roman law, peasants were increasingly excluded from participating in the judicial process.

The earlier school of historians played down even more the significance of peasant communities east of the Elbe after the rise of the landed estate. When eastern territorial states were studied, the emphasis was upon absolutism and the unique structure of indigenous manorial lordship; there was scant interest in communal institutions. Rustic servility in the form of expanding hereditary subjection was the focus of research; rural self-rule was considered to be of minimal importance. Indeed, peasants and village entities appear mainly as the objects of the territorial state's social concern in many provincial decrees and police edicts of the eighteenth century; they were simply regarded as incapable of autonomous action. From the viewpoint of absolutism accepted by historians of a later age, the village community was retrogressive and posed an obstacle to agrarian economic progress and efficient administration. Both estate owners and bureaucrats complained about the tendency of peasants and village bodies to cling to traditional ways and to resist innovations in justice, local government and the management of common lands. Nevertheless, it is fair to enquire whether peasant communities of the Early Modern era had really sunk to the level of total insignificance. We should also look at the topic from a European perspective and examine how communal institutions developed in general and how they were able to survive. Before we treat these questions, it will be helpful to sketch certain basic traits of the emergent village community.

Peasant collectivities arose in the principal countries of Central and Western Europe around AD 1100 and were a central component of old-fashioned European agrarian society from that time onward. The village community, at least in a distinct form, did not exist in Early Medieval times but appeared only in the High Middle Ages as a result of manifold changes in patterns of settlement, agricultural practices and legal systems. Because the latter phenomena were so divergent, it is impossible to discern common origins and structures. The theory of nineteenth-century legal historians to the effect that the Late Medieval village with its subdivided fields and commons stemmed from a Germanic 'mark association' or cooperative, which held land jointly and worked it as a team, is no longer tenable. Be this as it may, it seems that altered settlement patterns and new economic conditions played an important role in the birth of the village community.

Strong demographic expansion in the Late Middle Ages meant that land resources were more intensively exploited; another result was the appearance of conglomerate villages with common arable land. The desire to enhance the productivity of existing terrain and to increase grain yields forced ploughmen to shift to the multiple field system. The land that surrounded villages was divided into large tracts and in most instances farmed according to the three-field routine, that is, winter planting, summer planting and fallow. This innovation led to the formation of the village field association with its obligatory approach to cultivation and strict rules. Peasants were no longer permitted to plant crops according to a sequence they devised themselves; they now had to respect communally determined regulations. The transition to the three-field system or variations thereof took place in many parts of Western Europe between the eleventh and the fifteenth centuries. Multiple field practices were introduced to Eastern Europe only in the fifteenth and sixteenth centuries, indeed in some instances even later. In every region where the three-field system found acceptance it became the norm as time passed, and peasants were forced to work together much more than they had before. However, it did not prevail in those parts of Europe that were unsuited to intensive cereal cultivation. In such localities the ties between villagers were much looser, and individual households were far more autonomous than in grain-orientated communities.

The advent of the three-field system led to a plethora of statutes within the communities in question. Planting timetables had to be coordinated, rustics granted the right to traverse each other's plots and sown fields protected from grazing cattle by constructing fences. It was also necessary to regulate the collective use of fallow as pasture for village animals, to set compulsory deadlines for seeding or reaping and to agree upon a host of other matters in order to keep the level of conflict between neighbours at a minimum. The appearance of villages with binding field-use ordinances thus provided the framework for the evolution of a collective mentality and for the coalescence of local peasant families into a closely knit community. However, the genesis of communal life must be seen not only in terms of evolving settlement patterns and a changing rural economy, but also within the context of the High Medieval transformation of manorial lordship and the loosening of the bonds between seigniors and peasants – a subject discussed earlier in this book. As a result of the dissolution of the servile labour farm – the focus of which had been large-scale seigniorial involvement in an agrarian enterprise based upon compulsory peasant service – manorial lords had greatly reduced the amount of land they cultivated themselves and had therefore also largely released peasants from their work obligations. The trend towards commutation of rustic services into payments in money and kind enhanced the autonomy of peasant farms and accorded them the leeway they required in order to accomplish the tasks that arose in connection with a village economy and communal activities. During the twelfth and thirteenth centuries – that is, the period in which the chief traits of peasant communities were developed – the agrarian economic order centred upon the servile labour farm collapsed in most parts of Central and Western Europe, or at least in those regions where it had existed to begin with. However, even in localities that had never known this institution, manorial lordship evolved in the direction of more liberal terms of tenancy and less rustic subservience.

Finally, among the factors that affected the formation of the village community in the High Middle Ages, we must mention fundamental changes in the character of lordship. They had to do with a growth not of feudatories' power but that of the rustic population, which was now able to administer justice on the local level. The responsibility for keeping the peace within the confines of the village may be regarded as the culmination of the evolutionary process of communal autonomy, although the exercise of judicial authority is not *per se* an essential function of collective peasant life. The establishment of a local court certainly strengthened rural self-government, but it was not a prerequisite for constituting an autonomous community. Villages were legally competent and capable of acting on their own by virtue of their economic functions and already established rights. Unlike communities in long-settled parts of Germany, colonial districts in the central and east Elbian regions had magistrates' courts from the very beginning, a circumstance that much enhanced their freedom of action.

During the period of territorial formation in the twelfth and thirteenth centuries, small lordship districts emerged on the strictly local level; they often encompassed no more than a single village. This nascent, primal variety of ruling authority normally involved the right to issue commands or prohibitions, and this became the principal manifestation of collective dominion. Village precincts now formed the lowest category of lordship; they represented the smallest circuit within which a judge could administer the law. Thus the rustic community was not merely an associative but also a seigniorial entity. Local government bodies, especially municipal offices, were the concrete expression of this village dualism. The magistrate was simultaneously the symbol of lordship and the deputized spokesman of a corporate body. Lordship and community thus overlapped within the confines of village life and influenced one another.

From Late Medieval times onward village communities often had individual seals; sometimes they even sported escutcheons. Town halls were another feature; they often served as sites for staging dances and plays. In certain places local banners were hoisted on festive occasions. Villages were also legal personalities and had the right to initiate judicial actions. Rural communities appeared as parties in all kinds of trials. Sometimes disputes between them and other bodies or persons possessing seigniorial competencies were submitted to arbitration; if there was no agreement, the community appealed to higher courts. It likewise disposed of independent wealth and could endow chantries. Many villages supervised parish property and had the right to elect pastors. From the Middle Ages onward every community sought to have a church and a priest of its own in order to be able to exercise autonomy in the ecclesiastical realm as well. The individual identity of a secular corporation needed to be reinforced by associative forms of worship; village solidarity implied pastoral involvement.

The highest deliberative body in the Late Medieval and Early Modern rustic community was the village meeting, which everyone was required to attend. In most European countries such assemblies had the right to approve statutes, choose officials and appoint people to village posts. The frequency of such meetings varied greatly from country to country. In Bohemia and Hungary they were normally held only once a year, but in Denmark and northern France sometimes every Sunday. Elsewhere there were no hard and fast dates; people assembled when, as necessity demanded, the village magistrate called upon them to do so. Frequently, the pastor would announce the date from the pulpit. Business began when drums were sounded or the church bells rung. In many places the villagers met out of doors, often under a particular tree (oak or linden), in the churchyard or the square in front of the town hall. In Danish villages every participant was given a ticket to sit on a particular stone; the seats were arranged in a semicircle. Peasants stubbornly insisted on convening outside long after it became possible to assemble in closed rooms.

As already indicated, everybody who had the right to vote was expected to attend. Unexcused absences and tardiness were punished with fines, the amount of which was calculated on the basis of one's social status and the value of one's farm. Meetings were often tumultuous, punctuated by exchanges of insults and even accompanied by violence. Confusion seems to have been more or less the rule in Russia. There were no guidelines and no chairmen; anybody could participate and speak whenever he felt like it. Nineteenth-century travellers commented on the chaos they had observed on such occasions. If there was any agreement at all, it was owing to the intervention of the magistrate. An official report from the same era states that village gatherings often degenerated into wild drinking bouts. Those entitled to vote decided in favour of the person who supplied the most alchohol. Misbehaviour at meetings was not uncommon in other countries either, for certain individuals distinguished themselves by the volume of their voices and general combativeness. In Austria participants were forbidden to bring weapons with them; this rule was surely owing to the prospect of violent confrontation.

The leaders of village communities were men who had either been elected by fellow peasants or put in office by the local lord. Magistrates were known by different names from one country to another. In Germany the most common terms were *Bauermeister, Heimbürge* and *Schulze*. In Eastern Europe the office of village elder was frequently hereditary, and the prerequisite was possession of a particularly large farm. In Norway and Denmark it was customary for the job to be held by wealthier peasants on a rotating basis and for a limited period of time. The magistrate was the most important link between the village and its feudal superior. Municipal duties included making sure that local inhabitants fulfilled their obligations toward the seignior, who was often lord of the manor as well. Occasionally the magistrate was authorized to collect taxes; he was also responsible for maintaining roads and bridges. Inasmuch as he stood between the villagers and the seignior, he had all the advantages and disadvantages of a middleman. He not only had to carry out the instructions he received from the local lord and the state but also needed to remain on good terms with his fellow villagers. However, the office of magistrate was an honnour, and social prestige was often complemented by material benefits. In many communities the job exempted its incumbent, either partly or entirely, from the obligation to pay whatever he owed in the way of dues or services to the seignior, the state and the community itself. Sometimes he was granted additional land or special access to the commons. An unscrupulous magistrate could easily draw personal profit from his duties. It is thus hardly surprising that many local officials in France during the eighteenth century were thought to be corrupt.

In many cases the magistrate was assisted by a collegiate body which could include two, four or even twelve members. In certain instances he was subordinate to this council and needed its assent. The vestrymen had the right to act in the name of the parish and thus relieved it from holding too frequent meetings and the tedious debates they engendered. Village autonomy required the services of various employees; their numbers and functions depended upon the size of the community and its economic makeup. They included herdsmen, night watchmen, foresters and town clerks. Sometimes they were paid from the municipal treasury; on other occasions they were given a house or a piece of land and exempted from dues.

If one wishes to fathom the most basic component of village life, indeed the structure of the community as a whole, it is necessary to take into account the phenomenon of neighbourhood, namely, the everday realities of the proximity of human beings to one another. Neighbourhood pro-

vided an indispensable foundation for the evolution of peasant collectivities; everywhere in Europe it was an essential element of communal existence. Neighbourly ties depended on the degree of social contact,
and this varied from one set of circumstances to another. There would be
less association in the case of farmsteads scattered about the countryside
and more in the context of crowded village settlements. In the former
instance the link was looser, in the latter tighter. On the local plane
neighbourhood began as an imperative alliance of particular farms and
peasant households. Solidarity was based on the need to join forces against
hostile outsiders and to keep the peace internally. Families and domestic
collectivities that lived alongside each other in rustic settlements had to
exercise mutual deference and agree upon common procedures in working
the land and grazing stock. As time passed, these relationships became
more intimate; they matured fully in the milieu of densely inhabited
villages.

The propinquity of rustic homes within villages led to a special awareness of community, a circumstance summed up by the venerable phrase
'good neighbours'. The narrow range of geographic vision and the diminutive size of many villages meant that life in them had a very familiar
character; marriages and the resultant kinship reinforced intimacy. People
worked next to each other, attended divine service together and participated jointly in local festivities. Even if there were bitter internal feuds and
permanent enmities, solidarity towards the external world cemented individual relationships. The village seignior served as a common opponent;
the community closed ranks against him. Families were interdependent on
a day-to-day basis. If a barn was being raised, if older buildings needed to
be repaired or if tragedy struck a particular household, people knew that
they could count on fellow villagers. Neighbourliness was especially evident when specific kinds of chores were performed and when there had
been a fire or another case of misfortune: at such times concord and
collective willingness to help were even more noticeable than usual.

However, it is not our intention to idealize peasant village life. Rustic
community spirit was not a manifestation of utopia but rather the product
of common need, that is, of the bare fact that all inhabitants of a locality
depended upon each other. Close affiliation easily led to gossip and a lack
of respect for the rights of family privacy; altercations and even physical
violence could be the result. There were frequent conflicts between 'full
peasants', who constituted the social elite, and the mass of cottagers, who
suffered under restrictions on their access to pasture and complained about
the unfair division of privileges and responsibilies in the economic sphere.

Everybody belonged to the village community and was subject to its written and unwritten laws. As soon as someone arrived and settled down, he was bound by the rules. However, the right to live in a place was by no means automatic, and newcomers encountered obstacles when they attempted to strike roots. The object was to prevent overuse of the commons and to protect water resources, meadowland and woods. In many cases acceptance of strangers was conditional upon payment of a fee and the outcome of a public vote.

In Austrian villages recent settlers who wanted to use the commons were charged for the privilege – a fact to which written collections of precedent-setting peasant judicial sentences attest. In Denmark such persons first had to submit to an initiation ritual, the essence of which was to provide drinks for the whole assemblage. Acceptance into the community fold was thus often linked to an entrance toll in the form of an ample supply of beer and wine for one's new neighbours. The names used to describe this levy are partly indicative of its character: on the island of Fehmarn it was known as *Einspringbier*. If an outsider married into a local family, he was also liable for a tax. The amount was frequently set in advance, the proceeds being shared between the community and its lord according to a specific, mutually agreed formula. Departure from the village and hence also from the neighbourhood was also regulated. Many municipal ordinances required the person who was leaving to settle accounts with his fellow townsmen and the lord; if outstanding bills had not been paid, permission to go was not granted.

Birth, marriage and death provided the main occasions for ceremonies in which the whole neighbourhood was involved. Nuptials were the kind of festivities that allowed everybody to participate and contribute. They were associated with a host of customs and formed a time of genuine collective gaiety. Everybody attended most peasant weddings and entered fully into the spirit of the celebration, which sometimes lasted for several days. The rural judicial sentences and village ordinances mentioned above often concerned themselves with nuptial usages and the excesses to which they gave rise. Death and funerals also played a central role in the neighbourhood setting. Assisting the bereaved and presence at burials were at the heart of neighbourly responsibilities. In Westphalia all family members were relieved of the tasks associated with interment. Neighbours did everything that was necessary to prepare the bier. The closest one, the so-called 'death neighbour', washed and clothed the corpse; digging the grave and ringing the church bells was also the job of other villagers. After the obsequies were concluded, it was the practice to lay on a sumptuous funeral dinner, at which time the dead person was once more commemorated.

Next let us return to the question we raised at the beginning of this chapter, namely, what was the position of the peasant community in Early Modern Europe? Had it actually become a subordinate, meaningless institution within the fabric of absolutism? In this context we must introduce three historiographical catchwords: 'confessionalization' or officially mandated religious organization; 'social discipline'; and *Verrechtlichung* or the process by which bureaucracies imposed Roman-inspired concepts of law upon the public. These are the terms currently used to describe the incursions of the Early Modern European state. Governments monopolized the employment of legitimate force: this affected both villagers whose autonomy was undermined and city dwellers who were also generally unable to resist the onslaught of central authority. The same can be said of the landed nobility and the Church. All segments of society were increasingly subjected to administrative regulation. To be sure, the decline in the power of nobles and clergymen was a process that extended over several centuries. The nobility remained ensconced in its manors and was also in a privileged position with respect to securing bureaucratic posts, for which a higher level of professional qualification was gradually becoming indispensable.

The process of subjecting society to the dictates of princely government was most intensely felt in the rural setting. Although territorial potentates did all they could to concentrate authority in their own hands and delegate its exercise to submissive officials, rural communities managed to survive in a basic sense. Nevertheless, they were incorporated into the structure of the state as the lowest administrative unit. Peasant spokesmen received more and more commands from on high. Village juries and judges operating within the framework of local precedent became less important in an age of university-trained lawyers. Communities that sought to obtain justice had to resort to learned barristers. The negative facet of the *Verrechtlichung* of social relationships and, even more so, of conflict resolution was the devaluation of customary law; this trend was especially hard upon the inhabitants of the countryside. The practice of putting several villages under the authority of a single local bureaucratic entity headed by territorial princely officials, so-called *Amtmänner*, helped the establishment of central control over peasant communities.

In western Germany 'confessionalization' also led to a loss of rustic independence. The Religious Peace of Augsburg (1555) finally gave territorial rulers the right to decide whether their subjects should be Lutheran or papist. Ecclesiastical and communal visitations, i.e., official state inspection committees, as well as church ordinances issued by the princes and their advisors in such matters, now had the sanction of law and could be developed further. The impact of the new policies was obvious in both Protestant and Roman Catholic communities. Evangelical codes were particularly detailed; they regulated not only the liturgy and official Church acts within villages but also any other kind of local business that the state could somehow manage to control. Inasmuch as they had to report regularly about parish affairs, pastors also became adjuncts of the central administration. As a consequence of these developments, peasants lost the opportunity to engage in traditional, individual forms of devotion; there was no longer much leeway for shaping religion within the village environment.

Gerhard Oestreich has proposed the concept of 'social discipline' for yet another feature of emergent absolutism. By this he means the processs of all subjects of the territorial state being placed under central authority through the promulgation of laws and edicts. The bureaucracy cast a broad net: taxpayers, soldiers, producers and consumers were caught up in it. The two chief manifestations of social discipline in the countryside were the systematic collection of state imposts that no longer required the prior consent of manorial lords and compulsory service in a uniformed, regular, military force. Governments inundated rural districts with rules and regulations. Scarcely any aspect of peasant life was left untouched. The authorities intervened in matters of inheritance. They decided how communities should stage festivities, what arrangements should be made for retirees, and under what circumstances tax relief should be granted. The result was that many questions that country folk had previously settled on their own were now within the purview of the high and mighty agents of state power, the 'people on top'. However, the nabobs were hardly omnipotent: many decrees and orders were mere paper exercises. Territorial bureaucrats were often forced to yield in the face of obdurate peasant insistence upon respect for tradition.

Village communities and institutions did manage to weather the authoritarian storm. If they did not succeed in preserving all their rights everywhere, they were still alive and kicking in the eighteenth century. The functions of lower-level tribunals could only be limited by means of lengthy legal action. Arbitration and minor cases of criminal justice continued to be handled by local magistrates even east of the Elbe, as surviving court records make clear. In places where jurisdiction was exercised by legal personnel trained in urban and Roman law, rural justices and jurymen were gradually excluded from pronouncing judgements. Where communities were responsible for prosecuting disturbances of the peace and violation of commons ordinances and their role was sanctioned by existing law, local courts normally continued to operate. The range of their duties was quite broad: village ordinances contain rules relating to the use of arable land and forests, animal husbandry, fire-fighting, sale and purchase of property, employment of domestics and a variety of other matters.

The autonomy of peasant communities in east Central Europe was much more limited than in the west because of economic factors, particularly the spread of the landed estate. East of the Elbe peasants and villages were less exposed to the increasing pressures of the state than they were to the exactions of the nobility, who were seeking to maximize the yields of their properties. Rural settlements in this vast zone have thus become a synonym for communal subordination. In contrast to the west, eastern husbandmen had to spend most of the working day on the lord's estate. This circumstance alone left them little time to pursue their own lives and material interests within the village precincts. Nevertheless, even under such harsh conditions, 'a functioning rural community survived, however, weakly developed it may seem to have been in comparison to other regions' (Helmut Harnisch).[60] Although it is quite clear that peasant self-administration in the trans-Elbian zone had not been eradicated, the contrast with Western Europe cannot be overlooked. The powerful tradition of seigniorial dependency continued in the east even after the agrarian reforms of the nineteenth century, for most of the population earned a living not by farming for itself but by working for wages on noble estates.

The heterogeneous character of peasant communities in the various countries of Europe did not change during the Early Modern era. Economic, social and political influences at work in the rural world did not make themselves felt simultaneously; rather their impact was erratic, multifarious and of varying intensity. Thus any attempt at generalization is problematic. The French village – which we shall describe briefly – was still a basic component of country life. It owed its cohesion to the fact that rustics had to solve their problems jointly, whether it was a question of dealing with the seigneur or of regulating the use of commons. The most important institution was the town meeting. It was convoked as the need arose and normally picked one or two chairmen from its ranks every year. Their job was to make sure that the lump sum of taxes that had been imposed upon the community – the smallest fiscal entity in monarchical France – was divided as fairly as possible among their fellow villagers. They also presided over discussions regarding the maintenance of public buildings, roads and villages. Other matters that were settled under their supervision were elections for the job of school headmaster, rules for crop rotation within the framework of the three-field system, negotiations with the seigneur concerning collective manorial obligations and any question that related to the management of communal lands. As may be seen from surviving protocols of such meetings, the commons were the main focus of deliberations even in the eighteenth century. This was especially true when the proportion of collectively exploited terrain within the confines of a particular locality was relatively high.

The traditional character of village life and a decision-making process that involved all segments of peasant society remained more or less unaltered in mountain country and other remote places well into the eighteenth century. However, in other parts of France, such as the Toulouse region or Burgundy, there were signs of severe strain within rural communities, tensions that can only be interpreted as manifestations of profound conflicts of interest among individual rural groups. Well-to-do peasants incorporated common land, piece by piece, into their own farms and excluded the lower social stratum from participation in town meetings, in which they rammed through collusive agreements for grazing their usually very large herds on public meadows, thereby depriving cottagers of the necessary resources for raising cattle. Contrary to the interests of the latter, the big farmers began to lease or even sell sections of the commons in order to pay off community debts or finance new roads and municipal office construction. Moroever, influenced by the Physiocrats, the Crown sought from about 1750 onward to mandate the dissolution of commons although its efforts were largely in vain. A major reason for the failure of the royal edicts was surely the resistance they encountered in many villages. It was the poor peasants who offered the most tenacious opposition, for they clearly recognized that without pasturage rights they would be unable to survive economically.

The Russian village community (*mir, obshchina*) was in a class by itself. Even in the nineteenth century it retained essential characteristics of a distant past, and it was not finally done away with until Peter Stolypin's agrarian reforms of 1909. It was much more strongly marked by agrarian collectivism and the common possession of land than were its western European counterparts; it unquestionably represented the most extreme form of communal control over agrarian terrain anywhere in Europe. As late as the mid-nineteenth century more than 90 per cent of the land in Russia proper was in the hands of rustic communities rather than individuals. The mir predominated in the empire's mainly Russian heartland, especially in the interior provinces, but it did not exist in the Ukraine or Belorus. All that individual peasant families owned outright was a cottage or hut with a bit of garden. Every household had the right to use meadows and woods that belonged to the community and could also claim its share of arable land. The assignment of farming plots was a collective enterprise, whether this was done in a public meeting or by magistrates acting on behalf of the village as a whole.

The dimensions of the farms parcelled out by the community depended upon the size of particular families or upon the number of field hands a household could muster. Had there been a change in circumstances or had a new family been established, the village could reapportion terrain by reducing or increasing its size according to individual requirements. The regularity of redistribution evened out inequities that developed between households, prevented subdivision and made acreage available for recent arrivals or newly married couples. The system also guaranteed that rustic obligations towards estate owners and the tsarist government would be fulfilled, a factor that surely contributed to the historical continuity of the mir.

The intervals between redistribution varied. Meagre evidence from the sixteenth and seventeenth centuries allows us to conclude that it did not take place very often. By the eighteenth century it was increasingly common, and by the mid-nineteenth it happened periodically, mostly every twelve years. However, sometimes intervals were shorter: every six or three years and occasionally annually. Partial reapportionment was also possible if a new family had been founded or a household had become much larger. Villagers could insist that their absolute right to land be respected; even persons who had migrated to cities decades earlier could return and demand their due.

The mir's impact upon Russian agriculture is a controversial subject. One school of thought, which has stressed the negative features of the individualistic western European agrarian system, considers the Russian village community to have been a kind of paradise, arguing that the right of anyone to leave, return and reclaim land amounted to a solution of the question of social justice. The proponents of this theory have conceded that every agrarian technological advance and all other progressive measures met with opposition. However, in their view, even though innovations were implemented only very slowly, the opposite side of the coin was that the right to a piece of land was a progressive phenomenon *per se*. The other school believes that the mir constituted a terrible obstacle to the betterment of society; in the last analysis the reactionary tsarist regime was built on it. At all events, the very harmful effects of periodic land redistribution and the barrier it represented to progress in Russia's agrarian economy on the village level finally led to its abolition. In 1906–7 laws that Stolypin pushed through the Duma gave peasants the right to leave the mir under certain conditions and receive their fair share of land. This legislation was the beginning of the end for the institution in question: it disappeared forever a few years later.

If one surveys the arguments of both sides in the historiographical squabble we have outlined above, it would seem that scholars who regard the mir as having been incapable of reform are correct. We may cite the negative verdict that Max Weber pronounced long ago: 'Obligations associated with the land outweighed the right to possess it, and in every instance the community was held collectively responsible for payments to the estate owner.'[61] Moreover, there was a fateful connection in Russia between the village community and serfdom. Russian seigniors exploited peasants to such an extent that they were hardly able to use their stock of equipment for their own benefit; their horses and whatever other accoutrements they possessed were employed to work the estates of their masters. Land was either leased to peasants or directly cultivated by the lord, with teams which the rustics themselves were forced to provide. However, collective responsibility towards estate owners and serfdom existed only from the late sixteenth and early seventeenth centuries: obviously they were the matrix of the reapportionment system. The abolition of serfdom in 1861 and the dissolution of the mir in 1906–7 must thus be viewed as interrelated events that were the start of a long overdue reform of Russian agriculture. In Central and Western Europe improvements in farmers' lives and peasant emancipation had begun a hundred years before, as we shall see in the next chapter.

11

Emancipation and Reform

The liberation of the peasantry from seigniorial subservience was surely one of the most momentous events in modern European social history. Rarely have measures implemented by the state had so profound an impact on the structure of rural society and agriculture as the emancipation of the peasants and concomitant agrarian reforms did – events which took place mainly during the century from 1770 to 1870 and opened the way for an efficient, market-orientated style of farming. The fashion nowadays is to label many of the steps taken during these hundred years to abrogate the venerable feudal order of agrarian relationships the 'emancipation of the peasants'. However, the terms employed during the age in question varied. When rustics east of the Elbe were delivered from the yoke of their noble masters, the process was called 'regulation'. When ploughmen in the west were released from vestigial manorial obligations, it was a question of 'commutation' or 'acquittal of charges appertaining to the soil'. Only after the publication of a major study by Knapp in 1887[62] did the word 'emancipation' gain currency. This expression is succinct and easy to recall, but the advantage of a catchy rubric is sometimes outweighed by the risk of oversimplification. Certainly in the present instance the circumstances were varied and complex. The aura of liberal pathos associated with the concept of emancipation is quite unmistakable. We ought not to forget that our understanding of freedom is relative and subject to constant change. The single most important rallying cry of the masses in the French Revolution was *liberté*. This remained the case during the nineteenth century, an era in which political upheavals were inevitably accompanied by the slogan 'freedom and justice'.

How then should we interpret the phrase 'peasant emancipation'? What agrarian historical phenomena does it encompass? The answer is that it normally involves three reform processes: (1) commutation; (2) partition of common lands; and (3) separation. Commutation means the release of peasants from a broad range of manorial obligations and characterizes emancipation in the narrower sense of the word. The partition of common lands is more or less self-explanatory: collectively exploited terrain surrounding villages, the primordial mark, is divided among the persons who previously enjoyed access to it. Separation or coupling alludes to the concentration of scattered plots of arable land within village fields once collectively cultivated into a single larger tract of land which – since it is no longer subject to a strict, common regimen of crop rotation – can now be farmed by an individual peasant.

If severance of the age-old connections between lords and peasants was the focal point of nineteenth-century agrarian reforms, other issues needed to be addressed as well. Among the collateral problems, dissolution of the collective system of farming associated with the equally ancient institution of jointly held fields, meadows and forests was specially important. The abolition of binding field cultivation regulations and the creation of larger tracts of land by coupling enabled peasants to farm on a private basis, using improved techniques. The division of common fields and the end of collective exploitation of pasture meant that much new land came into the hands of individual farmers. It was, however, terrain that they first had to 'ameliorate', i.e., make arable by irrigating, levelling or building dikes. The process of emancipation involved two actions: terminating ties of manorial or servile dependency and annulling associative relationships. The new, nineteenth-century concept of freedom excluded both subjugation to a lord and involuntary membership in a collectivity.

It follows from this description that the expression 'emancipation' is justified on the dual grounds of practicality and substance. Division of common lands and separation in long established villages represented a genuine form of redemption for many peasants: they were freed from dependency upon one another. The large amount of land that had been farmed collectively and the common pasturing of stock had severely restricted the individual peasant's liberty of action. Had he wished to shift to new farming methods in keeping with advances in modern agricultural science, he would not have been in a position to do so. It is arguable that in some places the need to obey commons regulations was more of an impediment for peasants than seigniorial dependency. In addition, emancipation was closely linked to the far-reaching reform programme by which government and society were modernized during the early nineteenth century, the most outstanding example of which was Prussia. In reality, what occurred was not so much a matter of special agrarian political measures but rather a crucial political, economic and social transformation of the Prussian state as a whole – the direct result of the crushing defeat that Berlin suffered at the hands of Napoleonic France in 1806. Therefore emancipation must likewise be regarded as the first step in a process of modernization which has continued down to the present and 'which brought about the dissolution of a feudally defined, corporate society and transition to the industrially defined system of the modern world'.[63] In the last analysis, the goal was to incorporate country folk – still about 80 per cent of the total population in 1800 – into the nascent liberal political order of the nineteenth and twentieth centuries.

Major efforts to reform agriculture and to alter the rural economic system had been under way since the mid-eighteenth century. The Enlightenment, rationalism and liberalism were the driving forces. Two phenomena underlay this sequence of events. One was enormous demographic expansion in the principal countries of Europe during the second half of the eighteenth century: the numbers of villagers had grown so much that arable land and cattle herds barely provided adequate nutrition. The second factor in the reform movement was the desire to create a larger reservoir of taxpayers and increase the flow of revenue into the coffers of princely states. Flourishing modern agrarian science showed what could be accomplished: it had evolved the concept of 'rational agriculture' and set new objectives. The basic idea was to stimulate productivity. These plans not only required the abolition of feudalism but also measures that would encourage individual peasant enterprise such as the abrogation of pasturage rights, division of common lands, concentration of scattered plots into larger units, cultivation of fallow and stock-feeding in barns.

However, it was impossible to avoid calling for action against feudalism, as the barriers of seigniorial and collective subservience were intertwined. Natural law and the doctrine of a person's right to private property provided a solid intellectual foundation for advocating change: every member of society was entitled to personal liberty and economic autonomy. Thus it was that compulsory services, poor conditions of peasant tenancy and, above all, serfdom – which existed east of the Elbe in the guise of hereditary subjection, a late manifestation of primeval attachment to the soil – became the targets of criticism. Experts argued that the landed estate was most in need of legal regulation, but they recommended less radical intervention against western manorial lordship. The best example of the Enlightenment's attitude towards eastern European serfdom, which many polemicists equated with outright slavery, is found in the famous book by Adolf von Knigge, *Practical Philosophy of Social Life*:

> In most provinces of Germany the peasant lives under a kind of oppression and slavery that is truthfully much harder than serfdom in other countries. Overwhelmed by the burden of payments, condemned to render onerous services, under the yoke of cruel, hardhearted foremen, they are never happy with their lives. They have not a scintilla of freedom, nothing that they can call their own, and they do not work for themselves and their kin but only for tyrants. Whoever Providence has placed in the fortunate position of being able to help alleviate the lot of this persecuted class of mankind, oh, let him savour the sweet bliss of spreading joy within the tiny huts of country dwellers, and let him hear his name called blessed by their children and grandchildren![64]

Reforms that were carried out during the second half of the eighteenth century generally had little impact on existing feudal institutions. While enlightened monarchs did not limit themselves to reform measures on state domains but also promulgated edicts restricting the authority that the nobility exercised over its peasants, such steps brought about little improvement, with only a few exceptions. In 1771 a princely decree ended the feudal subservience of Savoyard peasants. In Austria Emperor Joseph II formally abolished serfdom. Such proclamations accorded peasants the status of personal liberty in a strictly legal sense, but they remained subject to manorial lords in a variety of practical ways. Moreover, in many countries the efforts of enlightened rulers to improve the lives of rustics were undermined by the nobility and the bureaucracy. On the eve of the French Revolution most European ploughmen were not much better off than they had been in previous decades.

The outbreak of rebellion in France in the summer of 1789 and the contemporaneous liberation of the French peasantry lighted a beacon that was visible across the whole of Europe. On 4 August, under the pressure of incessant rural disturbances, the National Assembly declared all seignieurial rights to be null and void. On 11 August another law was passed announcing the 'complete abolition of the feudal regime'. It provided for the abrogation without restitution of all rights based upon the persons of peasants, the rescission of all honourary prerogatives and authorized the commutation of annual manorial payments. Numerous gravamina and reports of peasant unrest submitted to the National Assembly had made it clear that the financial pretensions of ex-manorial lords were no longer sustainable. The outbreak of war in April 1792 necessitated further concessions; domestic law and order could not otherwise be maintained. A few months later the deputies decided upon the annulment without reimbursement of all feudal rights in so far as the former seigneurs were unable to present any evidence of the legitimacy of their claims. On 17 July 1793, after the uprising of the sansculottes in Paris, the National Convention unequivocally cancelled all remnants of feudalism, also without any kind of compensation.

A few weeks before this the Convention had approved important legislation relating to common lands. Village communities were allowed to divide collectively held terrain among peasants in a democratic manner. Partition was contingent upon the consent of one-third of the inhabitants and the allotment of equal shares to everyone. Forests, public squares and undrained wetlands were expressly excluded from the measure. Although the law was enthusiastically welcomed in certain places, it appears that subdivision did not go very far for quite some time. The reason for this was clearly the fact that many communities did not have common lands to any appreciable extent, and it was thus not worth the trouble of partitioning them. In mountainous areas, where living was hard and the extensive method of grazing cattle had long predominated, peasants had little interest in privatizing common pasturage.

It is quite correct to state that the principal success of the peasant movement during the French Revolution was the uncompensated abolition of all feudal prerogatives – a step that certainly went a long way towards accommodating peasant wishes and firmly linked them to the Republic. However, more recent investigation has shown that not all strata of rural society profited equally from the legislation of the era. In reality, the change benefited only those peasants who owned land. The destruction of feudalism proved to be a bitter disappointment for the great mass of tenant farmers and agricultural labourers. Many small peasants felt that they had been cheated by the revolutionary laws but were in no position to do anything about the situation in the face of the united front presented by proprietors. Nevertheless, a large proportion of French husbandmen did derive some advantage from the abrogation of manorial dues and became freeholders in 1793. The principal victors of the Revolution were the rustics who belonged to the uppermost stratum of rural society. Because of their economic predominance they stood out more than ever above the mass of their fellow peasants.

The course of events which peasant emancipation took in Germany was determined by the events in France that we have just described, but it culminated only at a later date. The turning-point in Germany was the

Napoleonic era, when the states of the Rhenine League were closely linked to France and were able to implement important agrarian reforms. While it is difficult to establish hard and fast dates for the Rhenish states, it is clear that the break with the past in Prussia occurred in 1810 and 1811. Friedrich von Raumer, a close associate of the famous reformer, Prince Karl August von Hardenberg, produced a memorandum that recommended full ownership of land for peasants with limited rights of tenancy. The proposal was sanctioned by the Regulation Decree of 14 September 1811. The document states, delicately but unmistakably:

> In keeping with the guidelines and conditions contained in the present ordinance, those rustic landed possessions which previously were not granted on allodial terms shall be converted into freeholds, whereas the services and pretensions that were formerly attached to them shall cease to exist in return for compensatory payment that is equitable to both parties concerned.[65]

Why was Germany's agrarian system transformed at precisely this point in time? The best evidence is provided by the Prussian reformers themselves. The shameful military rout at the hands of Napoleon was the reason why men with new ideas came to head the royal government. Complete defeat in battle against a revolutionary regime left no doubt that the corporate patrimonial state of enlightened absolutism was unable to confront changed political circumstances. The collapse of the Holy Roman Empire in 1806 removed the legal basis for corporate privileges and opened the door to reform. The principal resolution of the Imperial Deputation of February 1803 had already destroyed the old German national Church and incapacitated clerical elements. The territorial princes immediately exploited their new political leeway and began to alter the ancient feudal order and government relationships with the nobility. In the new political entities of the Rhenine League and in Prussia there emerged a modern, sovereign state which, having done away with obsolete estates, drew its strength from a young, professionally-minded bureaucracy bent upon reform.

In Prussia the news of martial disaster, which had revealed all the weaknesses of Frederick the Great's system, was the starting-point for thoroughgoing modernization. After new ministers had been appointed, a younger generation of officials and politicians came to the helm with the intent of reforming both the state and society. The newcomers had realized that Prussian absolutism still excluded burghers and peasants from any civil responsibility; they were mere subjects, upon whom the king could not rely in times of emergency. Therefore state and society needed to be fundamentally transformed in the manner suggested by reformers such as Hardenberg and Baron Heinrich Friedrich von Stein. Peasant emancipation was a major goal, along with a revival of municipal self-government. Stein became the leading figure immediately after the Peace of Tilsit (7–9 July 1809). On 9 October of the same year the royal government issued the famous decree entitled 'Concerning Easier Forms of Landholding and Free Disposal of Landed Property as well as the Personal Status of Rural Inhabitants'.[66] The edict abolished all subjection to estate owners; peasants became personally free and could henceforth enjoy full liberty of movement. To be sure, personal services and payments to manorial lords were preserved, at least for the time being. The difference was that they were no longer attached to individual human beings but to the plot of land in question. The proclamation also did away with all restrictions of a corporate character. Noblemen and peasants were free to learn a bourgeois trade, while burghers and ploughmen could transfer from one estate to another.

In 1808 Stein issued a new decree applying to peasants on state domains in East Prussia: it was the first genuine emancipation measure. The king's subjects were made freeholders but had to compensate the government. Somewhat later Stein was bold enough to extend his reform to peasants on the estates of the nobility. The Regulation Edict of September 1811 promised all peasants with weak rights of tenancy 'adjustment', i.e., the complete elimination of all service obligations and limitations upon their rights to land ownership in return for the cession of a third or a half of their current holdings. To comprehend the full significance of this law, one must take into account the fact that it did away with fundamental privileges of the nobility. The noblemen protested loudly, but the authorities did not bother to convoke the estates. The bureaucracy had won an important victory. It had introduced the modern concept of property and a free labour system. About half of the Prussian peasants who owned teams of draught animals – some 150,000 persons – were affected. For the time being, the reformers left many of the peasants who had to pay hereditary rentals untouched.

The agrarian system of the states that belonged to the Rhenine League was based upon manorial lordship rather than upon the institution of the landed estate, as was the case on Prussian territory east of the Elbe. The shift from a mere reform of existing feudal practices to a complete transformation of the rural world began even earlier than it did in the

Hohenzollern realm. In the newly created grand duchy of Berg all manorial obligations were abolished in one fell swoop (1808); the peasants did have to compensate the nobility. However, intially, not much changed in Berg or in the lands of the Rhenine League, at least in part because Napoleon decided that it was necessary to stabilize the somewhat shaky French position by buttressing the authority of the local ruling stratum. Moreover, the modernization process and socio-political reforms came to a standstill in the south German states that belonged to the Rhenine League. To be sure, here too the principle of emancipation had been enunciated with the clear aim of turning the nobility's peasant subjects into freeholders. What form commutation should take was a matter of controversy everywhere, since no realistic alternative to monetary compensation seemed to exist. The progress of emancipation in later decades thus did not depend upon theoretical considerations but upon whether or not political conditions within the particular states in question were favourable.

The process of emancipation tended to drag on in the manorial lordship zone of western and southern Germany in the period between the Congress of Vienna (1815) and the revolutions of 1830, not least because of the nobility's opposition. No serious attempts at continuing efforts to liberate the peasantry were made in the kingdom of Hannover; in Saxony consultations lasting many years did not lead to any action either. In Nassau and Bavaria too commutation laws remained a dead letter, since the peasants did not have the money with which to compensate their seigniors. Nowhere was there any deviation from the principle of voluntarism, and not a single government dared seriously to broach the problem of the complete elimination of the heaviest charge the peasantry had to bear, namely, ground rentals.

Events in Prussia east of the Elbe followed a differnt course even though the reformers had less influence during the Age of the Restoration than they had had prior to 1815. There was no fundamental reversal of direction; the policy first laid out by Hardenberg was retained. In 1816 a ministerial directive restricted the right of 'regulation' that had been granted to all rustics on landed estates in 1811 to those persons who possessed farms with teams of draught animals, i.e., 'full peasants'. So-called 'let-go' peasants – husbandmen with weak terms of tenancy – were outspoken in demanding that their service obligations be 'regulated'; as early as 1812 the officials entrusted with implementing changes had expressed surprise that precisely this category of ploughman was especially interested in agrarian reform. A few years later, in hard agrarian times, the advantages *per se* of a harsh yet clear-cut policy of using land rather than money to pay compensation became apparent. As early as 1831, 82 per cent of the farms in question had been 'regulated'. The comparison with southern and western Germany, where pecuniary commutation was making only very slow headway, was striking, to say the least.

Admittedly, the peasants lost a great deal of land. The half million hectares in question represented about one-third of the terrain that they had originally occupied. However, subdivision of the primeval marks, i.e., commonly held terrain, made up to some extent for failure in the manorial context. By 1831, 36 per cent of villages had already either begun or completed such transactions. Five years after the 1816 directive the government and the estate owners agreed upon conditions under which roughly 170,000 peasants subject to the hereditary rental regime – in other words, manorially dependent ones – were freed from the obligation to make payments and render labour services. In practice, the 1821 law allowed only those persons who had enough acreage to feed a four-member family to apply for commutation. While they could also compensate the nobility by ceding a part of their land, most of them chose to do so by paying an amount equivalent to twenty-five times the annual yield of their farms. Altogether, emancipation in Prussia proceeded at a rapid pace. By 1838 'regulation' had been terminated for all practical purposes, though the compensation mechanism continued to function for a number of years, and the subdivision of common lands required much time and patience.

In Germany west of the Elbe rustic emancipation was expedited in the post-1830 period, owing to generally more fluid conditions after the July Revolution and because of peasant uprisings. Reports of the insurgents' success in France and of urban unrest led to spontaneous rural revolts in certain German territorial states. In Saxony the chief malcontents were manorial peasants who felt oppressed by the nobility's refusal to agree to fixed terms for compulsory labour services, the obligation to furnish household help and an onerous level of dues. In Hessia many peasants in poorer districts rebelled and demanded that their burdens be reduced. The ploughmen found strong support in the diets, where the liberal opposition took up their cause. Ministerial committees of investigation sought to explain why all previous attempts to effect emancipation had suffered and why there had been so much delay: insufficient attention had been paid to the problem of financing. In succeeding years almost every German state passed laws that authorized the commutation of both ground rentals and tithes; banks were established to resolve financial difficulties. Saxony led the way in 1834 by establishing an agricultural lending society after the

English model. The fact that the state had intervened and was acting as a mediator between peasants and lords did much to relax rural tensions. Persons entitled to receive rentals presented their claims at the bank and received interest-bearing notes, whereas the peasants who owed them money could pay off their debt in instalments. The sums needed to cover interest and the necessary finance capital were provided by the state treasury. Thus new life was breathed into the process of commutation, and notable results were achieved.

The revolutions of 1848–9 constituted the final phase of peasant emancipation. As soon as news of the events in Paris and of similar occurrences in several German capitals reached the countryside, violent disturbances of a kind that had not been seen for many years broke out everywhere in Germany. Hessia, Baden, certain sections of Saxony, as well as other rural regions, were the scene of bloody uprisings. The reason peasants rebelled was their determination to end the delays caused by the indecisive agrarian policies of the governments in question. A new demand heard in many places was that all vestigial feudal rights be rescinded; indeed, there was even a call for confiscation of noble property – an indication that the rural poor were now also raising their voices. The causes and the objectives of individual insurrections varied. In Baden and Saxony the target of rebellious peasants was the nobility, many lords having failed so far to implement commutation procedures. In Nassau and Silesia the authorities were the object of protest.

This time the liberal ministers of the states that comprised the German Confederation acted quickly and consistently. In the spring of 1848 south German diets decided to abolish all remaining feudal dues and to set up agrarian lending societies, in so far as they did not already exist. The levels of compensation were now much lower than before, and commutation was effected more rapidly. Nevertheless, small peasants, agricultural workers and the indigent strata of rural society remained unruly, as their demands could only be fulfilled with great difficulty: they wanted land of their own, higher wages and collective rights. At the same time the Frankfurt National Assembly established a catalogue of basic civil rights in which all relationships of subservience and servility were abrogated. Likewise, all payments and services based upon land were declared to be commutable; patrimonial courts and personal payments deriving from the patronage relationship between peasants and estate owners were annulled without any provision for compensation. The right to hunt on the lands of other persons and compulsory service for the upkeep of hunting preserves – age-old practices that were especially hated by peasants – were also done away with. Finally, in March 1850, the Prussian government proclaimed laws which permitted less well-off peasants who owed menial services to commute their obligations by cash payment. However, parliamentary decisions by no means meant the conclusion of peasant emancipation as a practical matter. As far as commutation agreements with rural lending societies were concerned, it was the years after 1850 in which 'acquittal of charges appertaining to the soil' reached a climax. By 1865 the settlement process was essentially completed. To be sure, monetary transactions continued much longer, as instalment payments normally ran for fifty years.

The subdivision of common lands, the other facet of the Liberal agrarian reform movement, continued throughout the latter half of the nineteenth century in many places. In so far as an adequate legal basis had been laid, partition and separation were promptly executed. While coupling in the kingdom of Hannover required the consent of two-thirds of participating peasants up to 1856, after that date only 50 per cent of them had to vote favourably in order to implement procedures: the result of forcing the issue was that by 1869, 87 per cent of the ancient marks had been subdivided. Still, not much was accomplished unless the scattered plots of land in question were rearranged and concentrated into larger farming units. The first task in effecting coupling was to unravel the tangle of individual holdings and resolve the complexities of overlapping rights. After a thorough survey of existing circumstances, a new network of roadways and ditches was designed and staked out on the ground; everybody was entitled to reach his property without having to traverse another person's land. After the last objections had been overcome, the quondam mark was split into a number of bigger tracts, each of which was granted to a peasant family in accordance with its predetermined just share of the whole.

The subdivision of common lands was a hard blow for the lower rural social strata; poor villagers frequently failed to benefit from the change. If such persons had normally enjoyed access to marks in the past – although without legal entitlement – they were now out in the cold and had no basis for claiming rights and compensation. The husbandmen who had the law on their side placed a premium on expanding their farms and carved up the commons among themselves, to the detriment of small-time peasants, hired hands and cottagers. Thus, after the subdivision of the mid-nineteenth century, two unequal groups confronted each other within many villages: the less well-off, who could no longer graze their cattle, and affluent 'full peasants', who feared that their deprived neighbours might rebel. A proverbial comment of paid labourers in many rural communities during those days was: 'Commons subdivision has made the peasants into noblemen and us into beggars.'[67] However, the problems of poverty and population pressure within villages were overcome as the decades passed because of emigration to America and the opportunities for employment in urban industrial centres. The rapidly growing cities were able to absorb surplus rural workers and offer them a fresh start in life.

If the process of peasant emancipation from a broader perspective is examined, the fact that it took so long seems amazing. In Central Europe it stretched over fifty years, lasting – with some exceptions – from roughly 1800 to 1850. Commutation dragged on for decades since it was linked to the difficult issue of financing. The stubborn opposition of the nobility was another impediment to a prompt solution of agrarian problems. One reason for this resistance was an unwillingness to yield the power over peasants' lives that it had exercised for so many centuries. Another was that noblemen in the ex-zone of manorial lordship in western Germany had to stop living on rental income and once again become estate owners who farmed for themselves; thus they had to face the difficulties arising from a fundamental economic reorientation. East of the Elbe the 'regulation' imposed by the Prussian state meant that seigniors lost their traditional peasant work-force. There had to be a substitute for the services that peasants had once provided with their ploughs, teams and wagons, as well as for the manual labour of cottagers. Hiring agricultural workers often proved to be a complicated business.

What were the effects of peasant emancipation on the economy and society of the nineteenth century altogether? Certainly, one main consequence of agrarian reform was the incorporation of the rural population and agriculture into the new Liberal political and social order. The creation of a statewide citizenry – the goal of eighteenth-century enlightened despotism – ironically turned out to be an accomplishment of early nineteenth-century bourgeois revolutionaries. Even if – unlike the course of events in France – Germany's transformation was decades in the making, the result was the same: the ancient social order based upon corporate differentiation was replaced by a system of overall legal and political equality within the context of liberal constitutional polities. This meant simultaneously that all forms of personal dependency and peasant subservience had to be done away with; henceforth only relationships having to do with goods and chattels or legal indebtedness were admissible. The fact that new varieties of economic dependence – subjection conceivably even worse than rural bondage – might arise from the process of change was a risk that the reformers were willing to take. They were not deterred by their critics in the Conservative and Socialist camps. Seigniors, east and west, became mere landowners, serfs free peasants or agricultural labourers. The idea of property now had genuine substance. In effect, the Roman legal understanding of the matter had prevailed, for there was no longer any distinction between higher and lower forms of ownership. If we refer here to hoary medieval jurisprudence, we are also justified in concluding that the Middle Ages truly ended only with the emancipation of the peasantry in the nineteenth century.

As a matter of principle the vocation of agriculture was now incorporated into the market economy of liberalism; there were no longer any obtacles to real-estate transfers. Competitive forces would determine who acquired and exploited terrain. As agrarian specialists were wont to argue, the best qualified husbandmen would gain control of the land and poor farmers would fall by the wayside. The tendency towards market-orientated conditions had in fact been under way for quite some time and was especially prevalent in the vicinity of prosperous cities. However, only with the triumph of liberalism was a breakthrough achieved; only then was the economy allowed to operate on its own. Admittedly, certain protagonists of the older way of life – representatives of outmoded political, economic and social forces – managed to survive within the new economic and social order and make their presence felt. For example, the fact that the nobility had lost its legal prerogatives did not prevent it from assuming important leadership posts in the economy, politics and social life of the latter nineteenth and early twentieth centuries. While it is true that noblemen had lost some ground to the propertied middle class by 1900, they still occupied a strong social position, not only in Prussia but also in Bavaria and Austria.

The rustics too were still captive to an old-fashioned corporate mentality and could not become mere producers of agrarian commodities overnight. This was especially true of the 'full peasant' who remained exactly what he had always been in every region where the practice of bequeathing the farm to a single member of the family was retained – as was the case in Bavaria, the Alpine provinces of Austria and north-western Germany. His attitudes, ideas and modes of behaviour, as well as the linkage of other rural groups to his economic activities, remained unchanged in the context of his determination to uphold the ancient rules of inheritance. East of the Elbe, where the lord of the estate had become a proprietor, his formerly subject peasant neighbours had ascended to the same free-born status of landowner. However, here too the influence of the past was powerful. Moreover, the new Prussian system of local government – rural communes demarcated according to the pattern of the old seigniories – worked against change. The arrangements had a strong authoritarian flavour and, legal equality notwithstanding, there was a sharp social gap between the nobility and the peasant estate.

Seen from a broader perspective, once the problems of transition had been mastered, the peasants clearly did manage to consolidate their economic and social position. There were two reasons for this. One was that peasants had benefited materially from the breakup of the commons. The other was that they had also profited from the favourable agrarian market conditions that existed after roughly 1850 and had begun to enjoy higher net incomes. The purpose of emancipation – apart from the political objective of modernizing the state by depriving the nobility of its power – was decidedly economic, as the great disadvantages of limitations upon personal freedom and the exploitation of property had long been known. The goal of fostering agriculture and enhancing productivity was in fact achieved, despite the fact that peasants were burdened with heavy restitution payments. This was especially true of rustics who lived east of the Elbe, where we can see a substantial increase in efforts both to maintain farms and to invest capital resources in order to enhance productivity. Emancipation also led to strong population growth in this part of Germany: the number of inhabitants doubled between 1815 and 1871. Because of more acreage and better methods of cultivation it was not hard to feed more mouths, even though large amounts of grain were simultaneously exported. Undoubtedly, this extraordinary progress would have been impossible had there been no agrarian reforms. It was in precisely those places where peasant energies had long been repressed by seigniorial compulsion that their release led to the greatest outburst of activity.

Having considered developments in France and Germany in great detail, let us next direct our attention to the process of emancipation in other parts of Europe. Reform-minded princes, new economic trends and the unhappiness of peasants were some of the factors that brought about the modernization of the rural world. The military successes of revolutionary France and the abolition of feudal rights within the borders of the Republic at first had the effect of delaying the liberation of peasants in neighbouring countries. The victories of the revolutionaries exacerbated the fears of ruling elites elsewhere: afraid that they might be toppled from power by outbreaks of violence, they allowed many reform measures already initiated to lapse. In Austria the shock over what had occurred in France destroyed the spirit of reform engendered by Emperor Joseph II, who had faced powerful resistance on the part of the nobility from the start. It was only after the triumphs of the revolutionary host and Napoleon's forces that peasant emancipation was undertaken in the lands now subject to French rule. The crushing reverse that Prussia suffered at Napoleon's hands in 1806 made it absolutely clear to the country's leaders that they could not continue to tolerate the subservience of peasants to estate owners. The same thing happened half a century later in Russia: the tsar's defeat in the Crimean War (1856) forced his government finally to carry out fundamental reforms in the structure of the state and society and to lay the groundwork for the abolition of serfdom. The revolutions of 1848–9 were also a strong impetus and accelerated the pace of agrarian reform and emancipation in many European countries: wherever servile peasants could still be found, it was decided that they should cease to be tied to the glebe.

Almost a hundred years passed between the first edict announcing the emancipation of Savoyard peasants and the abolition of serfdom in Russia: this fact is clear evidence of how long the liberation process took. Many of the decrees and laws that were promulgated in various European countries during this period were formulated in different ways, but all were inspired by the same principles. Everywhere peasants were guaranteed the status of personal freedom, even though the authorities often established transitional intervals that would allow manorial lords to adjust to changed circumstances. The new legislation also accorded husbandmen equality before the law, along with all other citizens. Rustics could move about as they pleased and choose any vocation they wished. The hierarchical order of society – the institution of hermetically sealed estates – was abolished once and for all. The release of peasants from bondage and their acquisition of civil rights required a host of measures designed to transform existing political structures. Justice, public security, military service, fiscal practices, as well as the administrative apparatus on both local and central levels, had to be reorganized. Political and social change within individual countries proved to be a slow process and took decades to complete.

The first emancipation decrees, which were welcomed everywhere and created great expectations, did not immediately terminate peasant subservience: notwithstanding the enunciation of general principles of liberty, many forms of dependency remained. The edicts won public approbation since they laid the groundwork for the later triumph of the fundamental idea of freedom and provided legislative guidelines. Nonetheless, virtually everywhere many years passed before the vestiges of rustic servility were wiped away. The resistance of manorial lords, the obstructive tactics of members of the noble estates, the reactionary policies of many governments and the political inexperience of the peasantry were all factors that help to explain the long duration of the emancipation process. The intervals between the initial proclamations and the final passage of legislation that did away with remaining feudal prerogatives and manorial claims varied from one country to another. In Savoy it took 21 years, in Denmark 73 and in Prussia 43. Compensation payable to manorial lords for lost income, labour services and land was a common feature of most of the laws in question.

Differences between one part of Europe and another in the nature of peasant emancipation and the impact which it has had down to the very present are best illustrated by the case of Italy. The country knew three distinct agrarian systems at the beginning of the nineteenth century. In the south and on the islands of Sicily and Sardinia there was a mixture of feudal latifundia and tiny peasant farms. In central Italy and the hilly country of the north the predominant rural institution was the leasehold, which often left the peasant barely enough to survive. The third zone was the Po valley which – owing to a differentiation between landowners, intermediate tenants and day labourers, as well as the practice of intensive forms of cultivation – was one of the most progressive agricultural regions of Europe. The sole effect of the abolition of the feudal system in southern Italy by government decree was to create fluidity in the property market; the everday life of peasants hardly changed. The noble and upper middle-class figures who dominated government in northern Italy were also long disinclined to undertake strong action in the agrarian realm; the fact that they had regained their influence upon the Piedmontese monarchy had much to do with this attitude. Further economic and social modernization started only towards the end of the nineteenth century; only after the onset of industrialization were new reform measures put into effect. In contrast to Germany, a divided and incompetent bureaucracy was also responsible for the delay in bringing about badly needed change.

Our survey of the circumstances of peasant emancipation in the various countries of Europe has made it clear that there was no such thing as a uniform process of agrarian modernization or identical outcomes. Everywhere the decisive factor in the transformation of agriculture was the starting-point. What counted were pre-existent conditions, and they were in fact highly diverse. Emancipation led to favourable results only where property relationships were already relatively straightforward because of earlier reforms; this enabled the authorities to sort out legal claims to land without undue difficulty. In such instances agrarian reform also meant setting the stage for virtually instantaneous industrialization. The latter provided the impetus for overall economic expansion and permanently rising incomes, which in turn enhanced the social position of the peasantry.

Likewise, opportunities for the development of parliamentary and demo-cratic institutions depended in large measure on the manner in which agrarian reforms and peasant emancipation were achieved, as Barrington Moore maintains. In many instances the laws which were supposed to resolve the question of peasant emancipation once and for all did not help to end political and social discrimination against rustics. Ancient tradi-tions and behavioural norms, claims to precedence on the part of persons who belonged to the higher social estates, and deeply rooted disdain of the countryman were not things that could be made to disappear from one day to the next by the passage of a few reform bills. Moreover, the ruling elites were generally unprepared to renounce their antiquated privileges and unwilling to yield their powerful position in society without a fight.

Many peasants continued to be denied liberty of movement by a variety of means. They were put at a disadvantage in elections by devious polling arrangements or even excluded from the franchise altogether. In a number of countries the judicial authority of manorial lords continued in effect for decades – for example, in the Prussian administrative districts that corres-ponded to the former seigniories. In spite of all these inadequacies, the abolition of serfdom was the beginning of a new epoch in the history of the European peasantry: 'an era of freedom such as had never been known before'.[68] Emancipation did away not only with an obsolete system of compulsory services and financial exactions but transformed all aspects of rural life. A feudal form of existence was supplanted by individualism: marriage customs, occupational barriers, and various other inhibitions that had once characterized the village milieu fell victim to it. The equality of citizens before the law opened previously closed doors for rustics who now had an opportunity to get ahead in the world and make society recognize the innate dignity of their vocational estate. Freed from dependency and inequitable obligations, Europe's peasants developed into an influential segment of the population, which had its own political and economic agenda and was able to raise its voice within the modern industrial society of the twentieth century.

12

Survival in the Modern World

Industrialization and modernization

The industrialization of the nineteenth and twentieth centuries fundamentally altered the economy and society of Europe. For the most part the transformation had to do with life in manufacturing centres and rapidly growing cities and less with agriculture and the rural world which, however, did undergo a metamorphosis of its own. Change occurred in both the techniques of agrarian production and the structure of rural society: agricultural productivity increased enormously while, in comparison with the population at large, the proportion of persons engaged in farming shrank substantially. Especially impressive is the progress made by agriculture after World War II. If 60 per cent of Germans were employed in farming in 1800, by 1950 the figure was 25 per cent. The rate of decline then accelerated and by 1990 only 5 per cent of the population worked in the countryside. At the same time productivity expanded remarkably: if 2700 kilograms of wheat were harvested per hectare in 1950, by 1975 the amount was 4400. Overproduction had thus become a major problem for Europe's farmers.

What were the reasons for this amazing progress? During the nineteenth century agricultural production more than doubled. Its structure also changed, as the volume of meat production grew faster than that of field crops. The rise was due mainly to the following factors: new ways of preparing the soil, improved planting methods, a greater concentration upon stock-raising and the application of advanced technology. In the 1830s European agriculture entered on a new, almost uninterrupted growth phase that lasted four decades. As had occurred once before during the eighteenth century, demographic expansion and a concomitant increased demand for foodstuffs led to price increases. This time the trend was reinforced by the higher levels of personal income resulting from industrialization. Greater purchasing power first affected the market for groceries, since the nutritional requirements of the population were not yet fully satisfied.

As far as cultivation is concerned, the old-fashioned three-field system was improved and gradually yielded to permanent crop rotation: i.e., fallow was on the way out. The new three-field method consisted of two years of wheat followed by one year of fallow planted with clover, potatoes or beet. The elimination of fallow led to a significant expansion of arable surface and a corresponding rise in production (see figure 2). More intensive use of the soil required better fertilization since lost nutrients had to be replaced. Previously the sole source had been manure from barns, as imports to Europe of Chilean guano and nitrates began to increase only after 1840. As long as farmers had to depend upon natural supplies of fertilizer, they were caught in a vicious circle: they could obtain more manure only by raising more cattle, but this meant devoting more land to the production of feed and less to growing crops for human consumption. Vice versa, grain production could be enhanced only by reducing the emphasis on stock; smaller quantities of manure meant smaller yields per hectare. Productivity growth was possible only if agriculture could become less dependent upon natural fertilizer.

The credit for having solved the primary problem of pre-industrial agriculture and human nutrition has been quite properly ascribed to Justus von Liebig, who published his epoch-making study, *Organic Chemistry applied to Agriculture and Physiology*, in 1840.[69] Liebig succeeded in opening the way for mineral fertilization. Lime and bone meal were at first the

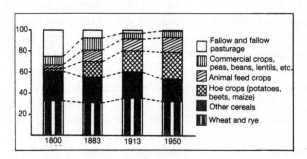

Figure 2   Changes in German farmland, 1800–1950 (after Abel, Agrarkrisen, *page 269)*

most important supplementary fertilizers, but it took quite a while for them to gain currency. Only during the second half of the nineteenth century did chemical fertilization with potash, nitrogen and phosphate derivatives become increasingly common. Phosphate production was greatly expanded as the result of the new ironworking process developed by Sidney Gilchrist Thomas: the slag served as the source of a by-product known as 'Thomas meal'.

Efforts to improve fertilizers were accompanied by systematic experiment in the field of plant breeding, with the objective of making new, more productive grain varieties and better seed-corn available to farmers. Even more important from the perspective of human nutrition was the expansion of potato growing. Potatoes became not only the chief food for the lower social strata but, not surprisingly, proved to be much to the taste of the pig population. The triumph of the potato as the basis of both human nutrition and stock feed went hand-in-hand with the disappearance of fallow. No less significant was the increasing popularity of sugar beet.

Stock-raising became more important in the nineteenth century as the result of growth in the number of animals kept by farmers, rising levels of milk production and better breeds. Systematic upgrading of herds through importing foreign strains and cross-breeding with domestic races was by no means a nineteenth-century innovation but merely a continuation of earlier attempts to improve the quality of cows, horses and sheep. Long neglected, pig breeding grew in importance after 1850, and pigs ultimately became the principal producers of meat. The enhancement of the quality of cows and swine meant that the population benefited from a greatly increased supply of animal products and meat.

The nature and the pace of change in agrarian technology during the nineteenth century differed from one European country to another. Whereas English agriculture stood out in the application of new methods and devices, mechanization proceeded only very slowly in France and Germany. Work productivity understood in terms of man hours increased but this was due mainly to the enhanced yield of cultivated land. Ploughs, harrows and wagons – which slowly improved from a technical viewpoint but were still drawn by animal power – remained the most important implements of French and German farmers. The most important labour-saving mechanisms introduced before 1914 included rotary tools, threshing machines and reapers. Since grain was the largest single crop, it is obvious that most efforts were directed to reducing the time and effort expended in sowing, harvesting and separating seeds from stalks. Threshing machines could soon be spotted on most farms, and by 1910 there was hardly a larger agrarian enterprise that did not possess one.

Mechanization of European agriculture really began in earnest only after 1945. Between 1950 and 1990 machinery and new technology permeated the farming world as never before in history. An agrarian revolution occurred during these four decades, like the one that had taken place in North America half a century earlier and had led to profound changes in country life, as well as a sharp decline in the number of persons involved in agricultural pursuits. The central feature of the increasing mechanization of most agricultural jobs was the tractor. It could be employed not only as a pulling device but also – because it could be used for exploiting the principles of hydraulics – hooked up to other implements and used for a variety of farming tasks. The numbers of tractors, as well as combines and milking machines, are the chief indicators of the size of the machinery plant within individual European countries. The harvesting of various forage crops, sugar beet, potatoes and, more recently, maize was also increasingly mechanized and carried out by implements capable of performing all individual operations. The consequence was a far-reaching substitution of machinery for human labour and animal power, as well as

10   *Tractors from 1890 and 1924. The one above is a steam tractor, which certainly provided great power but was hard to manoeuvre. Below is a petrol-driven tractor, which was easier to move.*

an improvement in the quality of farm work. Mechanization has also enabled Europe's peasants to attend to their chores at the most opportune moment and thereby minimize the risk of harvest losses.

There are a number of reasons for the delay in the mechanization of western European agriculture compared with North America. It is obvious that the overall economy of the United States and Canada was more orientated to technological progress as a matter of principle than was the case in the Old World – and agriculture was no exception. Moreover, climatic conditions in North America were better suited to the employment of harvest machinery, especially the combine. One must also take into account differences in the structure of agrarian enterprises. North American farmers, who cultivated much larger tracts of land, could rationally utilize capital-intensive technology, whereas their small and medium-sized European counterparts were less open-minded about labour-saving devices. Therefore the mechanization of European agriculture since 1950 has led not only to a decrease in the agrarian work-force but also to larger farms that are inherently better suited to the use of machinery. If there were still some 1.6 million agrarian enterprises in Germany in 1950, the number dropped to only 700,000 in 1986. The average size rose from 8 to 16 hectares (50 US acres). It should be stressed that as early as 1976 only about a half of the farms in question were full-time operations; the remainder fell into the category of part-time or supplementary income ventures. Work-force statistics are also significant. Enterprises of more than 50 hectares averaged four persons per 100 hectares, whereas the figure for those of 10 hectares was eleven.

The mechanization of agriculture in the industrial states of Western Europe since World War II is part of a larger process that most students of the subject have recently called the 'industrialization of the agrarian economy'. This concept describes a development that is characterized by the rapid advance of industrial forms of production within the realm of agriculture; the result is intensive working of the land. Phenomena such as the cultivation of large areas and animal husbandry on a massive scale have led to a radical transformation of the traditional structure of farming. Reactions to this far-reaching change among agrarian policy specialists diverge. One view is that the consistent application of advances in technology ought to be welcomed. The other response stresses negative social and ecological effects and employs invidious terms such as 'agrarian factories' and 'agricultural industry'. In reality the process of industrialization has given rise to a variety of problems which, at least in part, may be understood as symptoms of crisis.

What, we may ask, are the principal traits of the 'industrialization of the agrarian economy' as they have been uncovered by recent investigations in the field of agrarian science?[70] The industrialization of agricultural production refers above all to four developmental tendencies that run parallel to each other but are simultaneously interconnected: technological innovation, capitalization, sectoral and regional concentration of farming operations. Without any question technological progress, which has produced so many new approaches, is the main driving force behind industrialization. It encompasses above all incessant mechanization and the ever greater employment of chemical fertilizers – a process the origin of which lies in the nineteenth century and which has continued uninterruptedly down to the present. The introduction of mineral fertilizers, the invention of tractors and other auxiliary machinery, the use of chemicals to control weeds and insects, as well as the recent application of biogenetic insights to improve the quality of animals and plants, are among the major contributions of technology to the ongoing industrialization of agriculture. All this progress would have been impossible without the ever growing involvement of agrarian scientific research and the various disciplines that it includes. Indeed, it is difficult not to exaggerate the importance of the work that is being done in these fields.

Closely linked to agrarian technological innovation is a pronounced decline in the significance of the traditional factors of land assets and labour force that have taken second place to another catalyst – capital. Agriculture's growing appetite for capital is caused by never-ending mechanization that makes it easier and easier to substitute the power of machines for that of human beings. The number of persons employed in the agrarian sector has dropped sharply – for example, in the Federal Republic of Germany between 1950 and 1986 from 3.4 million to barely 800,000, a reduction of 77 per cent. Not only is it necessary to employ tractors and various types of combines for field work, but money must also be spent for equipment that is needed in the farmyard and barns, namely, silage installations, milking machines and other technical devices. Another factor in the capitalization of agriculture is the increased use of chemical fertilizers, as well as herbicides and pesticides. The increased use of grain and protein supplements (soya-bean, linseed and cottonseed meal) for stock-raising – frequently purchased in agricultural supply stores because a peasant's own production is insufficient for a larger number of cattle – is yet another indicator of growing capital investment. Farmers also need to buy efficient, meat-producing, hybrid animals such as poultry and pigs from wholesale breeders. The consequence of this trend is a fourfold increase in the amount of outside capital invested in German agriculture between 1960 and 1985.

Another feature of the industrialization of agriculture is greater concentration upon particular market sectors. Because small and medium-sized operations are increasingly unprofitable, the tendency is for production to be monopolized by highly specialized, large-scale, agrarian enterprises. What is known in German as 'farm death' is accompanied by growth in the average size of surviving units. A parallel development is a remarkable expansion in the number of persons engaged in farming as a sideline: peasants who are no longer able to work their land profitably on a full-time basis are forced to seek employment in industry or the service sector of the economy but spend their spare time farming. A special phenomenon is agrarian-industrial businesses or 'factory farms', particularly market-orientated facilities that concentrate upon the full range of meat production, especially the refinement or 'improvement' of livestock. Such activities involve industrial-style production techniques in the narrower sense of the word, as well as new methods of organization and management.

A final important characteristic of the industrialization of agriculture is a process known as agrarian-economic regional concentration. Geographical consolidation of the production and processing of foodstuffs is the hallmark of certain branches of the farm economy. Frequently called 'agrarian-intensive districts', they develop because of specific locational advantages – infrastructure, work-force and the quality of the soil – which encourage spatial convergence. They must be distinguished from 'agrarian-extensive districts' in which production tends to decline because of structural problems such as mountainous terrain, excessive distance from transport routes and poor soil. The Weser–Ems region in north-western Germany and the North Limburg region in the Netherlands are good examples of agrarian-intensive districts. They are renowned for their high degree of specialization and success in augmenting meat production – fattening of poultry and pigs – through greater capital expenditure. For better or worse, they are among the leading centres of food-processing within the wider European Community economic zone.

Agricultural industrialization and agrarian-intensive districts are in fact quite problematic: they have created a plethora of difficulties and caused much contention. The future of European farming is at stake. The main areas of concern are of a socio-economic and ecological nature. The principal socio-economic question is the threat to the existence of small and medium-sized farms; indeed, many of them have already vanished. Even greater pressure to intensify and concentrate operations under the motto 'produce or perish' obviously means that over the long haul only large agrarian businesses with major capital resources have the chance to survive. The grave social problems faced by peasant families that have been forced to throw in the towel require special mention. Conflict situations include the loss of work and income, the difficulties of vocational readjustment and not least the aggravation of personal tensions within rural homes. Government does what it can to alleviate the pain, whether by paying pensions to bankrupt individuals or through job retraining. The failure of many peasant farms has also had a deleterious effect upon village life and the rural world as a whole. The aging of the population, the departure of many inhabitants, the loss of many essential commercial services, such as stores and workshops, and the decline in the basic public infrastructure (schools, railways and post offices) are common occurrences. Measures to combat this trend, such as 'village renovation', are only partly successful, as they are often directed only to improving physical appearances and not to fostering regional economic development.

The ecological consequences of the industrialization of agriculture have long been an object of general interest. The dramatic aggravation of environmental problems as the result of agrarian activities has evoked great concern, not only within the scientific community and government but among the public at large. Ecological damage is especially worrying in agrarian-intensive districts that focus on meat production. Liquid manure pollution needs to be singled out. Because the density of the animal population is so high, there is excessive runoff; because it is so difficult to treat this form of sewage, the risk of environmental harm is very great. Intensive agriculture on arable land is the source of still other perils. The expansion of large-scale farming, combined with extremely heavy use of chemical fertilizers, weed- and insect-killers, has led specialists to conclude that intensive agriculture is the main reason for the rapid decline of many animal and plant species. A further issue – one that has particularly upset the public – is the possible contamination of animal and vegetable products with residual chemical and biological substances (herbicides, pesticides and hormones).

It follows that industrialized farming has transformed food production in north-western Europe in a variety of ways and has resulted in truly grievous problems. The main question is the social impact of large-scale agrarian-industrial enterprises. When we consider their economic and ecological implications, are factory farms really more efficient than modern peasant family farms? Do the former offer more social security than jobs in the manufacturing sector? It may be that the factory farm is more exposed to the ebb and flow of the economy than is the peasant family farm which has successfully withstood many crises in the past. Before we take up this issue in conjunction with the agrarian policies of the European Community, let us survey the development of agriculture in Eastern Europe, especially large-scale, so-called 'socialist' enterprises.

Collectivization and crisis in Eastern Europe

Eastern European agricultural development in the twentieth century has been characterized by collectivization, the establishment of large-scale enterprises and the destruction of the traditional peasant economy. What occurred in Russia between 1929 and 1930 under the dictatorial rule of Stalin and the Communist Party was the biggest and most brutal agrarian revolution in recent European history. The Soviet government almost literally flogged the country into mass collectivization without having made adequate preparations of an organizational and technological nature. In the summer of 1929 the central authorities ordered Party representatives in the most important grain regions to accelerate the pace of collectivization as much as possible. Moscow justified its sudden shift by arguing that a famine was in the offing and peasants were not fulfilling their delivery quotas. The Party took special pains to mobilize the small peasants against the kulaks – middle-ranking or well-to-do husbandmen – who expressed their vehement opposition to forced collectivization by slaughtering stock. Stalin ultimately put down the violent resistance to his decision by resorting to extreme measures: he ruthlessly deported and liquidated at least 5 million kulaks. By end of the first Five Year Plan (1932) 61 per cent of peasant farms had been collectivized; by 1936 the figure was already 90 per cent. How did this 'agrarian revolution from above' – a fundamental transformation of Russian agriculture – actually occur?

When serfdom was abolished in Russia (1861), peasants still accounted for 90 per cent of the country's population. The backwardness of the tsarist state was due in part to the delay in peasant emancipation that had been an important prerequisite for the social dynamism of emergent urban-industrial society in Western Europe. Temporal disparity between west and east

11 *A Soviet Russian propaganda poster from 1930, calling on peasants to volunteer to join collective farms. 'Go to the kolkhoz,' says the notice beside representatives of the old community who are trying to hold back a peasant girl from this step*

reflected the progressive nature of industrialization; accompanied by political liberalization, it spread stage by stage deep into the European land mass. The landed estate that predominated east of the Elbe – the material foundation of the indigenous ruling strata – was a mainstay of social retardation. In the European sections of Russia this agrarian institution represented a symbiosis between seigniors involved in producing grain for market sale and subservient, if self-sufficient, petty peasants. As had been the case in Prussia's eastern provinces, the dissolution of feudal ties – ultimately unavoidable from the viewpoint of Russian governmental policy – was linked to the question of compensating estate owners now dependent upon their own capital resources for their lost work-force, ensuring the economic survival of the emancipated ploughmen and finding other employment for a redundant agricultural labour pool. These multifarious difficulties could not be overcome prior to the 1917 Revolution owing to rapid population growth and low productivity per hectare.

Peasants in the central provinces of Russia did not become private owners of the land that was turned over to them in 1861. Rather, it was transferred to the mir mentioned before, which was made responsible as a group for compensating the seigniors and paying taxes to the state. The village community continued to allocate parcels of terrain to individual households and also apportioned financial burdens. Peasants went on cultivating their assigned plots until a few years had passed and land was once more redistributed. Emancipation had released Russian husbandmen from subjection to the nobility, but they were still ensnared in the collective web of the mir.

Poverty and land hunger on the part of a large proportion of village inhabitants remained the basic causes of social instability in rural Russia during the late nineteenth century. Growing proceeds from the sale of grain abroad stimulated the domestic market and capital formation outside nascent industrial centres, but vast tracts of countryside remained within the orbit of traditional rustic economic autarky. The rising discontent of the peasantry found an outlet in the 1905 Revolution, which was marked by many rural disturbances. Under the pressure of circumstances the government decided to change its position and set new goals for agrarian policy. If the previous autocratic regime had considered the mir a conservative force that promoted political stability, the course of events had shown that it was badly mistaken: there had been uprisings even in regions where the village community was firmly entrenched. The conclusion was that the mir should be allowed to expire and no longer block the development of efficient private peasant farms. The collective liability of village communities had already been rescinded in 1903; Stolypin's 1905 agrarian reforms provided for the abolition of much-hated restitution payments. From the autumn of 1906 every peasant could register his plot as a freehold without asking the mir for permission; this step did not affect his right to utilize common lands.

Stolypin's new agrarian policy aimed to free the Russian peasant from the chains of the village community; the idea was to enable him to increase production and expand his farm. Many rustics were disappointed by the reform laws. They had expected that they would be given more land – whether it came from estate owners, the government or the Church. All the peasants got was mere legal proprietorship of land that was already theirs. At the same time the redistribution system was destroyed: at least, so they reasoned, it afforded needy people a living of sorts. The state assault upon the mir unified many impoverished rustics and breathed new life into old traditions. Only in the western sections of Russia, where agrarian conditions were quite different, does Stolypin's prescription seem to have been generally accepted. However, in central Russia anyone who sought to leave the mir was likely to encounter opposition from his fellow villagers. The community responded with insults and threats, exclusion from meetings and various kinds of boycotts when rich, ambitious peasants broke with the redistribution system. Hence it is hardly surprising that, despite great expectations, the results of Stolypin's endeavours were modest.

A new chapter in Russian agrarian history began with the October Revolution of 1917 when the Bolsheviks, led by Lenin, used armed force to overthrow the middle-class government and established a new regime known as the Soviet of People's Commissars. It proceeded to confiscate the property of the nobility, the monasteries and the Church, as well as nationalizing industry and the banking system. The western parliamentary system was rejected in favour of a state comprised of soviets, i.e., theoretically democratic, elected government councils. Village soviets were established in the countryside and, together with workers' and soldiers' councils, became the backbone of the new political order. The expropriation of terrain belonging to the Crown, the Church and the nobility, as well as its transfer only to persons willing to work it with their own hands, were measures that fulfilled ancient peasant yearnings and especially benefited the lower strata of the rural population. Nevertheless, Lenin and the Party immediately declared that this more or less spontaneous land redistribution should be regarded as no more than a detour on the road to a socialist reorganization of village life. Deviations from this political line in succeeding years were simply tactical manoeuvres designed to ameliorate transitory problems in feeding the public.

As the result of bottlenecks in the food supply and the tenacious opposition of peasants to compulsory grain deliveries, there was growing domestic political criticism of the new agrarian arrangements. The

200 The Peasantry of Europe

breakup of large landed estates and the division of land among small farmers had led to a decrease in agricultural production, increased peasant home consumption and made it almost impossible for the state to plan for future needs in an orderly way. Also detrimental to productivity was a decision to apply the principle of mouths to be fed rather than the size of the work-force when land was distributed to peasants. Local autonomy in this regard was also a problem: since the amount of land available for distribution varied from one community to another, there were great disparities in the size of individual plots: this caused controversy between neighbouring villages. Another obviously negative feature was retrogression in the rearrangement of arable common lands initiated by Stolypin: farms that had been detached from the mir and rounded off by the purchase of additional property were forced to rejoin the redistribution system. Thus the old village community re-emerged and along with it all the disadvantages that resulted from an unstable pattern of landholding.

Although the renascent mir afforded no security of ownership, attempts to socialize agricultural production were largely abortive. The establishment of huge state farms (*sovkhozi*), worked by paid labour and designed to serve as models for the rest of the agrarian world, and the merger of peasant farms into collective enterprises (*kolkhozi*) were supposed to provide a solution to the dilemma faced by the Communist regime. While the land edict of 1917 had left peasants absolute discretion in deciding whether they would work the soil jointly or individually, the Soviet agrarian legislation of 1919 declared private farming in any form at all to be a merely transitional phenomenon: the future would belong to collectives. Strikes by workers, peasant uprisings, terrible food shortages and the disastrous overall state of the economy put an end to the previous policy during the winter of 1920–1 and led to a complete turnround. Lenin declared in March 1921 that the former approach had been a mistake and proclaimed what has gone down in history as the New Economic Policy (NEP), in effect a temporary peace accord with the peasantry. The grain requisition system was abolished and replaced by a tax: whatever peasants produced above and beyond the amount of this levy they were free to sell. For several years there was no more talk of a rapid transition to socialism. The small peasant farm – in keeping with the ideas of the then prominent agrarian scientist, Chayanov – continued to serve as the basis of food production, while the village community provided the setting in which agricultural activity took place during the 1920s. The new agrarian policy made it possible for the Soviet Union in emerge from the abyss: by 1925–6 the country had once more attained the levels of 1913–14.

Why, in the face of this very positive development, did the USSR undergo mass collectivization in 1929–30? The Communist Party had by no means renounced its revolutionary goals and in the mid-1920s – under its new general secretary, Stalin – was propagating the idea of 'building socialism' in Russia. The indispensable precondition seemed to be industrialization, above all the fostering of heavy industry; only after industry, agriculture and transport had begun to function on a genuinely massive scale would socialism have been victorious. In 1927–8 the Party approved the first Five Year Plan, the centrepiece of which was industrialization. Fresh difficulties that the government experienced in supplying grain during 1928–9 caused it to take draconian measures: cereals were once more forcefully requisitioned. The systematic terror of this campaign was the effective end of the NEP, which had guaranteed peasants both the right to work the land privately and free market access. Increasingly impoverished by the requisitions, the old Russian village had lost all hope of a better future. Once again exigency and misery pervaded the rural world. In such circumstances the only recourse was to join one of the collective farms which Moscow was now actively promoting and seeking to impose upon rustics with all the means at its disposal. Under duress the bulk of the peasantry began to accept the government stance in agrarian matters. There was no other way out: at least a kolkhoz would assure a family the bare minimum needed to survive. Peasants who resisted collectivization were defamed as 'kulaks' and driven from their properties. During the winter of 1929–30 hundreds of thousands of them were deported, condemned to forced labour or stuck into concentration camps. The deportations were carried out in so brutal a fashion that millions died in the process. The 'liquidation of the kulak class' was even legally sanctioned in 1930.

Collectivization was pushed especially hard from the summer of 1929 onward. Many local Party organizations attempted to collectivize whole townships in the shortest period of time possible. In the south, south-east and east of the country the movement assumed the character of an avalanche. Between July and September 1929 more than 900,000 peasant farms were incorporated into kolkhozes – almost as many as had been assimilated during the first twelve years of the Revolution. Between October and December 1929 the figure climbed to 2,400,000 or, on a daily basis, 30,000. The number of mergers grew from month to month, and the result was that advance planning proved to be inadequate. Economic distress, propaganda and direct pressure drove the peasants into the kolkhozes in such huge numbers that the movement slipped out of the authorities' control in many places. Conditions became chaotic, and it was virtually impossible to restore order. By early March 1930 there were some 110,000 kolkhozes including altogether 14.3 million individual farms (55 per cent of the total). Coercion and terror spread further throughout the countryside. A mood of bitterness and resignation prevailed among large segments of the rustic population. Despite resistance the government pressed ahead energetically with collectivization. By the summer of 1932 a total of 15,000 million peasant farms had been swallowed up. By 1935 over 80 per cent and by 1936 90 per cent of Russian agriculture was controlled by the state.

During the first years of collectivization the agrarian economy was in ruins; productivity sank below pre-war levels. The government pressed ahead with its policy of forced grain deliveries despite poor harvests. In the winter of 1932–3 there was an awful famine in which millions of people died. It took a number of years before the agrarian situation improved and production began to rise. Kolkhoz peasants were left with small plots of land which they were permitted to farm for themselves; they were also allowed to keep one cow and some smaller stock. Although this privately worked soil normally amounted to no more than 30 per cent of a hectare, it was enough to sustain a kolkhoz household, the survival of which could not otherwise be guaranteed. What the peasant earned on a collective farm did not suffice even remotely for this purpose. There was little change during the 1940s and 1950s. As late as 1958 a family still had to supply most of its food from its own minuscule plot: for vegetables, the figure was 95 per cent, for milk 98 per cent and for meat 100 per cent. Although the Communist Party constantly argued that large-scale enterprises were far superior to small peasant farms, it remained unable to corroborate its claims. Whether in terms of land area or work-force productivity, the socialist sector was never able to equal its private counterpart. In 1980 the latter was responsible for about one-third of overall agrarian production although it controlled a mere 3 per cent of all farmland.

When one considers that overcoming grain crises, fostering industrialization by means of enhanced agrarian productivity and demonstrating the superiority of socialism as an economic system were the official objectives of Soviet agrarian policy, there is no question but that collectivization was essentially a failure. During the early 1930s it pushed agriculture into a crisis that lasted for years and severely damaged relations between the peasantry and the state. It was very hard for the farming world to recover from the blows inflicted upon it. It is quite ironic that certain factors – the background of the mir and geographical circumstances – favoured a collective approach to the agrarian economy. Since the lives of the Russian peasantry were strongly influenced by the traditions of the ancient village community and the land redistribution system, the concept of private property was not as deeply rooted as in Western Europe. Moreover, most peasants were not as closely attached to a particular portion of terrain, since there was still much joint exploitation of local fields and pasture. Modern technology also seemed to speak for the concentration of scattered farming plots into large-scale agrarian enterprises, in which setting tractors and other agricultural machinery would make good financial sense. The wide steppe regions of southern Russia and the Ukraine, where the continental variety of climate needed the practice of extensive farming, were perfectly suited to traction vehicles and combines. Notwithstanding these positive factors, overhasty collectivization led to a virtually endemic crisis. Indeed, Russian agriculture never really escaped from the doldrums. Only during the 1950s did Soviet farmers again attain the productivity levels of the late 1920s.

The establishment of Communist dictatorships in the east Central European countries conquered by the Red Army at the end of World War II resulted in the socialization of their agrarian economies. Far-reaching land reforms and collectivization on the basis of the Soviet model ensued. By subdividing noble estates and other large landholdings the new regimes in Poland, Hungary, Romania and Czechoslovakia were initially able to win the support of the petty peasants who profited from expropriation. Many persons who belonged to the rural underclass and had little or no land of their own were inclined to join agricultural cooperatives. The confiscation process had left some of them with small farms, but they lacked the draught animals, agricultural implements and capital they needed in order to work their properties efficiently. However, after the authorities began to press hard for collectivization, the original satisfaction with Communist agrarian policy turned into bitterness and opposition. The rural population of Eastern Europe thus became hostile to Stalinist governments and on occasion even rebelled against them.

Notwithstanding resistance, collectivization was systematically implemented and produced results that were often disappointing from an economic, social and ecological viewpoint. Peasant discontent, poor central organization and inadequate material preparations led to only partial success. The difference between private and socialist agriculture was most evident in Poland, where much land remained in private hands and was managed more efficiently than state-owned enterprises. The reasons for the failure of collective farms included rotten organization, sloppy field work, slip-shod treatment of animal stock, much dissension between group members and bloated administrative staffs. The more that was spent on bureaucracy, the less likely the possibility of making money. Private farms made peasants feel more secure and gave them a chance to perform better by exercising initiative and working with care. They constituted the backbone of Polish agriculture and expanded their share of the overall agrarian economy in the 1970s and 1980s.

The partition of Germany and the emergence of divergent ruling systems in the Federal Republic and the Soviet zone gave politicians and agrarian scientists an opportunity to analyse the pros and cons of differing approaches to agriculture in territories immediately adjacent to one another. After the process of collectivization was completed in the German Democratic Republic in 1960 and almost all farms had been merged into cooperatives, it became possible to compare socialist management of agriculture on the basis of a highly developed industrial economy with the functioning of peasant family farms in an equally advanced, capitalist polity. The fact that the GDR did badly cannot be ascribed merely to shortages of tractors, machinery and other equipment. In the Federal Republic maintenance of the family farm was from the very beginning the declared goal of government agrarian policy. Another official objective was to assure peasants remuneration that corresponded to the wages of an industrial worker with equal qualifications. Peasants did see their incomes rise, but they were not as well paid as their urban counterparts. Moreover, many small West German farms failed because they could not compete effectively within the framework of a modern agrarian economy. In the east, the number of persons employed in agriculture was much higher, notwithstanding the prevalence of large-scale enterprises. Farms in the GFR of more than 50 hectares made do in 1973 with four workers per 100 hectares; this was only a third of the ratio in the east, 13.4 per 100 hectares. To the very end, the work productivity of socialist farmers lagged far behind that of their private West German counterparts, who set particularly high standards, to say the least.

After Khrushchev's agrarian reforms the situation of Russia's *kolkhozi* gradually improved. Further concession of limited rights to farm privately was no longer regarded as a temporary expedient or a disturbing relic of the past, but rather as an indispensable source of processed foodstuffs for the population at large. Moreover, the socio-political objective with regard to the rustic populace was no longer to achieve complete assimilation with the rural industrial work-force – in keeping with Khrushchev's idea of converting villages into agrarian cities – but rather to equalize the incomes of both groups. While collectivization had erased property disparities among peasants, the differences between them and other workers, town and country remained. The gap was apparent not only in wages and education but also in everyday life. To be part of a collective farm meant oppressively monotonous routines, lack of recreational opportunities, a limited range of consumer goods, poor medical care and inadequate schooling. Such circumstances provoked a massive flight from the countryside into the cities during the 1950s and 1960s. The only way the state could control the movement of the peasant population was to issue internal passports. The restriction of personal mobility was a clear indication that peasants had become second-class citizens.

The differences between daily activity in the rural and urban-industrial worlds remain. The life of peasants in Russian villages is still dominated by the passing of the seasons; mother nature and climate are omnipresent existential determinants. Nor should one exaggerate the degree of Russian agriculture's mechanization: glasnost under Gorbachev exposed the technological and economic weaknesses of the collective farm economy. The greatest dichotomy is found in the different personal lifestyles of the urban-industrial and rural-agrarian worlds. Kolkhoz peasants who live in villages are not basically agricultural workers but farmers and small entrepreneurs. The only things that matter to them are their land, homes and families. A patriarchal social order and traditional rustic attitudes prevail.

The Russian government has recently developed an agrarian policy, the objective of which is to increase output by systematically improving economic and social conditions in the countryside: a better life – so the reasoning goes – will result in stronger motivation and greater productivity on the part of the *kolkhozi*. Whether or not these efforts bear fruit will determine not only agricultural production and the amounts of grain that need to be imported from abroad but also the growth of Russia's economy overall and the future standard of living. Peasants need to be encouraged to work more efficiently and produce more; only thus will it prove possible to build up reserves that can be used for other branches of the national economy. The fact that in 1990, 20 per cent of the population on the territory of the ex-Soviet Union was still employed in agriculture – the figure in the European Community is 8 per cent and in the United States 3 per cent – shows how retarded the country is in comparison to the industrialized western world. Whether Boris Yeltsin's new government will be able to effect meaningful agrarian reforms, overcome the crisis in farming and make life easier for husbandmen only the future will tell.

The Community and the future

Hardly any branch of Western Europe's economy has changed as much in recent years as agriculture. If 15.2 million persons were employed in the agrarian sector of what was the Community of Six in 1960, by 1987 the figure had fallen to 5.2 million. After Spain and Portugal became members there were 5 million or so farmers. The new total amounts to 8 per cent of Europe's working population, but there are great differences between individual countries (see table 1). In Portugal 22 per cent of the people are involved in farming, but elsewhere the ratio is much lower; for example, in Great Britain, Belgium and Luxemburg it is under 5 per cent. Until 1973 the number of agricultural workers declined at a surprisingly rapid pace. The reason for this was the expansion of the industrial and service sectors, which were able to absorb surplus rural labour. From about 1975 overall unemployment began to rise, and this led to a pronounced decrease in migration from the countryside – another indication of the growing difficulties faced by husbandmen intent upon improving their lot in life.

The flight of peasants to the city stands in direct relationship to a striking drop in the number of agrarian enterprises. In 1960 there were some 6.4 million, mostly small farms; twenty years later the figure was only 4.8 million. At the same time the average size of a farm rose from 12 to 20 hectares. However, at present, within a Community of twelve

Table 1   European agriculture in 1986

	Size of farm	Number of hectares per agricultural worker	Agriculture as a percentage of Gross Domestic Product	Agricultural employment as a percentage of working population
	(ha)	(ha) (%)	(%)	(%)
Belgium	14.1	13.7	2.5	2.9
Denmark	30.7	15.9	5.0	6.8
Germany	16.0	8.9	1.8	5.3
Greece	4.3	5.6	16.6	28.5
Spain	12.9	15.6	6.1	16.1
France	27.0	20.5	3.7	7.3
Ireland	22.7	33.8	10.2	15.8
Italy	5.6	7.8	5.0	10.9
Luxemburg	28.6	19.7	2.6	4.0
Netherlands	14.9	8.2	4.2	4.8
Portugal	4.3	5.1	23.1	21.9
United Kingdom	65.1	30.1	1.8	2.6
EUR 12	8.9	12.8	3.5	8.3

member states, it is only 9 hectares, again with marked differences between north and south. If Portuguese peasants must make do with 4 hectares, the typical English farmer, with a long commerical tradition behind him, works 65. The migration of peasants to urban centres has thus led to a sharp drop in the number of farms, a rise in the average size of the remaining ones and more specialization. European Community agriculturalists are also concentrating on fewer branches of production, i.e., commodities and foodstuffs which, because of certain natural advantages or favourable market conditions, they know will bring a profit. However, the results of enhanced productivity are massive surpluses – nowadays the principal problem of Europe's agrarian economy. How did this situation come about, and what have been the goals of the Community's agrarian policy?

The objectives were surely quite ambitious from the very beginning. When the treaty establishing the European Economic Community was signed by the six founding members (France, the Federal Republic of Germany, Italy, Belgium, the Netherlands and Luxemburg) in March 1957, Article 39 defined them as follows: increase productivity, guarantee the rural population a decent standard of living, stabilize markets and ensure an adequate supply of food at a cost level acceptable to consumers. It follows from this that the intention is to accommodate the interests of both producers and consumers. It is also clear that there is an inherent contradiction and that conflict is inevitable: one party cannot be helped materially without injuring the well-being of the other. We must likewise consider the starting-point of the Community in the late 1950s: 17.5 million peasants farmed only 65 million hectares of land for an overall population of 150 million. In the United States 400 million hectares served to feed a population of 200 million persons. The average American farmer worked 100 hectares (250 acres), almost twenty times as much as his Western European counterpart; the US agriculturalist provided enough food for fifty of his compatriots and the Old World peasant only enough for ten fellow Europeans. The Community was able to supply roughly 85 per cent of its own nutritional requirements.

A major goal of European agricultural policy during its first phase was to equalize prices and promote the Community's self-sufficiency. Since the costs of production were higher than in other large agrarian states, prices also had to be above the world level; this was the only way European farming could be strengthened and protected. In order to increase competitiveness, agrarian structures also had to be modernized – without, however, damaging the peasant family farm. The focus of practical measures during the 1960s was market and price policy, i.e., uniform internal administration and identical rules for export. Common market strategies for the various individual branches of agriculture were gradually worked out and put into effect. Restructuring began somewhat later: carefully planned measures were implemented in order to even out the differences in production methods and farm size between individual countries. Thus the Community had a twofold aim. A common policy towards prices and markets regulated market conditions and set outer limits for the agrarian economy, whereas a systematic approach to structures fostered the effort to make European farms resemble one another more closely, in other words, encouraging symmetry.

The great economic success of the new Common Market also affected neighbouring countries: between 1957 and 1986 the Community grew from six to twelve members. The drive towards European unification led to the establishment of a new objective in the 1980s: the creation, by 1 January 1993, of an internal market, in which goods, services, people and capital could circulate freely. Agriculture is of course a central feature of this process, since it is at the heart of Europe's economy. What are the challenges to Europe's peasants? Differences between currencies, which the Exchange Rate Mechanism is supposed to harmonize, and conflicting fiscal regulations continue to hamper agrarian trade and are hardly in accord with the idea of a common internal market. Yet other steps of a harmonizing character are necessary if all obstacles to an integrated European agrarian economy are to be removed.

Enthusiasm for the internal market is all well and good, but a sober assessment seems more appropriate when one considers the extent of the difficulties that confront the Community's agrarian policy-makers. If we are truly hard-headed about drawing up a balance sheet of the current status of European agriculture, we can only say that the result of decisions taken so far is total failure. There are veritably massive surpluses, but almost half of Europe's farmers do not make a decent living. There are high subsidies, but only 25 per cent of the money goes to the peasants themselves. The rest is spent on storage, administration and miscellaneous other needs. The expense has become practically intolerable, as consumers and ecologists are more sceptical than ever. The result of excessively high prices has been to accelerate the accumulation of surpluses. The prices can be maintained only because the Community effectively bars imports and dumps surpluses abroad by means of high export subsidies. This approach has led to a increasing strain upon the European Community budget and has envenomed relations with other countries, especially those of North

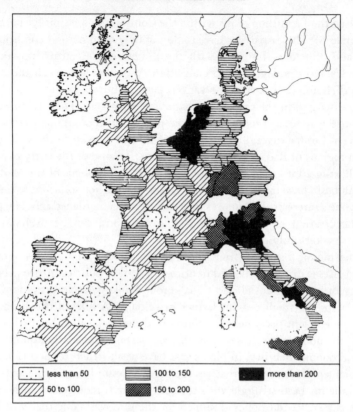

Map 8   Agricultural productivity within the European Community: average value of yield per hectare (after Die Lage der Landwirtschaft in der Gemeinschaft, *Report, Brussels, 1991, page 41)*

and South America. However, the objective analyst must also concede that there have been some successes. Increases in production have assured nutritional self-sufficiency, and the consumer has a wide range of choice at stable price levels. In many EC member states agriculture has evolved into a genuinely modern branch of the economy.

The problems of formulating meaningful European agricultural policies are due in large measure to highly divergent agrarian structures within the countries that constitute the Community – something that experts have pointed out from the very beginning. Because it is a handy term, people normally refer to 'European agriculture' as if it were a homogeneous whole to be defined in terms of statistical averages. However, the differences between the 12 million farms within the Community are simply enormous (see map 8). The disparities have to do not only with natural conditions – soil and climate – but also with the dimensions of farms, production methods and the degree of specialization. We must also recall the structural dichotomies between the various parts of Europe, which we have so often discussed in the preceding chapters of this book. The circumstances that affect agrarian production in the plains and mountainous terrain of Western Europe diverge greatly from those that prevail in the wide open grain regions of Russia and North America. Because of the entry of Spain and Portugal into the Community, the agrarian problems of the Mediterranean basin have taken centre stage and require policy solutions that serve everyone's interests. Differences in structure, often hardened into law prior to the creation of common farming institutions, can be overcome by policy-makers only gradually.

The mosaic resulting from the diffuse character of Europe's agrarian enterprises is directly reflected in price and market policies. A rise in cereal prices means substantial additional profit for large-scale operations but only helps the small peasant farmer marginally. A hike of this kind may assure inefficient petty peasants short-lived survival, but it has little effect upon the underlying causes – insufficient acreage and market quotas – of their economic debility. In places that have weak structures and lack non-agrarian employment alternatives the needy peasant has no recourse but to continue his hard struggle with the soil. What is required in such situations is a structural policy designed for the purpose – one that will both improve the facilities of individual farms and promote the development of the Community's disadvantaged regions altogether. In mountainous areas agriculture is often the single most important source of income for the local population. However, poor soils and unfavourable climatic conditions result in meagre harvests and extremely low earnings. It may not seem prudent at first glance to aid inefficient farmers, but it should be borne in mind that agriculture plays a crucial role in preserving the montane cultural landscape. Thus, in 1975, the Community decided upon a unique programme to subsidize peasants who live there. They receive special cost adjustment allowances that compensate them for the unusual production difficulties they face as the consequence of an unfavourable natural setting, as well as preferential investment assistance. Were it not for these measures, clearly they could not survive. The money provided by the Community undergirds the basic economic structure and thereby protects many centuries of man's cultural handiwork in the mountains.

The Community also furnishes special assistance to agriculture in countries with badly underdeveloped rural regions. In many instances it is a matter of improving both conditions on peasant farms and the general agrarian infrastructure. Funds are made available for constructing irrigation and drainage systems, improved road networks and cooperative marketing organizations. Special attention is being paid to Portugal, the agrarian problems of which are particularly acute. Considerable sums have been allocated to upgrade farms, as well as to modernize the country's agrarian economy altogether. It should be noted that the Portuguese programme is part of a broad trans-national undertaking that also encompasses backward regions in Mediterranean France, Spain, Italy and Greece.

Unquestionably, the major sticking-point of European Community agrarian policy is surpluses. Their growth, combined with mounting expenditure, falling peasant incomes and increasing tensions in international agrarian markets, represents the negative facet of the enhanced productivity of European agriculture. None of the many plans for reforming market and price policies has so far succeeded in winning the approval of all concerned and providing a solution to the scandalous issue of surpluses: there is no quick cure. However, there are two interesting if differing suggestions for a gradual cut-back in production. One is to establish overall quotas, and the other is a more strongly market-orientated price policy. Clearly, the Community has decided upon the second course of action and has devised a whole package of carefully synchronized measures. The key is a restrictive approach to prices – not sensational cuts but rather a progressive lowering of subsidies in the areas of surplus production, especially cereals. At the same time the principle of the co-responsibility of producers has been extended to all sectors of the agrarian economy. Collateral measures include programmes to remove land from cultivation, to encourage a shift to extensive farming and to improve the quality of individual agrarian commodities. Whereas the first programme has so far had only a limited impact, the emphasis upon extensive agriculture has begun to bear fruit. Peasants must substantially reduce production in one surplus sector without increasing it in another. As far as arable land is concerned, this means that they have to revert to less intensive methods of working the soil. The use of smaller amounts of fertilizers, herbicides and pesticides leads not only to a decrease in yields and surpluses but also limits the environmental damage that results from intensive farming.

The Community's reform plans to date have held fast to a leading principle of European agrarian policy: to foster a variety of agriculture characterized by the predominance of peasant family farms and heterogeneous forms of production. If the traditional social structure of rural districts and ancient cultural landscapes is to be preserved, huge tracts of land worked by only a few large-scale enterprises are obviously out of the question. However, does the peasant family farm really have any chance of survival? Is there any future for this kind of agriculture? Even though many peasants have given up in recent years and the number of small farms has shrunk dramatically, it is still possible to say that in the last analysis the agrarian economy of Western Europe is peasant-orientated. On the other hand, since the late 1970s the negative effects of the trend towards consolidation of farming enterprises and regional concentration have become increasingly evident. We need only mention the creeping destruction of the cultural landscape, the devastation of many priceless biotopes and the growing pressures upon nature and the environment caused by the presence of poisons and noxious substances. Dangerous residues in plants and other food products raise serious questions of public health, at least in some instances.

Individual peasant farms have tended to become increasingly modern, albeit in highly specialized ways. At the other end of the scale is the non-rustic 'factory farm', which depends not upon a large amount of land but upon imported feed crops that enable it to refine its products for sale on the consumer market. Practically all peasant family farms have meanwhile fallen victim to an existential crisis and face an uncertain future, whether they were once categorized by agrarian policy-makers as having economic potential or not. Farmers have to work more and consume less; feelings of insecurity also have a negative psychological impact upon family members. Price cuts have caused severe financial distress, and average peasant incomes have fallen dramtically. Economic decline has been accompanied by growing public criticism; indeed the social position of the peasantry has been called into question altogether by some commentators.

This difficult situation has recently given rise to a bipolar strategy: the problems of production quotas and environmental protection should be broached separately. Large-scale agricultural enterprises would be encouraged to produce as much as possible and as efficiently as possible. They would be made responsible for maintaining and improving public nutrition; they would assure both quantity and quality. Small and medium-sized farms would have to reduce their commitment to the intensive variety of agrarian production and be entrusted instead with the task of protecting nature and preserving the landscape. From an environmental and cultural perspective there can be no question that peasant agriculture is absolutely essential in many areas. It serves the whole of mankind in a way that no other force can, and up to now the remuneration has hardly been equitable. Recent agrarian policy takes this fact into account. The trend is to provide more support, especially cost adjustment payments in mountainous areas; the peasants who live there are compensated for their higher production costs. Subsidies of this kind contribute to preserving agriculture in problematic zones and guarantee protection of the cultural landscape.

Environmental conservation, within the context of agrarian policy, is undoubtedly of increasing importance to the public at large, for the harmful consequences of the rapid shift in the direction of intensive forms of agriculture can no longer be overlooked. Various steps have already been taken to make sure that farming is ecologically more acceptable. They include limits upon the nitrate content of drinking-water supplies and the banning of dangerous pesticides. The main – and very urgent – task of the 1990s must be to put an end to pollution and the damage to the natural environment caused by overemphasis upon stock-raising *en masse*, as well as excessive reliance upon fertilizers and chemical control of weeds and insects. Organic farming will play an important role, as it contributes disproportionately to protecting nature and the countryside. However, ecologically orientated peasants will not be able to supply all the agrarian commodities the public requires.

The idea of peasant farming that distances itself from 'factory farms' and the burden of ecological damage is finding increasing acceptance among husbandmen themselves. What we mean is a kind of agriculture that rests upon sure foundations, assures a satisfactory financial return for the labour it involves and fulfils multifarious social expectations. It is now clear, after decades of contention, that peasants and consumers have jointly arrived at a new and better understanding of their disparate situations. Cost-conscious consumers and the great majority of peasant family farmers agree upon four important political demands. The first is a form of agriculture that: (a) does not upset the balance of nature; (b) is tied to specific locations; (c) causes no permanent physical harm; and (d) preserves and protects the integrity and diversity of the countryside. Second, farmers must guarantee the population at large an adequate, stable supply of uncontaminated foodstuffs. Finally, whoever assumes the personal responsibility of working in agriculture should be treated in a socially just manner and receive appropriate remuneration for his efficiency in feeding the public.

Only the future will tell whether the peasant family farm will be able to survive within the European Community. The twelve centuries of rustic existence that have been described in this book show that husbandmen have experienced profound changes throughout their history and have had to adjust to a great variety of new circumstances. The latter include the rise of manorial lordship, the introduction of rigid rules relating to the use of common lands, assimilation into a free-market economy, mechanization of agriculture and a host of other phenomena. Despite all the challenges they have faced, Europe's peasants have always managed to safeguard their way of life. Perhaps this fact allows us to be optimistic about the future.

Notes

1   Riehl, *Naturgeschichte*, p. 221.
2   Marx and Engels, *Werke* (hereafter MEW), vol. 23, p. 528.
3   MEW, vol. 8, p. 199.
4   MEW, vol. 5, p. 471.
5   MEW, vol. 22, p. 502.
6   Tocqueville, *Oeuvres complètes*, vol. 1.
7   Gerhard, *Alte und neue Welt*, pp. 13–39, 159–72.
8   Wenskus, *Bauer*, pp. 13 ff.
9   Cf. Brunner, *Neue Wege*, pp. 199–212.
10 Weber, *Wirtschaftsgeschichte*, p. 77.
11 Cf. Wallerstein, *World System*, p. 320; Braudel, *Civilisation*, vol. 3, pp. 380 ff.
12 Fleckentein, *Ordnungen*, p. 2.
13 Hinze, *Feudalismus*, pp. 12–47.
14 Lütge, *Agrarverfassung*, p. 46.
15 Verhulst, *La genèse*, 135 ff.
16 Schlesinger, 'Die Hufe', pp. 41 ff.
17 Cf. Guérard (ed.), *Polyptique de l'abbé Irminon . . . de l'abbaye de Saint-Germain des Près*.
18 Cf. Ganshof (ed.), *Le polyptique de l'abbaye de Saint-Bertin (844–849)*.
19 Pirenne, *Mahomet*.
20 White, *Technology*.
21 Duby, *Guerriers et paysans*, p. 200.
22 Weber, *Wirtschaftsgeschichte*, p. 311.
23 Dopsch, *Herrschaft und Bauer*, p. 242.
24 Fossier, *Paysans*, p. 204.
25 J.C. Russell, 'Population in Europe 500–1500', in Cipolla: *History*, vol. 1, p. 36.
26 Le Goff, *Hochmittelalter*, p. 45.
27 Pirenne, *Sozial- und Wirtschaftsgeschichte*, pp. 29–42.
28 Fossier, 'La Naissance du village'.

29 Genicot, *Rural Communities*, p. 121.
30 Pirenne, *Sozial- und Wirtschaftsgeschichte*, p. 84.
31 Graus, 'Vom "Schwarzen Tod" zur Reformation: der krisenhafte Charakter des europäischen Mittelalters', in Blickle, *Revolte*, p. 13.
32 Russell, 'Population in Europe', p. 21.
33 Beresford, *Villages*.
34 Abel, *Wüstungen*, p. 25.
35 Abel, *Agrarkrisen*.
36 Abel, *Wüstungen*, p. 25.
37 Bois, *Crise du féodalisme*.
38 Cf. Genicot, *La crise agricole*.
39 Porshnev, 'Formen und Wege', pp. 440 ff.
40 MEW, vol. 7, p. 329.
41 Mousnier, *Fureurs paysannes*.
42 Blickle, *Revolution*, p. 21. The text of the Twelve Articles is reproduced in Franz, *Quellen in der Neuzeit*, pp. 14–19.
43 Schulze, *Bauernrevolte*, p. 38.
44 Blum, *Old Order*, p. 353.
45 Franz, *Quellen in der Neuzeit*, p. 310.
46 Wallerstein, *World System*.
47 For the Wallerstein controversy, see H.-H. Nolte, 'Zur Stellung Osteuropas im internationalen System der Frühen Neuzeit', *Jahrbücher für Geschichte Osteuropas*, 28 (1980), pp. 161–97.
48 Knapp, *Bauernbefreiung*, vol. 1, p. 72.
49 Ibid., p. 73.
50 Ibid., p. 75.
51 Hippel, *Bauernbefreiung*, p. 290.
52 R. Mols, in Cipolla, *History*, vol. 2, pp. 15–82; and A. Armengaud in ibid., vol. 3, pp. 22–76.
53 Cited by Abel, *Agrarkrisen*, p. 107.
54 MEW, vol. 2, p. 238.
55 Cf. Abel, *Agrarkrisen.*, pp. 241 ff.
56 Cited by Abel, *Massenarmut*, p. 255.
57 Franz, *Quellen in der Neuzeit*, p. 87.
58 Achilles, *Die steuerliche Belastung*, p. 26.
59 Chayanov, *Peasant Economy*.
60 Helmut Harnisch, 'Die Landgemeinde im ostelbischen Gebiet', in Blickle, *Landgemeinde*, p. 310.
61 Weber, *Wirtschaftsgeschichte*, p. 35.
62 Knapp, *Bauernbefreiung*.
63 Conze, *Quellen*, p. 11.
64 Franz, *Quellen in der Neuzeit*, p. 311.
65 Ibid., pp. 360 f.

66 Ibid., pp. 340 ff.
67 Knapp, *Bauernbefreiung*, p. 306.
68 Blum, *Die bäuerliche Welt*, p. 72.
69 Liebig, *Die organische Chemie*.
70 Cf. Hans-Wilhelm Windhorst, 'Agrarindustrie in den USA und in der Bundesrepublik im 19. und 20 Jahrhundert', in Pierenkemper, *Landwirtschaft*, pp. 237–49; and Pierenkemper, *Alternativen*.

Bibliography

Abel, Wilhelm, *Massenarmut und Hungerkrisen im vorindustriellen Europa*, Hamburg, P. Parey, 1974.

—— *Die Wüstungen des ausgehenden Mittelalters*, Stuttgart, G. Fischer, 1976.

—— *Agrarkrisen und Agrarkonjunktur*, Hamburg, P. Parey, 1978.

Achilles, Walter, *Die steuerliche Belastung der braunschweigischen Landwirtschaft und ihr Beitrag zu den Staatseinnahmen im 17. und 18. Jahrhundert*, Hildesheim, A. Lax, 1972.

Agricoltura e mondo rurale in Occidente nell'alto medioevo. (Settimane di studio del Centro Italiano di studi sull'alto medioevo, no. 13), Spoleto, 1966.

Altrichter, Helmut, *Die Bauer von Tver*, Munich, R. Oldenbourg, 1984.

Bader, Karl S., *Studien zur Rechtsgeschichte des mittelalterlichen Dorfes*. 3 vols, Weimar, H. Böhlaus Nachfolger, 1957–73.

Bäuerliche Sachkultur des Spätmittelalters. (Veröffentlichungen des Instituts für mittelalterliche Realienkunde Österreichs, no. 7), Vienna, 1984.

Baumgarten, Karl, *Das deutsche Bauernhaus*, Neumünster, K. Wachholtz, 1980.

Bentzien, Ulrich, *Bauernarbeit im Feudalismus. Landwirtschaftliche Arbeitsgeräte und -verfahren in Deutschland von der Mitte des ersten Jahrhunderts unserer Zeit bis um 1800*, Berlin, Akademie Verlag, 1980.

Bercé, Yves-Marie, *Croquants et nu-pieds: les soulèvements paysans en France du 16e au 19e siècle*, Paris, Gallimard, 1974.

Beresford, Maurice W. and Hurst, J.G., *Deserted Medieval Villages*, London, Lutterworth Press, 1971.

Bergmann, Theodor, 'Der bäuerliche Familienbetrieb – Problematik und Entwicklungstendenzen', *Zeitschrift für Agrargeschichte und Agrarsoziologie*, 17, 1969, 215–30.

Berindai, Dan and others (eds), *Der Bauer Mittel- und Osteuropas im sozio-ökonomischen Wandel des 18. und 19. Jahrhunderts*, Cologne, Böhlau, 1973.

Biskup, Marian, and Zernack, Klaus (eds), *Schichtung und Entwicklung der Gesellschaft in Polen und Deutschland im 16. und 17. Jahrhundert*, Wiesbaden, F. Steiner, 1983.

Blaschke, Karl, *Bevölkerungsgeschichte von Sachsen bis zur Industriellen Revolution*, Weimar, Böhlaus Nachfolger, 1967.

Blickle, Peter (ed.), *Revolte und Revolution in Europa*, Munich, R. Oldenbourg, 1975.

—— *Aufruhr und Empörung? Studien zum bäuerlichen Widerstand im Alten Reich*, Munich, C.H. Beck, 1980.

—— *Die Revolution von 1525*, 2nd edn, Munich, R. Oldenbourg, 1981.

—— *Landgemeinde und Stadtgemeinde in Mitteleuropa*, Munich, R. Oldenbourg, 1991.

Bloch, Marc, *La Société féodale*. 2 vols, Paris, Albin Michel, 1939–40.

—— *Les Caractères originaux de l'histoire rurale française*, 3rd edn, Paris, A. Cohn, 1960.

Blum, Jerome J., *Lord and Peasant in Russia from the Ninth to the Nineteenth Century*, Princeton, NJ, Princeton University Press, 1961.

—— *The End of the Old Order in Rural Europe*, Princeton, NJ, Princeton University Press, 1978.

Blum, Jerome J. (ed.), *Die bäuerliche Welt*, Munich, C.H. Beck, 1982.

Boelcke, Willi A., *Bauer und Gutsherr in der Oberlausitz*, Bautzen, Domowina, 1957.

Bois, Guy, *Crise du féodalisme. Economie rurale et démographie en Normandie du début du 14e siècle au milieu du 16e siècle*, Paris, Presses de la Fondation des Sciences Politiques, 1976.

Born, Martin, *Die Entwicklung der deutschen Agrarlandschaft*, Darmstadt, Wissenschaftliche Buchgesellschaft, 1974.

Bosl, Karl, *Europa im Mittelalter*, Vienna, C. Ueberreuter, 1970.

Braudel, Fernand, *Civilisation matérielle, économie et capitalisme, 15–18 siècle*. 3 vols, Paris, Armand Colin, 1980.

Brenner, R., Agrarian Class Structure and Economic Development in Pre-Industrial Europe', *Past and Present*, 70, 1976, 30–75.

Brunner Otto, *Neue Wege der Verfassungs- und Sozialgeschichte*, 2nd edn, Göttingen, Vandenhoeck und Ruprecht, 1968.

Chapelot, Jean, and Fossier, Robert, *Le Village et la maison au Moyen Age*, Paris, Hachette, 1980.

Chayanov (Tschajanow), Alexander (Aleksandr Vasilevich), *Die Lehre von der bäuerlichen Wirtschaft. Versuch einer Theorie der Familienwirtschaft im Landbau*, Berlin, Paul Parey, 1923.

—— *The Theory of the Peasant Economy*, Homewood, IL, Richard D. Irwin, 1966.

Cipolla, Carlo M. (ed.), *The Fontana Economic History of Europe*. 2nd edn, 6 vols, Glasgow, Collins, 1976.

Les Communautés rurales (Recueils de la Société Jean Bodin 40–45), Paris, Dessain et Tolra, 1982–6.

Conze, Werner, *Quellen zur Geschichte der deutschen Bauernbefreiung*, Göttingen, Musterschmidt, 1957.

David, Eduard, *Sozialismus und Landwirtschaft*, Leipzig, Quelle und Meyer, 1922.

Dawson, Christopher, *Understanding Europe*, London, Sheed and Ward, 1952.

Dipper, Christof, *Die Bauernbefreiung in Deutschland, 1790–1850*. Stuttgart, Kohlhammer, 1980.

—— 'Die Bauernbefreiung in Deutschland', *Geschichte in Wissenschaft und Unterricht*, 43, 1992, 16–31.

Dollinger, Philippe, *L'évolution des classes rurales en Bavière depuis la fin de l'époque carolingienne jusqu'au milieu du XIIIe siècle*, Paris, Société d'Edition Les belles Lettres, 1949.

Dopsch, Alfons, *Herrschaft und Bauer in der deutschen Kaiserzeit*, Jena, G. Fischer, 1939.

Duby, Georges, *L'économie rurale et la vie des campagnes dans l'Occident médiévale*. 2 vols, Paris, Montaigne, 1962.

—— *Guerriers et paysans, VIIe–XIIe siècle. Premier essor de l'économie européenne*. Paris, Gallimard, 1973.

Duby, Georges, and Wallon, A. (eds), *Histoire de la France rurale*. 4 vols, Paris, Seuil, 1975–6.

Elsenhans, Hans, *Agrareform in der dritten Welt*, Frankfurt, Campus, 1979.

Epperlein, Siegfried, *Der Bauer im Bild des Mittelalters*. Leipzig, Urania, 1975.

Fallers, Lloyd A., 'Are African cultivators to be called "peasants"?' *Current Anthropology*, 2, 1961, 109–10.

Fehring, Günter P., *Einführung in die Archäologie des Mittelalters*, Darmstadt, Wissenschaftliche Buchgesellschaft, 1987.

Finberg, H.P.R., and others (eds), *The Agrarian History of England and Wales*. 8 vols, Cambridge, Cambridge University Press, 1972–91.

Fleckenstein, Joachim, *Ordnungen und formende Kräfte des Mittelalters*, Göttingen, Vandenhoeck und Ruprecht, 1989.

Fossier, Robert, 1968: *La Terre et les hommes en Picardie jusqu'à la fin du XIIIe siècle*. 2 vols, Paris, Beatrice-Nauwelaerts, 1968.

—— *Paysans d'Occident (XIe–XIVe siècles)*, Paris, Presses Universitaires de France, 1984.

—— 'La naissance du village', in Dominique IognaPrat (ed.), *Colloque internationale: Hugues Capet (987–1987): La France de l'an mil*, Paris, CNRS, 1990, 162–83.

Fourquin, Guy, *Le paysan d'Occident au Moyen Age*, Paris, F. Nathan, 1972.

Franz, Gerhard, *Der deutsche Bauernkrieg*. 10th edn, Darmstadt, Wissenschaftliche Buchhandlung, 1975.

—— *Geschichte des deutschen Bauernstandes vom frühen Mittelalter bis zum 19. Jahrhundert*. 2nd edn, Stuttgart, Eugen Ulmer, 1976.

Franz, Gerhard (ed.), *Quellen zur Geschichte des deutschen Bauernstandes im Mittelalter*. 2nd edn, Darmstadt, Wissenschaftliche Buchhandlung, 1974.

—— *Quellen zur Geschichte des deutschen Bauernstandes in der Neuzeit*. 2nd edn, Darmstadt, Wissenschaftliche Buchhandlung, 1976.

Fumagalli, Vito, *Uomini e paessagi medievali*, Bologna, Il Mulino, 1989.

Ganshof, François, *Qu'est-ce que la féodalité*? Brussels, Office de Publicité, 1957.

Ganshof, François L. (ed.), *Le polyptique de l'abbé de Saint Bertin (844–849)*, Paris, Imprimerie Nationale, 1975.

Genicot, Léopold, *La Crise agricole du bas Moyen Age dans le Namurois*, Louvain-Leuwen-Gent, Centre Belge d'Histoire Rurale, 1970.

—— *L'économie rurale namuroise au bas Moyen Age.* 3 vols, Louvain-Leuwen-Gent, Centre Belge d'Histoire Rurale, 1974–82.

—— *Rural Communities in the Medieval West*, Baltimore, Johns Hopkins University Press, 1990.

Gerhard, Dietrich, *Alte und neue Welt in vergleichender Geschichtsbetrachtung*, Göttingen, Vandenhoeck und Ruprecht, 1962.

—— *Old Europe. A Study of Continuity, 1000–1800*, New York, Academic Press, 1981.

Gollwitzer, Heinz (ed.), *Europäische Bauernparteien im 20. Jahrhundert*, Stuttgart, G. Fischer, 1977.

Goody, Jack, Thirsk, Joan, and Thompson, E.W. (eds), *Rural Society in Western Europe, 1200–1800*, Cambridge, Cambridge University Press, 1976.

Graus, František, *Das Spätmittelalter als Krisenzeit*. Mediaevalia Bohemica (Supplementum I), Prague, 1969.

Guérard, Benjamin (ed.), *Polyptique de l'abbé Irminon ou dénombrement des manses, des serfs et des revenus de l'abbaye de Saint-Germain-des-Près*, Paris, Imprimerie Royale, 1844.

Gunst, Peter, and Hoffman, Tamas (eds), *Grande domaine et petite exploitation en Europe au Moyen Age et dans les temps modernes. Rapports nationaux*, Budapest, Akadémiai Kiado, 1982.

Halecki, Oskar, *Europa. Grenzen und Gliederung seiner Geschichte*. Darmstadt, H. Gentner, 1957.

Harnisch, Helmut, *Die Herrschaft Boitzenburg. Untersuchung zur Entwicklung der sozialökonomischen Struktur ländlicher Gebiete in der Mark Brandenburg vom 14. bis zum 19. Jahrhundert*, Weimar, H. Böhlaus Nachfolger, 1968.

—— 'Die Gutsherrschaft. Forschungsgeschichte, Entwicklungszusammenhänge und Strukturelemente', *Jahrbuch für Geschichte des Feudalismus*, 9, 1985, 189–240.

Hauptmeyer, Carl-Hans, *Annäherung an das Dorf. Geschichte, Veränderung und Zukunft*, Hannover, Fackelträger, 1983.

Hatcher, John, and Miller, Edward, *Medieval England: Rural Society and Economic Change 1086–1348*. London, Longman, 1978.

Heitz, G., 'Zum Charakter der "zweiten Leibeigenschaft"', *Zeitschrift für Geschichtswissenschaft*, 20, 1972, 24–39.

Henning, Friedrich-Wilhelm, *Dienste und Abgaben der Bauern im 18. Jahrhundert*, Stuttgart, J. Fischer, 1969.

—— *Landwirtschaft und ländliche Gesellschaft in Deutschland*, Paderborn, F. Schöningh, 1978–9.

Heuvel, Gerd van den, *Grundprobleme der französischen Bauernschaft 1730–1794*. Munich, R. Oldenbourg, 1982.

Higounet, Charles, *Die deutsche Ostsiedlung im Mittelalter*. Berlin, Siedler, 1986.

Hilton, Rodney H., *Bond Men Made Free: Medieval Peasant Movements and the English Rising of 1381*. London: M.T. Smith, 1973.

—— *The English Peasantry in the Later Middle Ages*, Oxford: Clarendon Press, 1975.

Hintze, Otto, *Feudalismus-Kapitalismus*, Göttingen, Vandenhoeck und Ruprecht, 1970.

Hippel, Wolfgang von, *Die Bauernbefreiung im Königreich Württemberg*, Boppard, H. Boldt, 1977.

Huppertz, Barthel, *Räume und Schichten bäuerlicher Kulturformen in Deutschland*, Bonn, L. Röhrscheid, 1939.

Jacobeit, Wolfgang, and others (eds), *Idylle oder Aufbruch? Das Dorf im bürgerlichen 19. Jahrhundert*, Berlin, Akademie-Verlag, 1990.

Jankuhn, Herbert, and others (eds), *Das Dorf der Eisenzeit und des frühen Mittelalters. Siedlungsform – wirtschaftliche Funktion – soziale Struktur*, Göttingen, Vandenhoeck und Ruprecht, 1977.

Janssen, Walter, and Lohrmann, Dietrich (eds), *Villa – curtis – grangia. Landwirtschaft zwischen Loire und Rhein von der Römerzeit zum Hochmittelalter*, Munich, Artemis, 1983.

Kaak, Heinrich, *Die Gutscherrschaft. Theoriegeschichtliche Untersuchungen zum Agrarwesen im ostelbischen Raum*, Berlin, Walter de Gruyter, 1991.

Kautsky, Karl, *Die Agrarfrage. Eine Übersicht über die Tendenzen der modernen Landwirthschaft und die Agrarpolitik der Sozialdemokratie*, Stuttgart, 1889.

Kellenbenz, Hermann (ed.), *Handbuch der europäischen Wirtschafts- und Sozialgeschichte*. 6 vols, Stuttgart, Klett-Cotta, 1980–90.

Klein, Ernst, *Geschichte der deutschen Landwirtschaft im Industriezeitalter*, Wiesbaden, F. Steiner, 1973.

Knapp, Georg F., *Die Bauernbefreiung und der Ursprung der Landarbeiter in den älteren Theilen Preußens*. 2 vols, Leipzig, Duncker und Humboldt, 1887.

Knigge, Adolf, *Ueber den Umgang mit Menschen*, Hannover, Schmidtischen Buchhandlung, 1788.

Kramer, Karl-Sigismund, *Die Nachbarschaft als bäuerliche Gemeinschaft*, Munich, Bayerische Heimatforschung, 1954.

Kriedte, Peter, 'Spätmittelalterliche Agrarkrise oder Krise des Feudalismus?' *Geschichte und Gesellschaft*, 7, 1981, 42–68.

Kuchenbuch, Ludolf, *Bäuerliche Gesellschaft und Klosterherrschaft im 9. Jahrhundert. Studien zur Sozialstruktur der Familia der Abtei Prüm*, Wiesbaden, F. Steiner, 1978.

Kula, Witold, *Théorie économique du système féodale*, Paris, Mouton, 1970.

Labrousse, Ernst, *La Crise de l'économie française à la fin de l'Ancien Régime et au début de la Révolution*, Paris, Presses Universitaires de France, 1944.

Ländliche Gesellschaft im Umbruch. Beiträge zur agrarsoziologischen Diskussion, Göttingen, Agrarsoziale Gesellschaft, 1988.

Le Goff, Jacques, *La Civilisation de l'Occident médiéval*, Paris, B. Arthaud, 1964.

——— *Das Hochmittelalter*, Frankfurt, G. Fischer, 1965.

Lehmann, Hans G., *Die Agrarfrage in der Theorie und praxis der deutschen und internationalen Sozialdemokratie*, Tübingen, J.C.B. Mohr, 1970.

Le Roy Ladurie, Emmanuel, *Les Paysans de Languedoc*. 2 vols, Paris, Imprimerie Nationale, 1966.

——— *Histoire du climat depuis l'an mil*, Paris, Flammarion, 1967.

——— *Montaillou, village occitan de 1294 à 1324*, Paris, Gallimard, 1975.

Liebig, Justus von, *Die organische Chemie in ihrer Anwendung auf Agricultur und Physiologie*, Braunschweig, Friedrich Vieweg, 1840.

Lorenz, Richard, *Sozialgeschichte der Sowjetunion 1, 1917–1945*, Frankfurt, Suhrkamp, 1976.

Löwe, Heinz-Dietrich, *Die Lage der Bauern in Rußland 1880–1965*, St Katharinen, Scripta Mercaturae, 1987.

Lütge, Friedrich, *Geschichte der deutschen Agrarverfassung vom frühen Mittelalter bis zum 19. Jahrhundert*. Stuttgart, Eugen Ulmer, 1967.

Maksay, Ferenc, Gutswirtschaft und Bauernlegen in Ungarn im 16. Jahrhundert', *Vierteljahrschrift für Sozial- und Wirtschaftsge-schichte*, 45, 1958, 37–61.

Marx, Karl, and Engels, Friedrich, *Werke*, published by the Institute for Marxism-Leninism of the Central Committee of the Socialist Unity Party (SED), Berlin, Dietz, 1958–

Mayer, Theodor (ed.), *Adel und Bauern im deutschen Staat des Mittelalters*, Darmstadt, Wissenschaftliche Buchgesellschaft, 1976.

Moore, Barrington, *Social Origins of Dictatorship and Democracy: Lord and Peasant in the Making of the Modern World*, 2nd edn, Boston, Beacon Press, 1967.

Mooser, Josef, *Ländliche Klassengesellschaft 1770–1848. Bauern und Unterschichten, Landwirtschaft und Gewerbe im östlichen Westfalen*, Göttingen, Vandenhoeck und Ruprecht, 1984.

Mousnier, Roland, *Fureurs paysannes: les paysans dans les révoltes du 17e siècle*, Paris, Calmann-Lévy, 1972.

Nitz, Hans-Jürgen (ed.), *Historisch-genetische Siedlungsforschung. Genesen und Typen ländlicher Siedlungen und Flurformen*, Darmstadt, Wissenschaftliche Buchgesellschaft, 1974.

North, M., 'Untersuchungen zur adligen Gutswirtschaft im Herzogtum Preußen des 16. Jahrhunderts', *Vierteljahrschrift für Sozial- und Wirtschaftsgeschichte*, 70, 1983, 1–20.

Patze, Hans (ed.), *Grundherrschaft im späten Mittelalter*. 2 vols, Sigmaringen, Thorbecke, 1983.

Pierenkemper, Toni, *Landwirtschaft und industrielle Entwicklung. Zur ökonomischen Bedeutung von Bauernbefreiung, Agrarreformen und Agrarrevolution*, Stuttgart, F. Steiner, 1970.

—— *Alternativen in der Agrarpolitik – ein Ausweg aus den Problemen?* In Hans-Wilhelm Windhorst (ed.), Die violette Reihe, No. 11, Vechta: Heimatbund für das Münsterland, Ausschuß für Umweltschutz und Landschaftspflege, Referate einer Vortragsreihe (Vechtaer Druckerei und Verlag).

Pirenne, Henri, *Sozial- und Wirtschaftsgeschichte Europas im Mittelalter*, 3rd edn, Munich, Francke, 1974.

—— *Mahomet und Karl der Grosse*, Frankfurt, G. Fischer, 1963.

Porshnev (Porschnew), Boris, 'Formen und Wege des bäuerlichen Kampfes gegen die feudale Ausbeutung', *Sowjetwissenschaft, Gesellschaftswissenschaftliche Abteilung*, 1952, 440–59.

Postan, Michael M. (ed.), *The Cambridge Economic History of Europe: The Agrarian Life of the Middle Ages*, 2nd edn, Cambridge, Cambridge University Press, 1966.

—— *Essays on Medieval Agriculture and General Problems of the Medieval Economy*, Cambridge: Cambridge University Press, 1973.

Puhle, Hans-Jürgen, *Politische Agrarbewegungen in kapitalistischen Industriegesellschaften*, Göttingen, Vandenhoeck und Ruprecht, 1975.

Raftis, James A. (ed.), *Pathways to Medieval Peasants*, Toronto, Pontifical Institute of Medieval Studies, 1981.

Raupach, Hans, *Wirtschaft und Gesellschaft Sowjetrußlands 1917–1977*, Wiesbaden, F. Steiner, 1979.

Razi, Zri, *Life, Marriage and Death in a Medieval Parish: Economy, Society and Demography in Halesowen 1270–1400*, Cambridge, Cambridge University Press, 1980.

Redfield, Robert, *Peasant Society and Culture*, Chicago, University of Chicago Press, 1963.

Revez, Lászlo, *Der osteuropäische Bauer. Seine Rechtslage im 17. und 18. Jahrhundert unter besonderer Berücksichtigung Ungarns*, Bern, Schweizerisches Ostinstitut, 1964.

Riehl, Wilhelm H., *Die Naturgeschichte des deutschen Volkes*, Leipzig, A. Kröner, 1935.

Rösener, Werner (ed.), *Strukturen der Grundherrschaft im frühen Mittelalter*, Göttingen, Vandenhoeck und Ruprecht, 1989.

—— *Bauern im Mittelalter*, 3rd edn, Munich, C.H. Beck, 1987.

—— *Grundherrschaft im Wandel. Untersuchungen zur Entwicklung geistlicher Grundherrschaften im süddeutschen Raum vom 9. bis 14. Jahrhundert*, Göttingen, Vandenhoeck und Ruprecht, 1991.

—— 'Bauern in der Salierzeit', in Stefan Weinfurter (ed.), *Die Salier und das Reich*, Sigmaringen, Thorbecke, 1991, 51–73.

Saalfeld, Dietrich, *Bauernwirtschaft und Gutsbetrieb in der vorindustriellen Zeit*, Stuttgart, G. Fischer, 1960.

Sabean, David W., *Property, Production, and Family in Neckarhausen, 1700–1870*, Cambridge, Cambridge University Press, 1990.

Schissler, Hanna, *Preußische Agrargesellschaft im Wandel*, Göttingen, Vandenhoeck und Ruprecht, 1978.

Schlesinger, Walter (ed.), *Die deutsche Ostsiedlung des Mittelalters als Problem der europäischen Geschichte*, Sigmaringen, Thorbecke, 1975.

—— 'Die Hufe im Frankenreich', in H. Beck and others (eds), *Untersuchungen zur eisenzeitlichen und frühmittelalterlichen Flur in Mitteleuropa und ihrer Nuztung*, vol. 1, Göttingen, Vandenhoeck und Ruprecht, 1979, 41–70.

Schneider, Karl H., and Seedorf, Hans H., *Bauernbefreiung und Agrarreformen in Niedersachsen*, Hildesheim, A. Lax, 1989.

Schulze, Winfried, *Bäuerlicher Widerstand und feudale Herrschaft in der frühen Neuzeit*, Stuttgart-Bad Cannstadt, Fromman-Holzboog, 1980.

Seibt, Ferdinand (ed.), *Europa im Hoch- und Spätmittelalter*. Handbuch der europäischen Geschichte, vol. 2, Stuttgart, Klett-Cotta, 1987.

Shanin, Teodor (ed.), *Peasants and Peasant Societies*, Harmondsworth, Penguin, 1971.

—— *The Awkward Class. Political Sociology of Peasantry in a Developing Society: Russia 1910–1925*, Oxford, Clarendon Press, 1972.

Slicher van Bath, B.H., *The Agrarian History of Western Europe, 500–1850*, London, E. Arnold, 1963.

Soboul, Albert, *Problèmes paysans de la Révolution, 1789–1848*. Paris: F. Maspero, 1976.

Tocqueville, Alexis de, *De la démocratie en Amérique*. (Oeuvres complètes, vol. 1), Paris, Gallimard, 1952.

Verhulst, Adriaan, 'La genèse du régime domanial classique en France au haut moyen âge', in *Agricoltura e mondo rurale* (q.v.), 1966, 135–60.

—— (ed.), *Le grand domaine aux époques mérovingienne et carolingienne*, Ghent, Centre Belge d'Histoire Rurale, 1985.

—— *Précis d'histoire rurale de la Belgique*, Brussels, Editions de l'Université de Bruxelles, 1990.

Wallerstein, Immanuel, *Capitalist Agriculture and the Origins of the Modern World Economy*, vol. 1, *The Modern World System*, London, Academic Press, 1974.

Weber, Max, *Wirtschaftsgeschichte. Abriß der universalen Sozial- und Wirtschaftsgeschichte*, 4th edn, Berlin, Duncker und Humboldt, 1981.

Wenskus, Richard, and others (eds), *Wort und Begriff 'Bauer'*, Göttingen, Vandenhoeck und Ruprecht, 1975.

White, Lynne, Jr., *Medieval Technology and Social Change*, Oxford, Oxford University Press, 1962.

Windhorst, Hans-Wilhelm, *Spezialisierte Agrarwirtschaft in Südoldenburg*, Leer, Schuster, 1975.

Wolf, Eric R., *Peasants*. Englewood Cliffs, NJ, Prentice-Hall, 1966.

Wolf, Eric R., and Cole, J.W., *The Hidden Frontier. Ecology and Ethnicity in an Alpine Valley*, New York, Academic Press, 1974.

Wunder, Heide (ed.), *Feudalismus*, Munich, Nymphenburger Verlagshandlung, 1974.

—— *Die bäuerliche Gemeinde in Deutschland*. Göttingen: Vandenhoeck und Ruprecht, 1986.

Zientara, B., 'Die Bauern im mittelalterlichen Polen', *Acta Poloniae Historica*, 57, 1988, 5–42.

Zimmermann, Clemens, *Reformen in der bäuerlichen Gesellschaft. Studien zum aufgeklärten Absolutismus in der Markgrafschaft Baden 1750–1790*, Ostfildern, Scripta Mercaturae, 1983.

Index

Page numbers in italics refer to illustrations or their captions

Germany (cont'd)
  attitudes to peasantry, 2–3, 4, 6;
  Bavarian uprising, 102; Black Death,
  68–9, 127; capital investment,
  193–4; Carolingian Empire, 31, 42;
  cattle raising, 28; changes in
  farmland, *189*; collectivization in
  GDR, 204; colonization, 50–1, 105;
  confessionalization, 165–6; diet,
  149; eastern landed estates, 108;
  economy, 111; employment levels,
  193; 'farm death', 194; farm
  numbers, 192; 'feudal quota', 119;
  feudal society, 47; July Revolution,
  179; land reclamation, 127–8, 131;
  landholding relationships, 60, 119;
  manorial lordship, 104; 'mark
  cottagers', 129–30; mechanization,
  190; nobility, 179, 180, 182, 183;
  peasant emancipation, 175–84;
  peasant living standards, 152–3;
  Peasant War (1525), 83, 87, 88–9,
  92, 93, 95, 96–101, *99*, 103, 116,
  118, 151, 152, 157; place-names, 49;
  population, 49, 126, 127, 147;
  Rhenine League, 176, 177–8; size of
  landholdings, 66, 116–17, 152–3,
  192; social position of peasants, 45;
  social reforms, 113; steward tenancy,
  117; tenancy rights, 81; Thirty Years
  War, 141, 147; village leaders, 162;
  vineyards, 75
goats, 23, 84
Gorbachev, Mikhail, 11, 205
Götz von Berlichingen, 93
grain: central and eastern European, 48;
  cultivation border, 26–7, 47;
  economy based on, 73; increased
  production, 30, 56, 62; prices, 61,
  67, 73, 75–6, 138, 144, 145–6,
  210; production, 22–3, 42, 196,
  198, 202, 210; seventeenth-century
  trade, *112*; varieties, 190; village life,
  159; yields, 148
grapes, 48, 56, 75, 140; *see also* wine

Graus, František, 165
Greece, 49, 211
Gubec, Mitija, 94

Hainault, 66, 82
Hannover, 105, 178, 181
Hanseatic League, 106, 110
Hardenberg, Prince Karl August von,
  176, 177, 178
Harnisch, Helmut, 167
harvest: combines, 192, 193; cycles, 62;
  dates, 22; failures, 64, 67; good and
  bad, 143-5; implements, 54;
  machinery, 54, *71*, 192, 193
hemp, 56, 136
Henry VIII, King of England, 121
herbicides, 193, 195, 211, 213
Hessia: abandoned settlements, 70, 74;
  emigration, 51; famine, 143; revolts,
  179, 180
hide: first appearance, 21; fiscal concept,
  117; importance, 21–2, 33;
  registries, 37; spread, 23; system,
  36–8, 43
Hildebrandt, B., 143
Hintze, Otto, 33–4
Holland, *see* Netherlands
Holstein, 104, 107, 113, 115
Holy Roman Empire, 52, 116, 176
horses, 53, 131, 190
houses: comfort, 146; construction, 62,
  150–1; layout, 126, 152
Hundred Years War (1339–1453), 78
Hungary: agriculture, 28; cereal prices,
  138; collectivization, 12, 203;
  feudalism, 34; land settlement, 50,
  131–2; landed estates, 116; nobility,
  110; peasant revolt (1514), 87, 94,
  95–6, 103; serfdom, 108; Turkish
  incursions, 21, 131; village meetings,
  161
Hussite Wars, 106, 107

inheritance: European traditions, 26;
  government intervention, 166;

inheritance (cont'd)
indivisibility of farms, 117, 129,
153, 154, 183; subdivision of farms,
66, 116–17, 153, 154
Ireland, 134, 150
irrigation, 23, 24, 48, 79, 211
Islam, 20, 23, 29–30, 42, 44
Italy: agricultural decline in south, 140,
141; agriculture, 79, 140, 211;
Carolingian Empire, 31; crops, 28,
48; decline in rents, 79; feudal
society, 47; landholding
relationships, 59, 119–20; peasant
revolts, 83; population, 49, 126;
rustic economic structures, 40;
sharecropping, 119–20;
transhumance, 139; vineyards, 75
Ivan IV (the Terrible), Tsar, 21, 25

Joinville, Jean de, 55
Joseph II, Emperor, 113, 174, 184

Khmelnitsky, Bohdan, 94, 101
Khrushchev, Nikita, 204
king: peasant concept, 90
Knapp, Georg F., 171
Knigge, Adolf von, 174
knights, 19, 20, 46, 76–9, 84
kolkhozi, 11, 197, 200–5
kulaks, 11, 196, 201

labour: compulsory service, 107, 113,
114, 117–18; division of, 57, 59,
111; servile, *see* servile labour;
shortages, 73, 76
labourers, 121, 181; day, 66, 153, 154,
155, 156; hiring, 182
Labrousse, Emile, 145
land: attachment to, 19, 107; clearance,
41–2, 49, 127–9; communal
regulations, 158–9; copyhold, 82;
enclosures, 121, 122, 129; freehold,
60; leases, 59, 60, 117, 119–23,
168; reclamation, 121, 127, 131–2;
rental, 36, 39, 59, 60, 63–4, 117;

revolutionary laws, 175; sale, 59, 60,
80, 121–2, 168; sharecropping, 59,
119; size of holdings, 40, 66, 107–8,
116–17, 129–30, 152–3; supply,
79; tenure, 119–23; waste, 70–4,
107–8, 127
landed estate: cartage, 114; communal
institutions, 157–8; compulsory
service, 113, 114; development of
system, 105–10; historical impact of
system, 123–4; peasant
emancipation, 171, 178–9, 184,
185, 196; regulation, 171, 178–9;
serfdom, 105, 107, 185, 196; size of
holdings, 107–8
law: courts, 160, 167; customary, 165;
Germanic, 50, 52, 105; land
agreements, 59–60; lawyers, 165,
166; magistrates, 160, 161–2, 166;
Roman, 157, 165, 166, 183; rustic
89–90; Slavic, 52
leases, 59, 60, 117, 119–23
Le Goff, Jacques, 53
legumes, 56, 135, 136
Lenin, Vladimir Ilyich, 199, 200
Liebig, Justus von, 189
linen, 66, 151
Lithuania: agrarian structure, 21–2;
emigration, 128; serfdom, 108
Lombardy, 58, 79
lordship, *see* manorial lordship
Lusatia, 104, 107
Lütge, Friedrich, 35, 61
Luther, Martin, 97, 101, 165

madder, 56, 136
magistrates, 160, 161–2, 166
Magyars, 40, 42
maize, 28, 139, 148, 191
Malthus, Thomas, 67
manorial lordship: changes to system,
58–61, 62; classical structure, 36,
39; comparison with landed estate,
104–10, 116–17; comparison with
Russian system, 25; compulsory

swamps, 140, *see also* drainage
Sweden, 48, 72, 123, 137, *see also*
  Scandinavia
Swedish-Polish War, 113, 138

taxation: bureaucracy, 166; calculation,
  117, 166; collection, 162; English,
  122; French, 82, 91, 101, 167;
  Norwegian, 122; peasant burden,
  119; peasant revolts, 85, 87–8,
  91–2, 101–3; Spanish, 91; territorial
  rulers' income, 77
technology, farming: American, 16–17;
  emancipation, 172; harnesses, 53;
  mechanization, 190–5; mills, 54–5;
  nineteenth-century, 188; plough
  design, 42–3, 53; revolution, 1;
  wagons, 53–4
tenancy: Early Modern, 91, 117–23;
  eastern European, 113; High Middle
  Ages, 59–61; Late Middle Ages,
  75–6, 79, 81; western European,
  117
Teutonic knights, 53
textiles: dyestuffs, 56, 75, 136; linen, 66,
  151; Low Countries, 66; peasant
  clothing, 151; spinning yarn, 56, 75;
  weaving, 39, 145, 151; wool, 66,
  129, 134, 135, 151
Thaer, Albrecht, 115
Third World: agrarian problems, 1, 7, 8;
  proportion of peasant farmers, 9;
  relationship with Europe, 124;
  studies of rural societies, 20
Thirty Years War, 92, 113, 126, 130,
  141, 147
Thomas, Sidney Gilchrist, 190
three-field system: changes, 136–7;
  development, 55–6; Eastern Europe,
  159; importance, 21–3, 53, 56; new
  method (no fallow), 148, 189;
  regulations, 62, 158–9; spread, 42;
  transition, 21, 23, 158–9
threshing, 17; machines, 190
Thuringia: abandoned settlements, 70, 74;

emigration, 51, 131; famine, 144;
  revolt, 100; social divisions, 152
tithes, 118–19
Tocqueville, Alexis de, 15
Tönnies, Ferdinand, 2
tools, 54–5, 148, 190
town halls, 157, 160
tractors, 191, 193, 203
transport, 17, 30, 33–4, 56
Tuscany, 69, 79, 120, 140
Twelve Articles, 98–100

Ukraine, 28, 109, 116, 203
United States: agrarian economy, 11,
  16–17, 205; comparison with
  European peasant farming, 14–17;
  farm size, 207; grain production,
  210; mechanization, 191, 192

vegetables, 28, 53, 75, 135, 137
vegetation zones, 27–8
Verhulst, Alfred, 36
Vikings, 31, 40, 42
village: abandonment, 70–4; autonomy,
  77, 95, 157, 162; ceremonies,
  164–5; community, 157–70;
  defence, 85; development, 61–3,
  158–60; employees, 162; leaders,
  162; legal status, 160–2; local
  government, 160–2; meetings, 161;
  new settlements, 49–50; newcomers,
  129, 164; North American patterns
  of settlement, 15, 17; ordinances,
  167; peasant identification with,
  94–5; relationships, 23, 163–4;
  renovation, 195; Russian mir, 26,
  168–70, 198, 200, 205; single-
  street, 51; solidarity, 162–3; soviets,
  199; views of society, 2–3
villatic system, 36, 39, 62, 84
villeins, 25, 40, 108

wages, 73, 75–7, 145–6, 155–6
wagons, 53–4, 190
Wallerstein, Immanuel, 25, 110, 111

warrior estate, 19, 20, 33–4, 38
wasteland, 70–4, 107–8, 127
water-mills, 54–5
weapons, 84–5, 93, 102
weather, *see* climate
weaving, 39, 145
Weber, Max, 18, 19, 23, 44, 170
Wendish Crusade, 51
Wenskus, Reinhard, 18
wheat, 27–8, 56, 134, 136, 140, 149, *see also* grain

White, Lynn, 42
Windish Rebellion (1573), 87
wine, 28, 38, 75; *see also* grapes
woad, 56, 136
Wolf, Eric R., 7
wolves, 84
wool, 66, 129, 134, 135, 151
work ethic, 17, 44

Yeltsin, Boris, 205